D1542748

Internal Control

Internal Control

A Manager's Journey

K.H. SPENCER PICKETT

ASSISTED BY JENNIFER M. PICKETT

JOHN WILEY & SONS, INC.

New York • Chichester • Weinheim • Brisbane • Singapore • Toronto

Library of Congress Cataloging-in-Publication Data:

Pickett, K.H. Spencer
    Internal control : a manager's journey / by K.H. Spencer Pickett.
        p.   cm.
    Includes index.
    ISBN 0-471-40250-8 (cloth : alk. paper)
    1. Industrial management—United States—Evaluation.   2. Auditing, Internal.   I. Title.
    HD70.U5 P52   2001
    658.4'013—dc21   00-068519

Printed in the United States of America.

10   9   8   7   6   5   4   3   2   1

Love and kisses to my wife, Jennifer,
for help, advice, support, and, more than anything, being there.

This book is dedicated to Master Lajos Jakab,
a man whose life involves teaching others that, with commitment,
dedication, practice, and hard work, one can achieve anything.

ACKNOWLEDGMENTS

THIS BOOK WAS devised on Sunset Beach in Montego Bay, Jamaica, and completed on Sarasota Beach in Florida. When you are able to relax on the beach discussing ideas with your wife, while your children, Dexter and Laurel-Jade, splash and play in the sea, you feel so in control of your life. It is aimed at people who need to know a little about managing risk and controls—in other words, everyone. We hope that you enjoy reading the book as much as we enjoyed writing it.

A special thanks to everyone who helped me maintain the energy to write, including my mother Joycelyn, my children Dexter and Laurel-Jade, Fredrica and Lloyd Livermore, Timothy Burgard, Nigel Freeman, Keith Wade, Sue Seamour, Jack Stephens (from Durham), Theresa Murray, Michael Livermore, Herbert and Elfreda Newman, Marianne, Lucie and Stella, Karron Stansell, Paul Moxey, Andrew Chambers, John Webb, and of course my mentor, Gerald Vinten. A very special thanks to the people of Jamaica, whose island inspired my words, including Reverend C.S. Wright, whose blessing remains with me.

K.H. SPENCER PICKETT

CONTENTS

ix

Internal Control

ONE

Taking Time Off

Our first chapter provides an insight into the board level responsibilities for reporting on internal controls and the pressure this creates for both senior managers and staff.

BILL REYNOLDS SAT in the doctor's waiting room and looked around. Waiting for test results was always difficult. He was an attractive, tall, slimly built man in his early thirties, with dark hair. He was not conventionally handsome, his lean features being too harsh and angular. However, his piercing blue eyes combined with the dark hair were striking.

Bill wondered if some mysterious illness lay behind the feelings of tiredness he had been experiencing lately.

The friendly young receptionist interrupted his thoughts with a cheerful, "Mr. Reynolds, please go straight through."

Bill was greeted by Dr. Todd as soon as he entered the consulting room. "Hello, Bill. Take a seat."

Seeing that Bill looked apprehensive, Dr. Todd began, "I'm pleased to tell you that all your tests have come back negative. You're basically fit and well. Having said that, let me check your

1

blood pressure as it's been a little high in the past. How are you feeling anyway?"

"Well, doctor," Bill said after some thought, "I'm still not sleeping well and to be honest, I feel tired most of the time."

Bill surveyed the examining room which, although bright and clean, was nonetheless formal in appearance. Various medical instruments sparkled from a nearby table. Not a very inviting room at all, thought Bill. For a man in his early forties, Dr. Todd, with streaks of grey throughout his thinning brown hair, looked a little tired. A good man though, caring and helpful; the perfect medical practitioner.

Dr. Todd meanwhile tested Bill's blood pressure and mumbled "Yes, yes, yes," in the reassuring way that doctors do. "Your blood pressure's still a lot higher than normal. Are you having any problems at work?"

Bill responded quickly. "Well, yes, as it happens. Things are terrible at work. We've had employment disputes, allegations of fraud, disciplinary action, and system crashes. There are currently twelve or so dismissal cases awaiting appeal hearings."

Dr. Todd nodded and said "Go on," surreptitiously checking his watch.

"In fact, Dr. Todd, we've just received an interim report from our external consultants indicating that our system of internal controls is inadequate. As a result, I spent two hours last week discussing this issue with the board of directors and we honestly don't know what to do. We're not even sure what the term 'system of internal control' really means, although none of us wanted to admit it. Meanwhile the main board is required to issue a statement on internal controls as part of next year's annual report and the chief executive's really worried."

"Okay," interjected Dr. Todd. "Let's take this in stages. When did you last take a break?"

"I've not really had any time off in three years," Bill replied.

"Right," said Dr. Todd. "You need to take time off to recharge your batteries."

"I can't do that. The board has to meet with the consultants next month to agree on the terms of reference for stage two of the review, where we deal with the problems."

"Right," retorted Dr. Todd, beginning to worry about the time this visit was taking. "I'm going to sign you off sick for a couple of weeks, because your blood pressure's far too high and I don't want you having a stroke. You can take some time off and approach your problems at work with a fresh mind, can't you? Look, what I am saying is, you must take a break and then tackle the problems that have led to the high levels of stress you've been experiencing. Take a vacation, hire a tour guide, and do some sightseeing. Doctor's orders," he added with a chuckle.

Waving aside the anticipated protest from Bill, Dr. Todd stood up, looked Bill straight in the eye and said slowly, "It is important that you take my advice, as in the long run, stress can affect your health and we must avoid this. Come and see me when you get back. Do you understand, Bill?"

Taking Dr. Todd's hand, Bill nodded and promised to go straight to the travel service.

What Bill had not told Dr. Todd was that he had been promoted to the post of head of corporate standards on the basis of a psychometric test that categorized him as a control freak. He was meant to deal with the problems that the chief executive felt were mainly caused by staff not following procedures. Having been in the new post for three months, apart from the new performance appraisal scheme that he was introducing, it seemed that the only hope for improvement was the work the consultants had done in rewriting the corporate standards manual.

Flicking through some travel brochures, Bill said to the waiting travel agent, "I need a short break for next week—anywhere hot and touristy where I can unwind."

"Right sir," came the reply. "It just so happens that I have a cancellation for Jamaica, flying out this Sunday, and returning the following Sunday. How does that sound?"

Showing little real enthusiasm, Bill asked for the details, which did sound attractive. Maybe this trip wouldn't be so bad after all. Since his wife had walked out on him three years ago, Bill hadn't bothered about travelling for pleasure, particularly if it meant travelling alone. But this was different—doctor's orders.

"Sounds fine," said Bill, wondering whether he could really afford to take a vacation, with the company in such trouble. "It'll do."

The travel agent wished all his customers were like Bill. Turn up, book a package, and pay straight away. However this was before Bill produced a detailed checklist of the travel and hotel arrangements he wanted. After an hour going through the timetables, tour details, hotel arrangements, and contact information, Bill finally agreed to the package and paid the amount in full. As Bill walked out of the shop, the travel agent stared at his back wondering why some people insisted on being so in control. A holiday was supposed to be fun, not a business project.

The next day Bill mentioned to the chief executive officer (CEO) that he would be taking a week's trip to Jamaica, which did not appear to present a problem as most people were booking a week or two's summer vacation at that time of year. The CEO, Georgina Forsythe, called Bill into her office late Friday afternoon and poured them each a glass of red wine. Georgina was a petite blonde, in her mid-forties with normally bright, mischievous green eyes, which had now darkened with worry, emphasizing the tiny lines around them.

"Bill," she began, "before you go on vacation I have to confide in you. I'm worried about the business. In fact, if things don't improve, I may have to resign."

Bill had known Georgina for several years and respected her as an honest and hard-working woman who really cared about all her employees.

4

"You see," Georgina continued, "we've built up the business over the years and provide what in my view is a quality product. But our systems have not kept pace and the latest project, the new automated document management system, has been abandoned as a failure. I pulled the plug on it yesterday. To top it all, I've been advised by the police that they intend to arrest our chief purchasing officer first thing tomorrow morning for tender fixing and accepting kickbacks. We'll have to go through yet another investigation and disciplinary hearing on top of all the others. When you get back, I'm going to recommend we establish a fully equipped compliance team to complement our two internal auditors. They can check and double-check on what's going on, in terms of breach of procedure and fraud."

"Shouldn't we wait until we've finalized the corporate standards manual?" Bill asked after listening carefully to Georgina.

"Yes and no. I want to be seen to be taking action, although, perhaps I won't recruit the compliance team until the new manual is ready. You know it's all very well saying we have no system of internal control and making me responsible for this failing, but so far no one can tell me what this system of internal control is, apart from checking everything. If I had everything we do double-checked, we wouldn't have time to get any work done at all. Anyway Bill, you have your break and let's tackle this problem head-on when you get back. We need to finalize our procedures manual and get staff to comply. Do me a favor and forget about work for a while. I need you fighting fit for this challenge."

With these words Bill felt a deep desire to meet this challenge and get these problems under control. He was tempted to cancel the intended vacation, but knew this would not be accepted. "See you in a week or so, Georgina. By the way, here's a contact number in Jamaica for emergencies."

Georgina frowned, "Don't be silly, enjoy yourself and forget about work for a while. Hang on a minute, Bill. I have a good friend who lives in Montego Bay. Jack Durham's a top business consultant whom I met when I studied for my MBA in Florida. He took a well-earned break from the rat race and settled in the Caribbean sometime last year. Would you mind taking over a gift from me? Just say it's from Georgie, his old study partner. He'll know what you mean. Give me your hotel details and I'll e-mail them to him."

It was humid and raining lightly as the taxi drove into JFK airport with Bill sitting in the back feeling as gloomy as the weather. He had been flipping through the first draft of the new procedures manual, which had taken up most of the space in his hand luggage. Georgina would kill me if she knew I'd taken this with me, he thought. I might as well review this on the plane going over. Checking in was straightforward and as Bill settled into his seat, he looked across at the various excited families and couples and felt a strange sense of isolation. Never mind, he thought, he had more important things to worry about. He spent the next hour skimming through the manual, which he decided needed very little alteration.

The flight itself was fairly relaxing, although as a control freak, Bill found it hard to sit back and let the pilot take care of the plane, even though Bill could not fly a light aircraft let alone a 747 passenger jet. The passenger sitting next to Bill, an older, rather round man with a large red face, was obviously enjoying himself. The man was enthusiastically disposing of glasses of wine and other complimentary drinks and laughing jovially with a woman who Bill assumed to be the man's wife. Much to Bill's annoyance the fat man kept looking at the manual with what looked like a slight smirk on his face. Bill, serious and concentrating on the manual, with the larger man enjoying himself and idling the time away, apparently without a care in the world, presented a stark contrast. Bill's worst fears were realized when the fat man started talking to him,

"What are you reading, son?"

6

"Oh, nothing interesting, just a new manual we have at work. Very technical you know," added Bill looking pleased with himself at this parting shot.

"If you employed good people, then you wouldn't have to write that boring stuff."

"Excuse me," mumbled Bill looking most offended at this comment from someone he regarded as an ignorant drunk. "I don't think running a large company is that simple. Compliance is the key."

Bill turned pointedly away from the man and resumed his reading. What a cheek he thought. Full of wine and merriment and wants to analyze my work. Cheek!

"Well," came the reply, in spite of Bill's obvious disinterest, "you may have got that wrong. For what it's worth you need to lighten things up at work, and maybe you need to lighten up a bit, too. That's just my view, son, nothing more."

Bill pursed his lips and remained silent.

"It's just," continued the fat man as he shifted his bulk in the seat with some difficulty, "you should give people a chance to shine, not just comply. You'd be surprised at the results." A loud burp followed this statement after which he apologized to Bill and burped again.

Grimacing at the man's antisocial behavior, Bill turned away and hoped his body language conveyed his displeasure. Bill looked at his watch and with a sigh, estimated the time left in the company of his newfound and unwanted advisor.

"Have a drink," continued the fat man with a friendly smile, as he passed Bill one of the small bottles of white wine that had been given to him by a generous air hostess. "Why don't you throw away that silly manual and start again?"

Ignoring the wine handed to him, Bill put his headphones on and feigned sleep.

The rest of the flight was uneventful and Bill eventually managed to read the entire manual. Boring stuff my foot. What would the world be like with no standards? Bill thought back to the previous night when he had written a comprehensive list of items to pack and meticulously placed everything in its right place in the suitcase. I guess I am a bit of a control freak, he thought. I can control everything except how people behave at work, which is frustrating. He asked himself silently, "Is compliance really the key to success? Does the fat man have a point? Is there any perfect answer?"

With these thoughts in mind Bill strolled through customs at Montego Bay and watched with some amusement as a group of calypso singers went through their welcoming routine. Collecting bags, taking a taxi to the hotel, and unpacking was all very straightforward. Resting in his room, Bill thought about the problems back home and the tropical heat lulled him into a short fretful sleep as he drifted in and out of dreams about the problems at work. The fact that a switch in the bedroom would have provided instant air-conditioning escaped him. After a shower, Bill found the hotel restaurant, which was very pleasant. The sweet smell of fruits, spices, and the delightful aroma of the delectable dishes being prepared added to the fragrant night air. A rum punch at the adjoining bar served by a helpful bartender put Bill in the mood for an early night to recover from jet lag.

The bartender who was a tall man and looked as though he enjoyed his food, topped up Bill's glass and inquired, "Is your wife joining you later?"

"No. I've travelled alone. I'm single right now. That is, I've not seen my ex-wife for years." Strange, thought Bill. It's really hard to explain to strangers that your wife walked out on you and simply disappeared with no explanation. Seven years of marriage down the drain. He still missed her company, but would never admit it to anyone.

"My name's Bill, what's your name?" he asked the bartender.

"I'm Byron, but people call me Bigga."

Completely puzzled, Bill asked, "Why do they call you Bigga?"

8

"You don't see how mi big?" the bartender replied.

"Oh!" said Bill. "Um . . . don't you find that offensive?"

Smiling, Byron said, with a good-natured chuckle, "Well, if I wasn't big I might be upset, but mi big, so it's okay. You don't think mi big?"

Embarrassed, Bill wasn't sure how much further to take this conversation, and instead of making a direct reply, ordered a final drink for the night. He was about to head for his hotel room when a door opened off the bar. A slim woman, smartly dressed in a light grey business suit entered the room. She had honey-colored skin and dark hair pulled back severely from her face, with striking hazel eyes framed by the longest lashes Bill had ever seen. She enquired, "Mr. Reynolds?"

Bill stared. He could not remember ever seeing a more attractive woman. He remembered his manners in just enough time to reply, "I'm Bill Reynolds, what can I do for you?"

She smiled, and said, "I'm Ruth Madoc, the manager here. You have a phone call. You can take the call here if you like."

The barman showed Bill to a phone behind the bar.

"Yes?" Bill asked, not really caring who it was, as he watched Ruth retreat back into her office. "Who is it?"

"Hello, it's Jack Durham. I'm a friend of Georgina Forsythe. She's asked me to contact you. Do you have any plans for tomorrow? If not, I could give you a tour of the area."

Bill vaguely recalled the name and, although on impulse he wanted to decline, he suddenly remembered Georgina's gift. "Yes, that's right. I'd like to do some sightseeing," he said in a noncommittal way.

The conversation, although stilted at times, ended with Jack arranging to collect Bill at 10 A.M. the following day, allowing Bill to catch up on his sleep and have a late breakfast.

Bill wondered if it had been wise to meet Jack so soon. Still, it would only be for the day, and afterward he could relax by the pool or at the beach and get through some of the paperbacks that he'd brought with him. Nonetheless, Bill did feel a little lonely and thought perhaps some company would be nice.

Jack turned up at 11 the next morning, and Bill, unable to hide his annoyance, indicated that this was an hour later than agreed. Jack was of medium height with short, cropped brown hair, which had been bleached by the sun. He had a powerful, muscular frame developed from many years training under the great Hungarian self-defense master, Master Lajos Jakab, reputed to have invented the most comprehensive self-defense system ever. Although stocky, Jack had a catlike movement, graceful and quick in spite of the growing heat generated by the tropical sun.

"Oh," mumbled Jack, "You're still on U.S. time. This is Caribbean time. It's a little more er . . . flexible."

Bill looked at his watch. Frowning and not bothering to reply, he got into the driver's side of the car before being asked to move across to the passenger's seat.

"Sorry," said Bill "Instinct, you know."

"Don't tell me you like being in control!" said Jack.

Bill started at the word "control" and smiled saying, "That word is banned for this week," not bothering to explain what he meant. Now they were even, since he had not fully understood Jack's remark about time.

Bill handed Jack a small package containing the gift from Georgina and they exchanged small talk about Georgina and how she had studied in the same MBA program as Jack.

Jack was a very informative guide, pointing out the sights along the way. The air-conditioning made the ride comfortable enough. Jack explained, "I'm taking you out to Safari Village where you can get some shots of the crocodiles and Princess, the tiger. This is where they filmed the James Bond movie—remember the one with the crocs in it? I think it was *Live and Let Die*."

"Fine," agreed Bill, sitting back and letting Jack take charge, which was quite out of character for him.

However, after a few minutes Bill could not refrain from taking control and inquired, "What brings you to the Caribbean?"

Jack replied. "Oh, I worked as a business consultant for many years, and basically set my own work schedule and salary. I decided to take time off last year and we, that is my wife and I, have settled here for a while. I'm supposed to be writing a book about my business exploits, which is taking longer than I thought to get going. Actually, the publisher was asking me last week for a completion date but it's not as simple as it looks. It's very easy to relax here and forget about work for a while. Very easy indeed."

"Anyway," Jack continued, "that's the boring bit over. You know, books and writing and such. Over to our left is Sunset Beach. The jets fly straight over this beach to land at Montego Bay Airport. It's quite an inspiring sight. Further along is Dead End Beach. According to local legend, this used to be a through road to the airport, until one day a jet flew in to land and the air gusts pushed a bus loaded with passengers into the sea. After that the road was blocked off and thereafter referred to as Dead End."

The sight of the sun shimmering off the glorious turquoise sea which flowed along the white sand coastline was quite beautiful to behold. Without taking his eyes off the road, Jack said softly,

Natural beauty, people, places
Vibrant energy, tranquillity

Sensing Bill's discomfort, Jack continued quickly, "I should tell you that I collect poems, articles, quotations, and any words that I feel should be noted for future reference. Although, I made this one up about this place. It's part of my mission in life . . . it's become a bit of a hobby."

A strange man thought Bill, wondering whether to continue this conversation further. Bill looked at the scenery. It *was* beautiful—the colors, flowers, coastline, and the people going about their business and work in the hot sun as his car sped past them.

"So what's this mission then?" ventured Bill thinking, "What the hell, we have to talk about something."

Slowing down to avoid a pothole, Jack looked at Bill as if wondering how much more to say. Finally, Jack remarked, "It's just that as part of my research for writing the book, I collect articles and book references."

Bill inquired, "What's this book about?"

"Oh," replied Jack, "I doubt you'd be interested."

After further cajoling from Bill, Jack continued, "As I told you, I was a business consultant specializing in companies that got themselves into all sorts of problems. This was after a career as an internal auditor. To try to provide practical business solutions, I'm writing a book on internal control."

Bill laughed out loud, much to Jack's consternation. Oh no. A consultant, and one who's studying controls—a living nightmare. Apologizing quickly, Bill exclaimed, "Sorry. No, it's just that this does interest me although . . . well, this is a holiday so let's not talk about work any more. Agreed?"

"Absolutely," agreed Jack.

Arriving at Safari Village, Bill noticed that Jack negotiated a suitable entrance fee of $200 Jamaican each, and winked at the attendant. However, a party of German tourists behind them in the queue were charged $400 Jamaican each. Bill wondered if these flexible charges fell in line with the flexible timing Jack referred to earlier.

"Let's move on to a small town called Falmouth just outside of what we call Mo'Bay. You know, Montego Bay," explained Jack after the tour had finished. "We can get a meal in the shopping precinct and you can pick up some souvenirs if you wish."

Falmouth proved to be an interesting town, busy with the hustle and bustle of market day. After several rather hot and sticky hours, armed with a newly acquired oil painting of a local sunset scene, they were on the road again, heading back to Mo'Bay.

As they drove along, Jack announced, "I'm now going to introduce you to Irie FM, a radio station dedicated to reggae music."

Thereafter, a soothing beat flowed through the car speakers. After downing a couple of bottles of local beer called Red Stripe that Jack had bought earlier, the car journey became almost magical for Bill, as the countryside and coastline flashed by, along with overtaking cars.

Bill became more relaxed and, as usual, his conversation turned to the problems at work. Little by little he relayed to Jack the trouble, control breakdowns, poor performance, and scandals that were an everyday feature of the workplace. Jack listened like a trained therapist nodding slightly and mumbling, "Yes. I see," in all the right places.

Bill drifted off to sleep and upon waking demanded flippantly, "Well, what's the solution to my problems then?"

Quick as a flash Jack replied cryptically, "Seven squared, I think."

Like the good friends that they were fast becoming, Bill retorted instantly, "Very funny, I don't think," and laughed. "Come on, what *is* the answer?"

"Well," started Jack, swallowing the last piece of a mango he had been eating. "There aren't any real solutions. It just depends on the situation and what you're trying to achieve."

"Okay," snapped Bill now getting into the conversation, "You're just like all the consultants I've ever met. No answers, just the usual mumbo jumbo."

"You go too far," jested Jack. "There is a solution," Jack continued. "Look, your hotel's just around the corner so I'll be quick. You need to establish a corporate internal control facility, or better still, a corporate internalized control facility. Get it? Internalize controls and get people to take charge of themselves."

Tired, Bill looked at Jack and wished him good night as they drove into the hotel forecourt with the daylight fading into an orange sunset. As he got out of the car, Bill thought again about what Jack had just said and held the door open saying, "Look, Jack, let's do some more touring tomorrow and continue this conversation. I know, you bring your reference file, the one full of quotes and let's explore the issues. Perhaps I could take some notes for my new manual. To be honest, I need to launch the company's new standards manual when I get home and would be glad of any help. I'd get much more from my vacation if this were added to my tour across the island," continued Bill. "I know, I'll bring my dictaphone and we can record our conversations. That way, we'll have a record of this concept of internalized controls that you talk about and you can have some material for your book. What do you say, Jack?"

"It's your vacation, Bill, and if that's what you want, I'll be glad to help. As we say in Jamaica, *No problem*."

TWO

Concepts of Control

This chapter provides the information needed to understand what control means, why it is important, and the type of control models that exist. Both managers and staff will be able to appreciate the impact of controls on their working life and why this can no longer be seen as a specialist topic.

"**G**OOD MORNING, BILL," said Jack and this time Bill did not bother to check his watch or comment on Jack's timekeeping.

"I thought we might take a trip to Boston Beach in Portland. They sell the best jerk pork and chicken in the world. Bit of a drive, but well worth it."

"Jerk pork being . . . ?" inquired Bill as the car pulled out.

"The pork is seasoned with pepper, salt, garlic, and various herbs. After marination, it's smoked over an open fire until cooked. They use a special pepper sauce to bring out the unique flavor."

"Mmm . . . sounds delicious," Bill mumbled. "You know, I was talking to Ruth, the hotel manager, this morning and she was saying how she really likes sweet mangoes. I think they're called Julie mangoes. But they're really hard to find in this area. Apparently she buys a bag each week and many of them are no good. Maybe we can get some to bring back to her."

"Fair enough. Oh, by the way, I know the manager of your hotel. She's a friend of Sharon, my wife. Lovely young lady. Anyway, we'll drive back to Falmouth," Jack said, "straight through St. Anne's Bay and into Ocho Rios, the famous tourist resort. People here call it *Ochi*. We can stop there and get a snack and a drink if you like. Then we'll hit the main road to St. Mary, into Portland, and then past Port Antonio and on to Boston. There's a small district in Portland, just past the border of St. Mary called Windsor Castle. If you wish, we can pick up some Julie mangoes from Miss Luna, a feisty old lady I know who lives there."

OCHO RIOS AND BACKGROUND TO CONTROLS

The car swept on through miles of winding roads and countryside sparkling in the sun, which danced through the trees and foliage. Meanwhile, Jack relayed the history of the island and its varied population. Bill learned that the island's first inhabitants were the Arawaks, who crossed the Caribbean Sea to Jamaica around A.D. 500 and that the current population is quite varied, hence the national motto, "Out of many, one people." Jack glanced at Bill who appeared to be drifting off, lulled into sleep by his slow and deep voice. Noticing this, Jack changed tack and said, "Let's talk about controls!"

"Yes." replied Bill, suddenly brought back to consciousness with fresh enthusiasm. "Yes, I'd like that. Before you start, Jack, I'll turn on the tape." Bill wondered whether Jack was aware of his capacity for talking at length on almost any subject imaginable. He said, "I should tell you that my company apparently has inadequate systems of internal control and I find this annoying. Business unit managers cannot spend all their time checking on staff. This isn't what modern management is about. We're going to set up a compliance team, maybe as part of an internal audit, and they'll carry out these checks, leaving managers to manage and not policetheir staff."

Bill paused and wondered why he became so emotional when talking about controls; it was such a negative subject. Maybe it wasn't such a good idea to spend his vacation discussing this concept. He would probably end up having a stroke by the time he got back to New York.

"Why do you feel compliance teams are the answer?" Jack asked.

"Well, control is about checking up on past performance and assessing whether standards are being adhered to. Managers are more interested in coaching staff for future performance and encouraging development. So, it makes sense to let the auditors do this after-the-event checking."

Jack was silent as he swerved to avoid an overtaking Lada that had cut in front of him just as an oncoming Leyland truck thundered past them. The next few moments would probably set the tone for the rest of the day. Would it be best to let Bill go on about his plans, or should he tell Bill about some of the theories he'd developed over the years? What the hell, thought Jack, he'd go for it and win Bill over. He'd turn a control freak into an internal control freak. Or, more correctly, an internalized control freak.

"There are those," Jack launched into discussion mode as he glanced at the small tape recorder whose red light indicated that it was recording everything, "who feel we are overaudited."

"Ah hah." retorted Bill. "What about accountability and transparency? These things underpin control and ensure regularity surely. I shouldn't need to tell you, Jack, you used to be an auditor. Checks and balances, checks and balances."

The brief silence allowed a moment's reflection for both of them. Jack continued, "Let me see if I can remember a quote from Michael Power:

Face to face accountability has been displaced by trust now in the audit process and compliance regulations promote obscurity not transparency.(1)

"So control isn't achieved through extensive checking and double-checking. It's more about having clear objectives and ensuring they're achieved. There's more. Our activities must be constrained by an ethical framework, which is really where the concept of compliance comes in. The other key point is that we can only make sure objectives are achieved insofar as this is possible. There's always a degree of uncertainty that must be accounted for. Nothing is perfect."

"Mmmm . . ." mumbled Bill, "You sound just like my old school English teacher. Always had a quote or two to hand."

Bill reached for a thick folder that lay on the backseat and flicking through it, noticed that it contained articles, diagrams, and references loosely connected to the topic of internal control. "Let's stop for a beer. I'm thirsty," said Bill.

"I've got a better idea," suggested Jack. He stopped the car beside a group of young men who stood around a wooden cart. "Ice cold jelly?" called Jack. He purchased a huge green coconut with its top sliced into a spout. Bill watched Jack drink deep from the coconut's spout. "Try some, it'll stir your heart and quench your thirst at the same time." Growling, Jack wiped his mouth with his handkerchief.

Bill asked for a straw and drank from his coconut, and trying to copy Jack's deep growl, ended up stifling a choke instead. "This man really needs to be defrosted," thought Jack, he's too tense.

"Right," said Bill slowly. "Let's set some ground rules. I guess it would be best to speak clearly so the tape will pick up the precise meaning of these things. We should also say where a quote comes from. You'll need to give each diagram a reference number so that you can use it when you write your book."

As they got back into the car, Bill said, "I've found your extracts from the *Collins English Dictionary* (2). I'll read out the definition of control:

1. To command, direct, or rule.
2. To check, limit, curb, or regulate; restrain.
3. To regulate or operate.
4. To verify by conducting a parallel experiment in which the variable is held constant or is compared with a standard.
5. To regulate financial affairs, to examine and verify accounts.
6. Power to direct or determine: under control.
7. A means of regulation or restraint.
8. A device or mechanism for operating a car, etc.
9. A standard of comparison used in a statistical or scientific experiment.
10. A device that regulates the operation of a machine.
11. A dynamic control is one that incorporates a governor so that it responds to the output of the machine it regulates.

It says the control chart is:

a chart on which observed values of a variable are plotted, usually against the expected value of the variable and it's allowable deviation, so that excessive variations in the quantity etc. of the variable can be detected.

While a controller is a person who directs, regulates, or restrains . . . ."

"Hold on, Bill," Jack said, "forget the technical detail. It's so boring. Let's start at the beginning. You suggest that control is primarily about constraining things."

"Yes," agreed Bill, "it's about holding back and stopping things from going wrong. Like the brakes on a car."

Jack interjected, "Okay. But my view of control is based on a more dynamic concept that ensures objectives are achieved, as far as they can be. As such, control is not a case of holding things back but of driving them forward. Making sure the car goes where it's supposed to go."

"But it must also act as a fail-safe mechanism that stops problems from escalating out of control, you know, speeding out of control," Bill replied.

Jack sensed that they were now entering the real journey, one even more exciting than the views and colors that flashed past the car windows as they drove along the winding coastal road. "Right," Jack replied, "let's take the control chart that you referred to in the definitions. This chart in its most basic form sets an upper and lower limit within which everything should fall. I have a diagram in the reference file." (See Figure 2.1.)

"We can argue that control is about keeping all things within these two limits as we move from left to right, or we may suggest that the top bar constrains activities while the bottom one acts more as a driving force. A form of push-pull strategy, making good

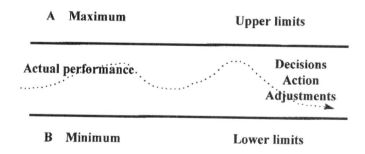

Budget versus actuals = Variances

Figure 2.1 Control chart.
(See also Figures 3.9 and 6.13)

things happen while at the same time stopping any bad things. Meanwhile, our efforts are simply directed toward comparing actuals against budgets, or standards, and then correcting variances that move you outside the A and B limits."

Bill retorted, "I accept this, which is why I say that we let the auditors measure these activities and ensure they meet set standards. The control chart belongs to them while managers can work on providing services or outcomes. This is quite straightforward and I really don't see control as *the* corporate issue. It's just an added nuisance, that's all."

Jack continued his line of argument, "Let me deal with your view of control as merely a nuisance by pointing out three things: First, society now demands some degree of corporate governance, you know, standards about the way larger organizations are directed and controlled and, as such, argues that your board of directors is responsible for the task of reporting back to shareholders on any efforts made in this matter. Second, control can be about life and death."

Seeing Bill's raised eyebrows and smug smile, Jack continued, "We've said that control is about setting and achieving defined objectives. It's also about effective procedures. Some call these control activities that help manage risks. But just as important, controls must be flexible and innovative. Do you agree? I've written this down. It's in the file as Figure 2.2."

"Well, yes, I guess we can call this model CEFI for short," mumbled Bill.

"Okay, if you insist." Jack launched into the debate while steering, with one hand only, around a rather steep bend. "What is the primary objective of regular Pap tests for women?"

"To detect cervical cancer early so that it can then be dealt with," answered Bill after some thought.

"Okay." said Jack. "I read a heartrending case reported in the newspapers about a widower whose wife had died of this disease

Figure 2.2   The CEFI model.

after receiving the all-clear from a Pap test. Read page 6 of the file you have in your hand."
Bill read:

John was puzzled to find an envelope on the doormat addressed to his wife. He picked it up and opened it. Inside was a letter calling her back to the hospital because it was suspected her test had been wrongly graded. A lump stuck in John's throat: His wife had died two years earlier of cervical cancer. Slowly the true extent of the tragedy dawned. Not only had he had to endure losing his wife, leaving him to look after their two children, but he now began to realize that her death had been unnecessary.(3)

Jack continued, "Apparently she wasn't alone and as the tests were rechecked, many women had to be recalled for treatment. This is the real impact of poor controls. Mistakes were made, procedures were poor, and work wasn't properly checked by the hospital in question. The key objective failed and if you read John's story, you cannot help being moved."

"Exactly what is corporate governance?" Bill asked while raising his eyebrows.

"It's what I said. The way organizations are directed and controlled. My work is all about the control side and why employees should appreciate what it's all about. There's an entire industry looking into the other bit of the corporate governance equation, that is, directing the organization. The need for standards on the role, appointment, remuneration, and assessment of the performance of directors is important to good overall control. Due diligence and what's called the tone at the top has been subject to a great deal of research. The relationship between the board and key stakeholders is crucial both to success and accountability. Again, the whole question of independent directors brings into play many issues about boardroom accountability. To be honest, I can't really go into this. It's outside the scope of my work. I'm really interested in managers and staff and how they fit into the big picture."

Bill was silent, which was a good enough signal for Jack to get to his third point, "The final point concerning controls is that if they're too limited we'll miss everything that falls outside of the control chart limits. That is, everything both good and bad."

Unknown to Jack, Bill had spent a little time reading up on business controls when this issue first came up on the corporate agenda. Nonetheless, these ideas had not appeared in his reading material. "And just what do you mean by that?" he asked.

"Well," Jack continued, "We need to think about what's in front of us and what we can't see. You know, stuff that's out of bounds. If we go back to the control chart, we can draw a circle around these out of bounds areas." (See Figure 2.3.)

Bill absorbed these arguments and responded softly, "If we're not careful, we'll return to your earlier suggestion that there are no real answers to the control question. In fact, I'm surprised to hear

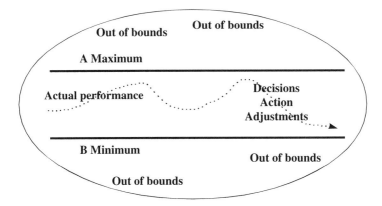

Figure 2.3   Out of bounds.
(See also Figures 6.1, 6.14, and 6.15)

control consultants speak about breaking the rules." Feeling a little smug Bill continued, "I can give you a quote from Monty Python's Flying Circus, you know the British comedy show from the 1970s. One sketch summed up accountants, and I presume auditors as well. Let me see now, I spotted it in your file somewhere. Yes, an accountant turns up at a recruitment agency and is told:

> In your report here, it says that you are an appallingly dull person. Our experts describe you as an appallingly dull fellow, unimaginative, timid, spineless, easily dominated, no sense of humor, tedious company, and irresistibly drab and awful. And whereas in most professions these would be considered drawbacks, in accountancy they are positive boons . . . ."(4)

"Hmm, I'm amused," mumbled Jack. "However, going back to the main argument, you appreciate that there aren't many chief executives who can provide definitive statements for the board on internal control and there are fewer external auditors who will issue positive statements on this matter, particularly where they relate to nonfinancial controls. It would mean that they effectively assume liability for anything major that goes wrong with the company thereafter. We have then a clear expectation gap. Society wants these statements while no one knows how on earth they can be issued without such heavy qualifications that they're meaningless."

Bill found the arguments interesting, but wanted to take part in an active debate and not just listen to a monologue. He said, "Our external auditors are excellent. They have introduced value-added audits where they encourage us to adopt process reviews and a wider view of audits outside the old tick and check model."

"I accept this," Jack was saying, "but I still say that executive management is responsible for internal controls, and they can only discharge this role by making all persons who work for, or have contact with the organization, also assume some responsibility. This is why I would recommend some form of control facility. What I mean is, a small team that helps employees appreciate the importance of good controls and assists them in living up to these newfound responsibilities."

Remembering his brief research into controls, Bill said, "What about the standard control models used in management theory in Figure 2.4? So you set standards, measure performance, and correct variances using a feedback loop."

Jack responded, "There's nothing wrong with this and other similar models. They comprise suitable techniques—part of the armory of control concepts. What I'm looking for is a model that explains the whole thing, including the need to ensure change and creativity. I promise that by the time you return to work, you'll have all my ideas. In a way, our discussions are helping me develop my own thoughts about control."

"This is just as much a journey for me," admitted Bill.

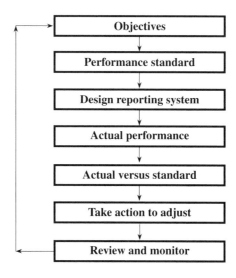

Figure 2.4 Standard control model.

"Look," suggested Jack, "we'll be in Ochi in a few minutes. Let's recap. What have we said about controls? We agree that it's high on the corporate agenda and that it's difficult to make definitive statements about how matter affects an organization. The feedback loop in Figure 2.4 and control chart in Figure 2.1 are good techniques that can be used to promote better control. We've suggested that standard definitions of control as restricting behavior may impair creativity within organizations. I think we should dedicate today to control concepts and this first part of the trip to Ocho Rios is about background material. The next stage, up to Boston Beach, I think should be about reviewing these concepts of control and then we can tackle systems because this goes hand in hand with control. In fact, your consultant's report talks of poor systems of internal control, doesn't it?"

Bill agreed and said, as they entered Ocho Rios looking for a suitable place to park the car, "True. I guess I need to put some of these ideas into my new standards manual."

"Yes, Bill. Start your manual with a background to control and the importance of control standards. Get it down in a simple way that everyone will understand. We'll get a draft together back at the hotel this evening. If this format works out, you can use it as the basis of awareness workshops back at work. That's the way forward, Bill. Give people a chance to get into a new way of thinking at their own pace and on their own territory. Come on, let's eat."

LUNCH AT OCHO RIOS

Bill and Jack sat around a table outside a small restaurant eating a plateful of ackee and saltfish each. Jack explained, "This is a famous national dish in Jamaica. Ackee is a small fruit that bursts through its skin when ripe. The yellow fruit is cooked with salted fish and looks a bit like scrambled eggs as you see. Mmm . . . delicious. Anyway, back to work. I don't want you to think I view controls as the highest form of human thinking. They can be very basic at times." Jack reached for his folder and read,

"Right, that's settled then," said Pete. "We're getting on. Now about saving up for fireworks."

"We'll all bring what we can as we usually do," said Barbara. "I've got a bit of money in my savings box already that I can bring. Who shall be treasurer?"

"Better vote for one," said Pete. He took out his notebook and tore the page into seven neat strips, and handed a strip to each person. "Everyone got a pencil?" he asked.

"You haven't, Pam? Well, take mine for a minute. Now, write down the person you think would be a good treasurer—someone to hold the money for us, and keep it safe, and count it each time we bring any. They'll have to keep the figures in a book, so that we know what we've got and who brought it. Ready? Write the name

down then of the one you want. It must be someone good at figures, of course. We don't want a muddle made of our money." They
all sucked or chewed their pencils, and frowned. A good treasurer?
One who could manage figures well? One who would not make a
muddle? (5)

"That was taken from a children's book, and I think it's basic internal controls at their best: agreed roles and responsibilities, documentation that is verified, a record of income and accountability,
segregation of duties, a review and monitoring committee, custo-
dial security, and frequent checks. Moreover, there is a key objective of saving to buy fireworks. How about that! Do you remember
our simple model, CEFI, of control involving clear and effective
procedures, flexibility, and innovation?"

"Not bad," Bill chuckled. "I do remember reading Enid Blyton's
The Famous Five, but not *The Secret Seven.*"

Bill tried an ice cold drink called Supligen, which he sipped
slowly. "What's your definition of control then?" he asked between sips.

"To be honest. I feel it's a cop-out to use a basic definition of
control along with a hundred-point criterion, because in the end, it
becomes too general and meaningless. I could easily argue that
controls are mechanisms to ensure objectives are achieved. If I had
to pull a list from my back pocket, it would read that they should be
flexible, clear, economical, understood, communicated, useable,
adaptable, agreed, accepted, meaningful, fit the culture, based on
exception reporting, supported by information systems, promote
excellence, be promulgated by top management, protect assets,
promote compliance, secure value for money, be in line with defined risk criteria, and so on and so forth. The problem is that
this list doesn't really add to our understanding, because it's only
a series of catchy words. More than that, it's a turnoff. It sounds
boring and people can't tune into it at all. What I want is a sexy

way of promoting controls. Something that clicks with everyone. This is my mission. To be honest, Bill, I really can't write the book until I've cracked this problem."

Jack continued, "I guess the starting place for controls is to decide what you really want to do. Everything else flows from this. I've noted a famous quote from Winston Churchill that illustrates this point. He said in one famous speech:

> You ask "what is our aim?" I can answer in one word: "Victory!" Victory at all costs, victory in spite of all terror, victory however long and hard the road may be: for without victory there is no survival.(6)

"This basic aim set the foundation for the many years of struggle that was the Second World War. I guess that control is about having an aim, making sure you have the means to achieve it, and managing those risks that can impair your ability to get there. It's a driving force that moves you in the right direction, but it sets your energies within a framework of policies, guidelines, ethical rules, and accountability. It seeks to promote achievement but also depends on compliance with these policies. Also, it should provide safeguards against fraud and corruption and make sure value for money is secured as we strive toward excellence. It's concentric in nature as the circles starting from the middle consist of you, your team, your section, and then your department, all bound together by communication and values. Right at the heart of these circles is your soul, where control starts—from self-control: self-awareness and an appreciation of what the organization is trying to achieve and how you can best contribute to this task. I've put this in Figure 2.5."

Bill listened, laughed, then said, "You ever thought about becoming a preacher? Okay, so your view of control is as a holistic concept, rather than an additional process superimposed over business processes."

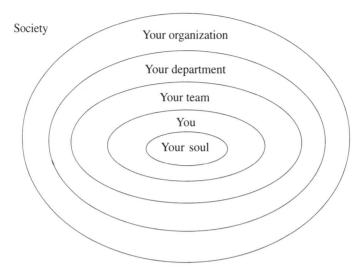

Figure 2.5 Concentric self-control.
(See also Figures 6.10 and 7.6)

Jack nodded and said, "Yes, which is why I believe you merely need to facilitate the spread of this concept throughout your organization and develop these control circles. The problem is that control starts with self-control, and stress is very dangerous because it results from seeking control where it's not actually possible. This equation cannot be reconciled so the body cannot feel comfortable with the mind."

The stilted silence that followed convinced Jack to leave this topic for a later stage in their discussions and he added, "Right. Let's get back to basics. Most agree that control is based around three key concepts. That is,

1. It's a process that runs throughout the organization.
2. It's based around people and how they behave at work.
3. It can only provide reasonable, not absolute, assurance that objectives will be achieved.

"You know, the term control was first used by the certified public accountants who broke it down into accounting and administrative controls. It's now embedded in the Foreign Corrupt Practices Act for publicly owned companies. Some consider that controls are required to achieve objectives, whereas others take a narrower view where it's needed to achieve what we call control objectives. That is, achieving efficiency, effectiveness, compliance, accountability, and regularity as well as our set goals. These and similar themes run throughout the control debate. Apart from giving a few examples of basic accounting controls, most published material doesn't seem to go much further. The problem is that this material doesn't capture the imagination of busy managers. Anyway, enough of this. We need to digress and concentrate on the idea of systems, because the next part of our route takes us into the journey through systems theory."

A nearby craft shop caught Bill's eye. He stared at the sculptures and paintings under the watchful gaze of the shop assistant who suggested they finish their meal and come and view the goods in more detail. After several minutes spent negotiating a suitable price for an oil painting depicting a peaceful river scene of the north coast of the island, they embarked on the second leg of the journey.

ON TO BOSTON AND SYSTEMS

They were on the long winding road again, through the bypass toward Oracabessa. "Right." Jack began. "Your organization suffers from poor systems of internal control."

Bill replied, "Well, yes. But the consultants call this a poor *system* of internal control, implying that only one such system flows through the organization. Do you think this is feasible?"

Jack responded, "There's one difficulty about systems theory that we need to get around from the start, which is, that systems can comprise a whole or a million subsets, depending on how you wish to view them."

Bill was pretty much getting used to these open-ended comments from Jack. This idea was so far from his view, which, in the final analysis, demanded a straightforward answer to all things. It was all very well floating around a tropical paradise armed with a bunch of generalized theories, but Bill needed real solutions to real problems, not just lots of hot air.

"My view of systems," Jack continued, "is that it starts from the soul, which is deep within the person and all other things are related to comprise a whole. That whole is defined as such for that moment in time, and changes through time, and from different perspectives. Corporate communication then binds these fragments into the whole that is the organization."

Noticing Bill's look of skepticism, Jack stopped and thought about the best way to get his message across. "Bill, let's explore some of the things that have been written about this subject."

This was the cue for Bill to start leafing through the reference file on his lap. Jack stopped at a gas station and went inside for chewing gum while the attendant filled the tank. Bill took the opportunity to select the references that were filed under the heading "Systems."

As they got back on the road, Bill read through the quotes. "Right. Here's one from Harold Geneen:

> The soul of a business is a curious alchemy of needs, desires, greed, and gratifications mixed together with selflessness, sacrifices, and personal contributions far beyond material rewards.(7)

"I guess this makes it a little difficult to set a system of control within this hotbed of emotions."

Jack retorted, "But an organization is a series of emotions—controlled emotions in the sense that they're directed toward business goals. Emotion drives one's energy, and energy in turn drives the business."

Jack concentrated on a series of tight bends, not helped by a huge oncoming tanker that swept past them at great speed. He removed the habitual grimace that he wore when negotiating a difficult stretch of road and continued, "You get the point. Systems are all interrelated. I've scribbled an image of this idea in the file as Figure 2.6. These systems bind and tie in everything that goes on in an organization from start to finish. My current interest is in SuperString theory, which suggests that the entire universe is connected by an invisible thread that has a complicated dependency chain that both affects it and allows it to affect other things. Therefore we must view an organization as a series of systems. Control is about getting these system components to recognize their respective responsibilities for contributing to the organization and managing risk in a defined manner. We cannot simply set standards and get a team to look for compliance with these standards. Most externally imposed control is resisted. I think there's a philosophical debate over the ethical rights of a person or, for that matter, a company to exert control over its people. Do you remember you used the dictionary to define the controller as a person who directs, regulates, or restrains? What we really need is control facilitation that ensures people are able to direct, regulate, or restrain

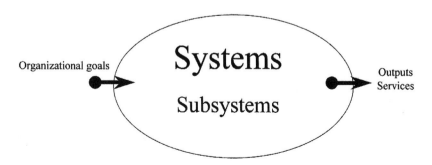

Figure 2.6   Where systems fit in.

themselves. They need to understand why control is important, how it can be achieved, and how one's role relates to others, or how one's processes relate to other processes and wider corporate procedures. One aspect of systems theory that I find particularly useful is that of synergy."

Bill said, "You mean the old two plus two equals five routine? Meshing individual sections into one and coming out with a super organization."

"Correct, although I can see you're not convinced. I explain this concept by pointing out that the components of a motorcycle lying on the ground are each valuable in their own right. They cost money to buy and store, obviously some parts more so than others. But, having put the individual components together in line with the manufacturer's recommendations, we have something entirely different. We have a transportation system, capable of taking people and things from one place to another. This is synergy at work, where the end result is of much greater value than the sum of the individual components as in Figure 2.7.

"There's more. We need a rider, fuel, a road system of sorts, a destination, knowledge of the route, insurance, good riding conditions, and so on for the transportation system to be of any use. We may have all these things, but if the rider feels tired and cannot operate the bike, it won't go anywhere. Or if the rider hasn't been taught how to ride, there will be problems. In fact, the number of things (that is, systems or subsystems) that underpin the transport concept are infinite. If the rider carries an important report a hundred miles and then finds that the document could have been E-mailed in a matter of seconds, the journey has little value. If the objective is to get the report to the client as soon as possible, then this goal has not been met by using the motorcycle. If the objective is to get the client to act on the report, then the rider may deliver it and present its findings, which may make e-mail inappropriate. In this case, the use of the motorcycle is justified and the systems ob-

Figure 2.7 Transport system.

jective is met. It all depends on what you're trying to achieve and how you go about it. The owner of a company may wish to use the motorcycle because he just enjoys the ride and the excitement of biking. It's his company and if this is what he wants to do, the objectives have been met. Again, it depends on your definition of a transport system. Risks exist in terms of what may go wrong or what could be done better. One risk is that the bike may break down halfway there. Controls are part of the way these risks are managed, once they have been isolated. In this example, controls would include things like a planned program of maintenance.

"The concept of entropy is also important. Entropy is the tendency for systems to decay and fall out of synchronization with their environment if not maintained. Whenever an organization becomes inefficient and starts to fail, it's because of this principle. Systems of internal control are similar. They must reflect the realities of organizational life and so be relevant and up-to-date. If not, they too will fail. Using the motorcycle example, it may be better to stop relying on maintenance work and buy new motorcycles each year because of the need for reliability. Or it may be that traffic congestion makes biking an inefficient mode of communication.

"A system is what you want it to be. If it's meaningful to you, then it's important, and this in its own right means that you see it as a system. To someone else, your system may be seen as a small part of a wider system, because it has less importance to that person. This can be seen clearly when you ask someone what is most important about their job. It may be to get rid of each customer as quickly as possible and deal with the next one, rather than provide a quality service. The greatest challenge to organizations is to get staff to adopt common perceptions and so ensure their efforts are coordinated and have meaning all around. This has to happen because of the nature of systems' interdependencies. If the mailroom doesn't work, then our manual correspondence fails to arrive, causing problems. If the mailroom is staffed by incompetents, checks may get lost and important documents may disappear or be interfered with. Most organizations don't see the value of the mailroom and the way it interfaces with the rest of the organization. This principle applies equally to electronic communications systems. Again, an agreed definition of systems, processes, and links would greatly assist an organization's efficiencies. We would still have different perceptions of reality, but we need to understand each other's personal systems before we can move on. Have you ever had a conversation with someone yet it feels as if you're both talking about two different things? That's what I mean about different perceptions of what's important."

Bill responded, "But didn't you say that control is about setting systems objectives and achieving them?"

Jack looked thoughtful, "Yes, but business is about moving through the process of achieving objectives. Life isn't based on a zero-one formula where we have either succeeded or not. It's a journey that moves us toward our objectives with no natural start and finish."

Bill interjected, "This makes it a bit hard to set up performance appraisal if we need to set targets, measure the extent to which they have been met, and so judge performance."

"Fine," Jack agreed, "but the focus should be on where you're going in terms of performance and not what you were able to do last year or last month. What we've learned from last year's experiences is important only to the extent that it might help us meet new challenges. So we should be proud of what we've achieved but eager to reach new targets."

Bill was listening with his eyes half closed. After a few minutes, he stirred and mumbled, "We can view control as a complex concept but surely we must try to keep it simple. The mind likes to work on one basic thing at a time. That's why most people get turned off by the subject."

Now wide awake, Bill continued speaking, "You've been playing around with ideas and viewing systems as ongoing relationships. But how would you view the staff performance appraisal scheme within this concept of systems? I'm having real problems trying to establish a corporate scheme. People are very skeptical and I overheard someone suggesting that it would be used as a way of deciding who to get rid of when we implement budget cuts later on in the year."

Jack glanced at Bill. "I told you that this journey is *not* about simple solutions," he said. "I can't be pressed into this."

"Just as we make progress you back off," Bill interjected. "I still think that consultants spend their time writing reports that really make little difference at all. If they can't provide solutions, then why employ them?"

"That's unfair. Anyway I'm no longer a consultant, at least not for a bit, so you can't use that argument with me. Look, Bill, the key point with systems theory is that you can't consider one corporate issue, such as performance without looking into the organization as a whole. Simple solutions are called quick fixes. Check out that reference from Ralph Kilmann:

> A single approach that attempts to "fix" a problematic situation by influencing only one point and inadvertently or purposely ignoring all the interrelated aspects is doomed to fail.(8)

"This is where I think you may be going wrong. Being in control is like a balancing act, where you weigh everything and use performance appraisal to help drive through the required changes. Remember performance appraisal acts as a control that helps manage the risk of poor performance from staff. Unfortunately, it's essentially about communication systems. If managers cannot tell staff what they think is important, how they're doing, and help them in this task, then it'll fail. It's also about mutual trust and the ability of corporate management to set clear direction. Again it goes back to people and how they behave. Some argue that people act in a way that brings them closer to their perceived goals. The problem is getting everyone to understand and work toward the same goals—not an easy task. Again, much comes down to good communication. You start establishing performance appraisal schemes by reviewing your communications and ethical values and ensuring they work. These are all systems in their own right and together form a corporate whole. As I said, good performance appraisal is a control, as long as it fits in with the organization's cultural base."

"Okay," Bill said. "What about an automated documentation system that failed as a computer development project? What do you think went wrong there?"

"It's not possible to diagnose a problem without carrying out a review, you know that. What I can say is that these big projects won't work unless top management is behind them and users are fully involved in deciding what's required and how it's delivered. Controls over the project in the form of set procedures are also essential. People will support a project where they see clear benefits. Document management systems will appear where the organization pushes for efficiency and people feel comfortable working within a paperless environment, while being dependent on computerized systems. Where these risks aren't isolated and dealt with, these new initiatives may be resisted. You'll probably find that your document management systems fell short somewhere along the line. Probably it relates to an overall lack of a control culture that we know is a problem in your company. It's mainly due to people being scared to take responsibility for fear of being penalized. This fear isn't helped by adopting a compliance environment. You said that your board was reluctant to make a statement about internal controls and, unfortunately, I imagine that this position would set the tone for the rest of the organization."

"What about fraud and corruption, Jack? Any advice here?"

"Let's leave that subject for another day," Jack replied. "I don't want to keep going on about systems of control and systems theory. This subject is found in all good textbooks on management and auditing. What I want to get across is a basic view of human activity. This is, that systems both push and pull. Managers use both carrot and stick and our world is full of driving and resisting forces. We have problems working out how to use systems processes because of these inherent conflicts. We want to push ahead at work and try to avoid the pitfalls, but there's always some risk involved. This was well put by Blake and Moulton in their management grid(9), where they assessed whether managers were more concerned about the welfare of their staff or the system outputs. Where they can achieve both, we get what's called 9.9 managers—a great basis for success. But, we cannot always have it both ways. One view of management is that it's about managing business processes and then managing the problems these processes cause employees. That is, driving forward and solving problems on the way. We'll come back time and time again to this problem. I'm convinced that it comes back to the fundamental conflict between science and art. The science of control is straightforward and is based around our control chart. The problem is that the very opposite of what you want to happen happens where you adopt this approach too rigidly. The art of control recognizes this but veers toward chaos where staff reinvent processes in a search for success. I think chaos is defined as the random repatterning of systems as a response to forces that support change and innovation. To say that it equates to good control is a somewhat strange argument. Your compliance team solution falls on the scientific side of control.

"The organic adaptive model is now gaining ground under the weight of the many critics of the traditional command-control models that don't allow us to cater for change and enlightened management. I argue that this balancing act requires a great deal of skill and doesn't sit well with the growing call for better corporate governance. We'll revisit this issue many times before your vacation is over."

Bill threw back his head and laughed, "What on earth do you mean by the organic adaptive models and command-control ones? How on earth can I write a standards manual and talk about the organic adaptive model to my staff? They'll think I'm mad. It's too difficult and boring for your average everyday employee."

"Point taken. What I mean is the sexy model of control. The *can-do will-do* model. You know what I mean, Bill."

"Well," replied Bill, "you'll have your work cut out to convince employees that control can be a sexy word," and laughed even louder.

Bill settled down and watched the landscape of the parish of St. Mary flash past, through Port Maria, along past the huge banana plantations and then into Annotto Bay, a busy town centered around the local police station.

"We can get your mangoes further down in Windsor Castle," said Jack.

After a further fifteen minutes drive, they arrived at a small grocery store and Jack asked the whereabouts of Miss Luna. Shortly thereafter, a small elderly woman emerged from the back of the store and Jack introduced her to Bill. Miss Luna wore a large-brimmed straw hat and had an abundance of white hair visible around the sides and back of her hat. Looking at her weathered face and lines around her eyes, Bill assumed she was around seventy-five or eighty years old. Despite her obvious years, she moved quickly but gracefully. As they all headed toward the fruit market near the town center, Jack explained that they were after sweet mangoes.

"Miss Luna, how are the mangoes today?" asked Jack, trying to keep up with her.

"We'll soon find out," replied Miss Luna with a smile.

As they walked past the various stalls, they followed Miss Luna's example and studied the fruit and inquired about the price. Jack asked, "What about these mangoes, Miss Luna?"

"You have time!" came the response.

"What about these?" grinned Bill as he held up his selection.

"You have time!" again came the response from Miss Luna as she wrinkled her nose and marched quickly on through the market traders.

Walking alongside Jack, Bill whispered, "What does she mean by that?"

Jack, looking sorry for Bill every time he had to replace a bag of mangoes that looked reasonable to him, laughed and whispered back, "It means it's too expensive or the mangoes are no good. My control over buying mangoes is to get Miss Luna to vet them and choose the best deal. She's respected locally and is, in my opinion, one of the best negotiators on this side of the island."

Eventually they found a good buy and left Miss Luna with many thank-yous and handshakes.

"You've just seen a system at work," continued Jack as they got back in the car. "That is the acquisition of mangoes from start to finish. Bill, view this as a system. Consider the inputs—you, me, Miss Luna, and money. The process is finding, viewing, and negotiating for the fruit. The output is the fruit itself and maybe an enjoyable time spent shopping. You know that most things can be viewed as a system. The system follows a defined order: We meet, agree what to buy, find the market, select the fruit, buy it, then take it home. That's the other point about a system; we can break it down into a process with clear steps. Enough of that, Bill. Let's get through Port Antonio and into Boston. There's still some way to go before we get there."

Some time later, they arrived at Boston Beach and ate spicy jerk pork, washed down with a soda. The beach had the most glorious white sand that Bill had ever seen, set against a picture postcard blue sea. Unlike the North Coast, the water was quite rough and Bill could imagine a good day's surfing on a day like today. The nearby jerk center looked like a giant outdoor barbecue, with groups of men using long machetes to cut up large slices of pork that were cooking on wooden slats placed over the burning coals. The return trip was quite relaxing as the car swept back through the sights and sounds of the colorful green countryside. After several minutes, Jack, looking thoughtful, said, "We need to talk through three more issues to conclude our discussion on control concepts. They are:

1. Controls should be directed at high-risk areas.
2. Control in the form of a foreign body.
3. Control frameworks."

Bill didn't bother to try and guess what these issues were about but stared straight ahead and continued to enjoy the scenery. "Jack," he said suddenly, "stop the car a minute. This bay is absolutely wonderful."

Jack stopped the car halfway down a hill as a classic view of a sandy cove with palm trees arching toward the blue sea appeared in front of them. On one side, hibiscus and oleander bushes added color to the hill. On the other side, detached houses, some painted white, some pink, were safely out of reach of the sea. What struck Bill was the effect of the white and purple bougainvillea vines that cascaded down the boundary walls of the houses. The profusion of color was breathtaking. It looked so peaceful. Bill sat on a large boulder and watched a group of older men sitting on the edge of a fishing boat anchored on the sand, close to the sea and listened to the barely audible voices that drifted up toward them. "Who needs business controls when you have all this tranquillity," said Bill.

"That's the point, Bill. This is a picture of control. Once things are in their right place, you can relax and stop worrying. It makes it all worthwhile. Anyway, let's get back on the road. There's still a way to go."

RISK AND CONTROL

Back on the road and making good progress, Jack continued, "Let's get back to my points on control. They are related to risk and views concerning the form that control takes. The first issue . . . ."

Bill finally took his cue to take part in some more verbal sparring. "Yes," he said, "risks. My reading suggests that controls are directed toward areas that represent high risk. High risks being the dollar amount at risk times the likelihood of this amount being lost or depleted.

"For instance," he continued, "if a purchasing system is established, the system objective would be to acquire and pay for supplies and services used by the organization. The control objectives would be concerned with doing this in a way that promotes value for money, compliance with procedure, and deterring fraud and corruption." Bill had remembered this idea from an auditing book he'd read, when he first came up against the control problem. He went on, "We then establish the type of risks that may mean control objectives won't be achieved, say for example high pressure selling, and then tackle these by the use of controls. Or what our auditors might call control mechanisms. Risk then drives controls and in this way real problems are dealt with."

"Excellent." said Jack. "There's not much to add to your analysis, but I have a slightly different slant to this equation. Let's start with the diagram I developed in Figure 2.8.

"The model you've described Bill, means controls are located at point A. Here, we tackle high-risk areas that can be controlled through the use of sound control mechanisms. We may go on to

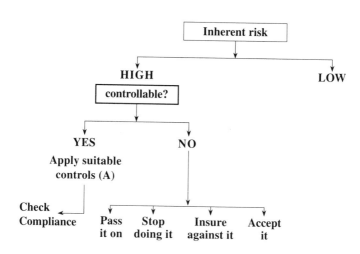

Figure 2.8 A model of risk.

make sure these controls are being complied with. However, my view is that the entire risk management model in the diagram is in itself a key control over managing an organization and part of its control framework. The perceived risk rating as high or low should also be subject to control, as this rating will change as new information or altered circumstances dictate. Control also needs to be exerted over the strategies whereby we seek to contract out problems or insure against them happening and so on. These all form part of the overall control process and not just the various control techniques applied at point A, such as a central point for contact with suppliers to prevent pressure selling. So we adopt a wider view of controls as something over and above a series of one-off techniques in the form of an overall control framework.

"The other thing," continued Jack, "is that risk assessment includes considering the opportunities that may be taken advantage of. So, if we identify a risk area, we have three main options as I've put in Figure 2.9.

"So you see, Bill, it may be that we wish to push for more risk in the form of new opportunities, rather than just see it as something that's bad and needs reducing through better controls. It may be that we've got it about right and the middle option, accept the risk, makes good sense. Or, we may need more controls in place. This balance is so important and it's not simply about having contingency

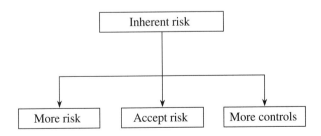

Figure 2.9   Risk: The three options.

plans to cover us when everything goes wrong. You know, too much risk is bad as it means things will probably go wrong. It's what I would call pure gambling. Too much control is just as bad because there will be no progress, just stagnation. Accepting the risk means keeping an eye on things and making sure we know enough about the issues and changes. What we think is low risk may actually be a high risk that we don't know enough about. The federal sentencing guidelines mean we are exposed if we don't have suitable controls that help prevent, detect, and report crime. Good control against risk makes it less likely that we, that is the organization, will be punished where our people have been involved in crime. The risk of not having due diligence and not adhering to our controls may not be fully recognized by our executives."

Bill did not object to this discussion. "Okay," he said, "point taken. I need to get this into my standards manual. But what about your second point concerning views on control as a foreign body?"

CONTROL AS A FOREIGN BODY

"The other point that I think we need to consider is that many people see control as a foreign body superimposed over business processes. For example, many still state that it's all about information. If we give managers the right information, then they will always be in control. Again, I believe there's nothing wrong with these views, it's just that I'd add more bits to make it more dynamic."

Bill was obviously not taking all of this in. "What's your problem here, Jack?" he asked, frowning.

"Well, I've developed two separate models of control to illustrate these differences. Let me see, you have them in the file under Figures 2.10 and 2.11.

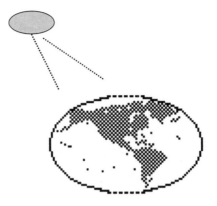

Figure 2.10 Control beam.
(See also Figures 2.11 and 6.7)

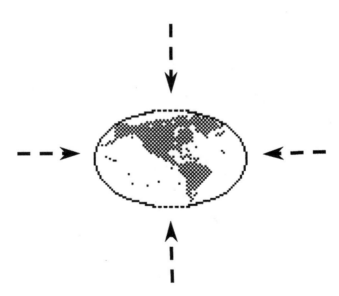

Figure 2.11 Gravitational model.
(See also Figures 2.10 and 6.7)

"In Figure 2.10, control is seen as a foreign body beaming down information on Earth, or for our purpose, the organization. This model highlights problems, noncompliance, and general trends. We set up this satellite control and it tells us what's going on. A process that's seen to be superimposed over an operation. The Foreign Corrupt Practices Act of 1977 requires companies registered with the Securities and Exchange Commission to have systems of internal control. This is a requirement but shouldn't just be seen as such. We should see good controls as naturally beneficial. Figure 2.11 comes closer to this concept.

"In my preferred model, control is more of an invisible but dynamic force that's akin to a gravitational pull over planet Earth (i.e., the organization). It instills order and respective relationships between components that sit on the surface of the planet. It's internalized and in one sense not noticed, as it pulls things together and stops people from spinning off in all directions or disappearing into space, never to be seen again. I know what you're going to say, and I agree, people still want to jump, swim, fly, and fight gravity. They even want to break the bounds of gravity and travel to other planets. This is fine, but gravity is still the principal force and structured efforts to break free simply reinforce its importance. As such, control becomes invisible and dynamic and affects us all in a natural way that we don't even notice."

The miles whizzed by and as if by mutual consent, they both fell silent and enjoyed the rural scenery.

After some time Bill said, "I appreciate your point that control isn't a device, it's a concept that has no right or wrong answer. But, I really must get something more concrete before we leave this discussion. You suggest that being in control is an art and not a mechanical matter that can be set out through a defined checklist and a fixed model. You feel that it's invisible but dynamic, ever present perhaps. Nonetheless, I feel that the day would be incomplete if we didn't form some sort of concrete model and framework that could

48

be used to capture the essence of control. Unfortunately, my personality type needs this result to function; so I can control the idea of controls, if you see what I mean."

Jack gave this idea some thought as he negotiated the winding roads. "Okay," he finally said. "Let's take it from the top. There are many useful models of control including what we've called the control chart and the feedback loop. You know, where we set standards, review performance, and obtain feedback on whether the standards have been met. There's also a criterion that sets a framework for control that we listed earlier. My study of control is like a journey, viewing the subject as an art, not a science. I've no final solution and that isn't the point anyway. The current trend is toward downsizing, empowerment, increased delegation, process reengineering, and coaching as a replacement for supervisory management. These trends give a different control perspective, where old command/control models based on top down instructions are being replaced by more fluid ones. Superimposed over this is the constant change factor that means past performance and past activities are no longer good measures of future success. The upside is that newer, interactive information systems mean there's less delay in getting the right information for decision making. Against this background, the only real control model we can use is one of self-control.

"All else moves too fast for systems to follow staff around and spy on them much as a closed circuit TV system might. One interesting model I can give you of embedded control is where each business unit manager is required to understand and apply what I call a managerial control system, a series of processes that together form a complete system comprised of interlinked subsystems. It's in the file as Figure 2.12.

"Here, directors, senior business unit managers, line managers, team leaders, staff, in fact, all employees are expected to hold clear objectives and put together a strategy (based on effective

Figure 2.12   Managerial control system.
(See also Figures 4.1, A.4, and D.1)

decision making) for achieving these objectives. They then need to ensure that an appropriate mechanism is used for employing staff or other resources that fall under their responsibilities. The human resources should be secured and developed in the best way possible to work to the stated objectives, and this is where procedures come in as a defined way of performing and reviewing the work that this strategy entails. The operational process itself must be managed so that it adheres to quality, security, and procedural standards. Marketing ensures that the product or service is available to and meets the needs of users and stakeholders. Superimposed over these processes are information and communication systems that give feedback and let people know what's going on and what decisions are being made. Innovation, leadership, and motivational and change management techniques would be employed as parts of the driving forces that make this model work. If everyone in an organization were trained to adopt this model, or parts of the model that relate to their responsibilities, then the organization would be in control. That's not to say that the uncertainties that confront all organizations and processes would not exist and there would be no problems or mistakes. These would also have to be managed. But it does mean that a basic system of control would be in place and ready to be applied. We can ask for nothing more and this is what the board would report on in any annual report on internal controls."

Luckily Bill had not fallen asleep but was listening with interest to these remarks. He eventually asked, "Do you have no time at all for some principles that could be applied to control concepts?"

Jack relented, "We can have a go at this if you like. Let's list some of the examples of more basic control standards:

"**1.** We need good *segregation of duties* where necessary. Having said this, empowerment means not separating tasks for artificial reasons."

Bill glanced at Jack and asked, "How would you define segregation of duties?"

Jack replied, "We're coming into Buff Bay. Let's stop for some Coco bread. We can have this bread with fried fish later on. I tell you what—you buy a few of these."

Bill went into the bakery, paid the cashier, secured a receipt, and on producing it, received his Coco bread from one of the store workers at the main counter. Jack continued on where he had left off, "You've just witnessed segregation of duties where cash handling is separated from stock movement (i.e., the stocking and handing over of the various baked products). This system means the manager can reconcile the receipts for the day with the movement of cakes, bread, and so on. It also means that the shop helpers have no contact with cash. Cash goes to the cashier only. It's a basic example, but segregation is essentially about not allowing one person to control an at-risk process. An at-risk process here involves the movement of cash and stock from start to finish. In this case the shop manager has decided that the cash is at risk if taken by the baking staff and not a dedicated cashier.

"If, in the bakery you just visited, each of the workers baked bread, stored it, sold it, and received cash for the bread, there'd be no way to ensure these transactions were being accounted for properly. The owner would never be sure his resources were being used properly or that he'd received all the cash due to him." Jack went on, "Let's continue the list.

"**2.** We may need to seek *authorization* of important transactions that have a high value. The act of authorizing brings out another concept, that of internal check, since another person will get involved where necessary, to ensure the transaction is correct and proper. In the bread shop the receipt you got from the cashier authorized you to collect the bread you paid for.

"**3.** *Security* is another key control where we keep unauthorized persons away from valuable items, or for that matter, information as well. Physical security is self-explanatory, whereas logical security is used by computerized systems, where say, passwords and other devices are needed to access the various databases. Again, staff other than the cashier can't access the cash register and you can see that the store itself is protected by the security grill between the staff and customers, which acts as a preventive control.

"**4.** *ID codes* log the person who accesses a computerized system, and that brings into play the concept of audit trails. Where possible, we trace who did what in any transaction. Physical access devices can also log individuals. We can then get reports that show whether the patterns are regular, or if necessary, carry out investigations into someone's activities, if we later find problems to do with regularity. Go back to the receipt that you were given. It contains the initials of the cashier and is countersigned by the person giving out the bread. So we could trace this transaction back to these two people if we wanted to. A detective control.

"**5.** *Verification* is another important concept that depends on being able to check that something that should be there is there. Stock checks, inventory reconciliations, inspections, asset checks, and regular callbacks for assets used outside the office mean we have control over attractive and portable items. Cash-ups may be seen as a form of verification, where we ensure the money we should have taken does exist and agrees with our records. Again we can guess that the shop will carry out stock checks on the bread and other foodstuff, perhaps at the end of each working day.

"**6.** *Control totals* can be used to aggregate transactions and compare them with a separately held total to trace the movement of transactions through a system to ensure that they're present and correct. The cash register probably incorporates this type of control.

"**7.** *Supervisory review* is another good control. We ask that managers and supervisors satisfy themselves that work is up to standard before it goes out. The way this is done is up to them but we can set standards in this respect. Organizations such as yours with poor disciplinary records normally have failings in this aspect of management. Either managers don't know what work is done so they can't review their people's work, or they just don't care. You notice how the bakery manager was present in the shop, essentially, keeping an eye on things and helping staff if they're having any problems.

"These are only very basic examples and if I were to discuss ethics, good human resource management practices, information systems, and so on, I would simply be repeating what's in the managerial control system (MCS) that I described earlier. I've put together lists setting out attributes, risk, and best practice on each aspect of the MCS in Appendix A of the file. Some call these directive controls in that they drive the business forward as best they can.

"If we put these things together and direct them toward high-risk areas, they form what can be called a system of internal control. More than anything, we would want to establish a control culture where people in the team want to get things right."

Bill was experiencing an overload of information. He made no response to Jack other than to nod his head slowly and smile in basic agreement with these words. Well, you did ask, Jack thought to himself.

They fell silent as they listened to the reggae music coming from the radio. Shortly after, they stopped at a rum bar in Port Maria, where Jack introduced Bill to several friends who insisted on buying them drinks.

CONTROL FRAMEWORKS

Back on the road again, Jack asked, "Bill. You okay?" while tapping Bill's arm to get his attention, "Let's get one more thing in the bag today. Have you got anything in your standards manual on control frameworks?"

"Let me see . . . not really. I guess we need to beef it up anyway. You know there's quite a lot to cover to sell the control concept to my people. That is, without putting them off at all."

"There's still a bit missing," Jack said. "We need to talk about my third point, frameworks that can be used to cover the entire organization. We've already mentioned the managerial control system. Anyhow, the two most popular models are called COSO (Figure 2.13) and CoCo (Figure 2.14). It won't take long. These models have been developed to cover the infrastructure and culture that should be in place to underpin the concept of control. The people who most need them, that is, executive management, tend to ignore them whereas people like accountants, who are generally well versed in control culture tend to understand them better. This is a

Figure 2.13   The COSO model.

shame. Again, it goes back to the view that controls are a boring subject. Certainly, it's really hard to persuade busy executives to take an interest."

Bill pursed his lips and assumed a rather pleading tone, "Jack. Is there really a way of getting the control message across in an interesting way? I've got to get these ideas in my manual and it's not easy. I myself quite like talking about this subject, but how do I get the material down in a way that impacts my organization? You know, the ordinary operational workers and line management."

"It's a challenge all right and it's what's stopping me from writing my book," Jack said. "Anyway, let's get the control frameworks down on tape. COSO was prepared by the Committee of Sponsoring Organizations of the Treadway Commission(10) some years ago. The framework they developed consisted of five main components that together make up the control infrastructure common to most organizations. It's in Figure 2.13.

"Imagine the owners of the bread shop back there asking whether they've got the right control environment (or culture) in place; do people, starting from the managers, really care about getting things right? They would then ask whether an assessment of risk has taken place and so sort out where problems are likely to affect the business. They would then go on to manage these risks and establish control activities where need be, say directed at the movement of cash and stock and toward good customer care. They would also ask whether they have the right sort of information to judge whether controls are working. Finally, there would need to be a monitoring mechanism to ensure the owners and investors can rely on management reports and accounts on the business. This is control in its widest sense.

"CoCo is a model devised by the Canadian Institute of Chartered Accountants(11) that sees control as an experience that moves one forward in terms of learning and progressing through a cycle of setting objectives, that is, a purpose, ensuring capability and commitment to this task, then monitoring, learning, and adapting as a process of continuous improvement. The learning element of CoCo in Figure 2.14 makes it a really dynamic concept that's becoming quite popular.

"These frameworks are really useful in viewing the control concept at a corporate level. You'll need to put summaries of them in your new manual. So long as the key components of the chosen models are in place, the board can review and report on them. Over and above this should sit an independent audit committee

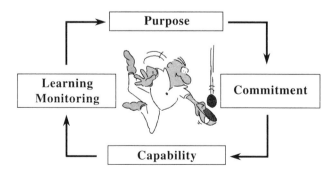

Figure 2.14   The CoCo model.

that can oversee the effectiveness of the applied control framework. This is all part of the monitoring role, to ensure the organization is meeting its obligations in this respect. I guess this falls in line with getting control on the boardroom agenda, which isn't such a bad thing. In the United Kingdom, the 1990s saw the Cadbury report, which provided a great deal of material on the role of directors, shareholders, the board, audit committee, and some of the components of good governance. Again there's a lot of really useful material here aimed at senior directors of companies listed on the London stock exchange. Back home our public companies are also required to have proper systems of internal control. In one sense, the board are sold on the idea of control because they are responsible. Accountants and auditors are trained in this matter and so have no problems here. There are other people in the risk business, say, specialist staff such as insurance, health and safety, and information technology (IT) security managers, project managers, and legal compliance officers who tend to appreciate the importance of risk and control. It's all the other people who work for an organization, including managers at all levels, who are left in the dark. They get no training, no one tells them about control, and they tend to view it as a specialist subject. Sorry, Bill, I'm getting on my high horse again. You must be tired. Bill?"

Jack saw that Bill had drifted off and was quietly snoring with his head tucked into the gap between the headrest and the car window. Yes, it could be a tiring topic thought Jack and how on earth could he write an entire book on business controls when even interested people like Bill fell asleep when it was being discussed? What to do, what to do? Jack had left the States to concentrate on this book on controls and so far had produced exactly nothing. How could he get the message across? The message was important, he knew that. But how could he get it down in an interesting way?

Both men spent the rest of the journey in silence. Bill with a fixed smile on his lips as the drinks and music combined to make him feel more relaxed. It started to get dark and Jack opened the car windows and turned off the air-conditioning to let in the cool evening air as the sound of noisy crickets echoed outside the car. Bill was now in a deep and pleasant sleep, while Jack was thinking wistfully about the book that might never be written.

"You're home," said Jack as they drove into Bill's hotel. "Let's have a final drink and agree on the first part of your standards manual. You need to say something about controls, what they are, why they're important, and something about personal responsibility. Control simply means making sure you get to where you need to be without too many problems. Or to put it another way, by recognizing potential problems and ensuring there are procedures to deal with them."

AN EXAMPLE—CONTROLS IN ACTION

"Okay," said Bill, "what you say is really based on theory. There's nothing wrong with this but I need practical examples that I can sell to my staff, of control in action. People just won't read my standards if they can't see how they make their job easier or if it's just too dry and boring. I appreciate your efforts, but you do see my point don't you?"

"Let's get a drink first and then wrap things up. Take out the mangoes you bought today, Bill, and let's have a look at them. I know. How about we use the task of buying mangoes to illustrate control models. What's the objective of this task?"

"Buying mangoes?" ventured Bill, trying to hide his surprise at this question.

"Agreed," said Jack, "but we need to refine this and define what we can call control objectives. That is, buying mangoes that are reasonably priced, taste good, without undue delay, and without undue hassle. We need then to achieve these control objectives to enable us to meet the prime objective, that is buying good mangoes. You know that control objectives tend to revolve around quality, time, and cost in that they try to deal with the inherent conflicts within these three factors. They also cover compliance with procedure, accountability, and protecting assets. So you really also have to consider these things as you go about achieving your objectives. If there were an embargo on buying imported mangoes, we would have to adhere to this ruling. In fact, embedded controls mean that we should really incorporate control objectives within our main goals and restate this as buying good mangoes without too much cost and hassle. We then determine what could go wrong (i.e., the risks to the achievement of these objectives). What could mess us up and how much more could we achieve? We can assess the impact of these risks and how likely they are without controls in place. Then we can work out how to ensure these risks are managed, including more focused controls as one option. That is, where the risks cannot be accepted. I can see you're not convinced, Bill."

"I like it," Bill replied, "It's just that I need a simple way of getting the message across. Ahh. Here comes Ruth now. Ruth, here are the mangoes you wanted. A gift."

Somewhat embarrassed Ruth explained that she could not take gifts from a guest. But, as Jack suggested they could be a gift from him, she eventually accepted the huge bag of mangoes with thanks, and went through to the kitchen saying she would return in a few minutes. The bar was set out in the open and various green plants made it a pleasant place for a quiet drink. A tall coconut tree stood in the middle of the patio, surrounded by potted plants and flowers. The aroma of distant wood fires added to the fragrant night air as Bill sat back waiting for Ruth to return while Jack was at the bar buying their drinks.

"What does Ruth drink, Bigga?" inquired Jack as the tall barman stroked his beard.

"Well. You can get her a bottle of Dragon stout. I know she'll drink that. I'll take out a cold one."

When Ruth joined the two men she had nothing but compliments for the mangoes and the fact that Bill had gone to so much trouble to get them from the other side of the island. As the small talk diminished, Jack rubbed his hands together.

"Ruth," he asked, "do you think buying mangoes is a hard task?"

"Not really. It's just that you have to be careful if you want good ones."

"Okay," continued Jack, "let me take you through a system for buying them. You don't mind, do you, Ruth. It's just that I've been working on some ideas with Bill that we need to finish off. Bill, let me write down a control model we can use in Figure 2.15.

"Can you see what we've done?" asked Jack trying to ward off a series of giggles from both Bill and Ruth, who found the entire exercise rather silly. "I've taken the objective of buying mangoes as a system that entails certain risks. These risks are assessed and managed in a way that makes sense and fits the stakeholders' concerns. Ruth, would you have been disappointed if we'd returned with a huge bag of spoilt mangoes?"

"I guess so," Ruth admitted still trying to take the whole thing seriously. "But you know, it's against company policy for staff to accept gifts from guests. Even if it's for the hotel."

Looking at Bill's crestfallen face, Ruth added quickly, "But thanks anyway Bill, even if they were from Jack."

Bill returned her smile and suddenly felt like a shy teenager.

"Bill," continued Jack. "Can you see what's happening? If you'd set out and simply bought a bag of mangoes, much could have gone wrong. Come on, work with me folks, and stop laughing. You wanted a simple example that brings out the concepts, and this is what we've done. If you multiply the impact scores (1–3) with the likelihood scores (0–1) you get a final risk score or what we call the exposure. The individual devices that we have in the last column of

60

System objective: Buying mangoes

Control objectives: Reasonable price

                          Good quality (undamaged)

                          Without too much delay

                          Without too much hassle

Control objective	Risks	Impact H M L (3) (2) (1)	Likely with no controls (0-1)	Risks managed (score)
Reasonable price	Price inflated artificially	M (2) Prices are low anyway	0.5 Bill and Jack look like tourists	(1.0) Not a big issue. Get an idea of usual price range and then haggle
Good quality (undamaged)	Fruit appears good but is of poor quality	H (3) Guests will complain	0.9 Past experience of poor fruit	(2.7) Major risk. Need outside expertise—Miss Luna
Without too much delay	Good fruit hard to find	L (1) No real time pressure	0.2 Mangoes not hard to find	(0.2) Accept this low-level risk
Without too much hassle	Unpleasant arguments over price	M (2) Supposed to be a vacation	0.3 Most vendors are pleasant	(0.6) Avoid certain traders (e.g., from isolated side roads)

Figure 2.15   Buying mangoes.

the table are individual controls, aimed at the higher risk-score areas. If we put them together into a risk management strategy, it becomes a system of internal control. The entire approach to making these assessments and reporting to you Ruth, as the key stakeholder, is what we can call the control framework."

"A very fruity example, Jack," retorted Bill, getting into the spirit.

Jack continued, "The point is, if we'd bought a bag of rotten mangoes and also got into a distasteful argument with a vendor, we could still use our control framework and risk assessment to show we had done our best, even if it didn't work out in the end. Also, where the cost of controls is too great, then it may be we have to accept the risk anyway. Say we couldn't afford to use a specialist mango buyer, then so be it. No matter how careful you are, there's still some judgment involved and so like all things, it can still go wrong. Or not completely as planned."

"This is great and I see how it all fits together, but how can it help me with my manual?" inquired Bill.

Before Jack could answer Ruth interjected, "Gentlemen. Sorry to be a spoilsport. But I have to get back to work. Tell you what. I'll do a risk assessment of the hotel systems sometime," she said jokingly. "Maybe you can help, Jack." With that, Ruth disappeared back into the office with what sounded like a final giggle as she left the boys to continue their game.

"This is a lot to think about," Bill said.

"I know." Jack replied, "But say in our mangoes example you didn't take a risk-based approach and head office simply issued a procedure for buying fruit. A compliance team may come around and check that you're sticking to the rules. You lose self-assessment and you get overcontrol, which is just as bad as undercontrol. Right, Bill, it's getting late. Let's sort out your manual. What have you got in it so far?"

"Well, the manual mainly consists of material on our financial regulations. You know the rules for making orders, getting new stocks, and things like expenses and travel claims. You know we tend to concentrate on the finances first. There's a little bit on receiving gifts and hospitality and then some material on health and safety, security, and customer care. And then lots of operational stuff."

Jack finished his drink and said, "Fill 'em up please, Bigga."

Bigga brought over the fresh drinks and inquired whether they would want to play dominoes with another pair of customers who sat in the corner.

"No, Bigga," Jack said, "we're all right. We've got work to do. Well, it's not really work as such but it's just that my friend, Bill, relaxes by working. He's a workaholic."

Bill frowned but decided not to rise to the bait.

"Anyway, Bill, the new manual. First, we need to expand our view of controls to get outside of the financial arena. This is old hat. We're used to financial controls and accounting for income and expenditure and auditing it. That's not a big problem. The challenge is when we see systems of internal control as important to corporate business and not just accounting. This is when we make progress. You need to define controls, systems of internal control, being in control in terms of managing risk, and wider control frameworks such as COSO. Then we move on to systems and how work can be viewed as both a system and as part of other systems. Then I think you provide illustrations such as the control charts and buying mangoes. Well, perhaps not mangoes, but something simple that drives home the point. The types of basic controls that we mentioned—remember, supervision, authorization, and so on, can be covered and explained. Then you're more or less there in terms of basic concepts of control."

"Right. Sounds simple," Bill said in a slurred voice as his eyes started to close with sheer weariness. "But, I'll have to rewrite the whole thing," he added.

"Don't worry," Jack went on, "I'll do a presentation pack that covers what we discussed today on concepts of control. I can do it on PowerPoint and you can use it to set the first part of the manual and for control awareness seminars back at work. It won't take me too long. Tomorrow we'll visit Negril and the next part of our journey will take us into the world of office procedures."

Bill agreed. As he said his good nights and armed with a bag full of Coco bread that he had no idea what to do with, he made his way toward his suite.

THREE

Negril and the Art of Using Procedures

After reading this chapter, the reader will be able to appreciate the role of procedures (the accepted way work is performed) and how they are derived from risk assessment to form control standards. Included is a policy on procedures and numerous tips on design, implementation, and review. This chapter can be seen as a self-help guide with all that is needed to get staff to design, document, install, and monitor operational standards.

"GOOD MORNING, BILL." Jack's familiar greeting brought a smile to Bill's lips and he thought about the pattern that had developed between them. Driving, sightseeing, exploring the country's cuisine, and the discussions that had been a feature of each trip so far. Jack continued, "We'll take a trip along the other side of the north coast and visit a seven-mile strip of white-sand beach that contains the beautiful holiday spot called Negril. Have you brought your swimming gear?"

"Oh, yes," Bill confirmed, without bothering to mention the bag he carried with him on each journey containing trunks, towels, a medical kit, various paperbacks, and other items on his checklist of travel gear. Jack would only use this information to support his view that Bill was the last of the control freaks.

"Remind me—what's today's topic of conversation?" Bill asked, rubbing his hands together and trying unsuccessfully to hide a faintly ironic smile.

"Procedures," replied Jack emphatically. "This control is important because people need to operate in an acceptable way and there's much to explore here. You know, doing things right is the key to good control. Even in your private life, you must have a clear way of doing things. Like my old school teacher (Figure 3.1) used to say."

The car pulled out of the hotel parking area and swung along the coast road, this time going in the opposite direction so that the sea was to their right.

Bill, feeling particularly enthused, decided to take the initiative this time and launched into his thoughts on the subject of procedures. Once again, he had been glad that his research into controls had included material on procedures. The consultant's report had made reference to this issue as particularly lacking throughout the organization.

Bill said, "If you like, I can describe my approach and I will probably be able to give you a comprehensive checklist of attributes of good procedures. A model showing attributes and the pros and cons of using procedures in an organization and I believe that will be that. We can put this subject to bed quite quickly and relax for the rest of the trip." He looked at Jack with a sense of triumph and clicked his fingers for emphasis.

"Sounds good enough," Jack agreed. "Before you start, let me test you on something. Do you recall the words, 'There is a lack of formally documented procedures and this issue must be addressed by management to ensure good systems of internal control' . . . ?"

Figure 3.1   Getting into procedures.

Bill turned to the window and watched the white surf spray on the sparkling blue sea. A trick question perhaps. Well, let me see he thought . . . Finally, he said, "That reminds me of the sort of thing the consultant's report on controls said. How do you know this? Have you read the report?" He stopped suddenly, realizing that this question was silly. How could Jack know anything about his company?

Jack replied, "I'm basically repeating what most consultants' reports say at some point. This comment is what we call a throw-away comment. I don't encourage these bland statements because they are meaningless to management. Management agrees with the auditor's comments. The auditor disappears and a year later nothing has happened. I've seen it happen time and time again. In fact, on one high-risk audit, we asked the section manager if we could view his operational procedures, and he said he'd let us have them next week. It turned out that over the weekend he managed to put together a few rough pages setting out how his staff worked and submitted these as his procedures. When I realized this I had a heart-to-heart with him and we spent the remainder of the audit advising him how to prepare and implement good procedures."

"Okay." Bill interrupted, eager to get on with his lecture. "I hear what you're saying and this is fair enough. Now let's return to the model I mentioned earlier. However, before we get to it, I'll argue the importance of procedures." Bill stopped and, licking his lips, realized that this situation was much like being at work and delivering one of the formal presentations that he had become used to performing over the years, the difference being that this task was enjoyable and stress-free.

"Anyhow, let's turn on the tape," Bill continued. "I've noted that work flows in organizations are becoming more and more complicated. At times no one really knows how an entire process works as it crosses sections and departments. My company is working on an initiative whereby managers can come to grips with work flow management. It may be possible to get them to draft diagrams that set out the flows and who is affected, as an aid to understanding, and share this knowledge across sections. Here procedures become important so that people know what they're doing and what goes on elsewhere in the organization. This concept was supposed to be integrated into the automated document management system, until the project crashed. Anyway, where was I? Yes, procedures. Procedures are there to help direct staff and lend consistency to our operational processes. They form the basis for defining activities and I'd like to think they have a key role in the type of internal training programs that the organization uses.

"In your file here, Jack, you have a note about work done by Carolyn M. Zimmerman and John J. Campbell(1), where they argue that procedures consist of a set of instructions that describe a task or process. They go on to suggest that the three main parties involved in developing procedures are the writer, the reviewer, and the users. A simplified version of their model for preparing procedures suggests that we need to plan, draft, review, check if it's okay, then finish. To get this into perspective they reckon that 40 percent to 60 percent of the time spent developing procedures is spent planning them."

"Excellent," Jack said sincerely. "I suspect that you've made a study of this matter. That correct, Bill?"

Bill shrugged his shoulders and laughed, refusing to be drawn into an admission. Instead he went on, "I also said that we can make a list, you know, a formula, that, if applied, to the development and use of procedures, would ensure that they work. In fact, such a list could be used by my new compliance team where they could check up on the use of procedures and assess whether they've been properly installed. This list will go a long way to sorting out our problems with poor internal controls. Agreed?"

"Absolutely," agreed Jack. "Let's stop at Lollypop beach and have a bite to eat."

They parked and entered a brightly painted café set beside the sea front and enjoyed the refreshing breeze gathering off the sea.

Over a cold Red Stripe and a meal of fried chicken and rice, the conversation continued. Jack suggested they take turns compiling a comprehensive criteria for good procedures and the list ended up looking like this:

Jack	Bill
Clear	Simple
Accepted	Workable
Communicated	Formally documented
Integrated with other procedures	Reinforces quality
Cross-referenced	Structured
Fits culture	Part of performance appraisal
Well written	Adds value to process
Allows good judgment	Standards well presented
Not too bulky	Automated where possible
Reviewed	Flexible
Makes sense	Reflects roles
Consistent	Complete
Agreed with users	List of abbreviations
Used in-staff training	Compliance reviewed
Mandatory bits made clear	Allows departures
Promotes accountability	Doesn't stifle innovation
Not overly technical	Prepared by experts
Users fully consulted	Signed off by management
Dated	Makes people responsible
Entails reviewing processes	Not seen as a hindrance
Staff happy to refer to it	Not excessive
Complies with legal matters	Bottom-up approach

As they came toward the end of the list, Bill felt that he could start to conclude these discussions and said, "We have a model. We have a list of attributes that we could expand on in some detail if need be. I think we've done a lot of useful work on this subject. Now, Jack, you normally like some form of philosophical quote to close don't you?"

Jack smiled.

"How about this one from your file by Chuang Tzu," continued Bill.

> The purpose of a fish trap is to trap fish, and when the fish are caught, the trap is forgotten. The purpose of words is to convey ideas. When the ideas are grasped, the words are forgotten. Where can I find a man who has forgotten words? He is the one I would like to talk to. (2)

"So documents are words that are only relevant where they assist you in what you're doing. Once we understand them, we don't need the words, agreed? I'll finish by suggesting that procedures must convey ideas, hopefully the ideas or visions that the organization has for its future, its goals, and how it wants staff to behave and perform. You can get that in your book—one more chapter down, eh?" Bill pursed his lips in the self-satisfied manner that he had when he felt things were in their right place.

This conclusion was good enough to prompt a return to the car and continuation of the drive on to Negril. Driving along winding roads and past small districts, several people waved as they recognized Jack's car. From time to time, Jack would stop and give someone a ride or just engage in small talk, which gave some light relief from the long car journey.

After two hours they arrived at Negril and swam freely in the warm sea, returning to their shaded tables and chairs from time to time. Bill tried several cups of fish tea during these rest periods as suggested by Jack. Fish tea was really like soup in a cup, as Bill discovered much to his delight. The sun glared along the white beach and made everything appear brilliant and somewhat dazzling. Bill became reflective and started to look forward to a relaxing drive home since they, or more correctly, he, had dealt with the day's topic of conversation. He asked a young man working for a nearby hotel whether they could use a sun bed, as the sun had dipped low enough to sunbathe without burning. The attendant explained that the beds belonged to the hotel and were for use of guests only. Having said this, he gladly offered them.

IS THERE MORE TO PROCEDURES?

"You have just seen a technical breach of procedure," Jack observed. "We aren't supposed to use the sun beds but were given them anyway. Do you feel the young man should be punished, Bill?"

Bill responded, "Not really. There must be some leeway. He's encouraging tourists to feel at ease and that must be good for everyone. The hotel he works for, the tourist industry, and us, who can use the facility."

Jack said, "This is where a compliance team can also go wrong. Where they see procedures as a fixed set of rules that don't take on board the risk within the environment in which they operate."

The rest of the time was spent swimming, relaxing under the shade of palm trees scattered around the beach, and taking the occasional cold drink from the beach bar. The sunset over the coast showered rays of pink and purple hues which deepened as the evening progressed. This marked the end of the day at Negril and grudgingly, they agreed to get back to the car and embark on the long drive home. Taking one last look at the purple sea, Bill settled down in the car and Jack revved up the car engine. To Bill's surprise, Jack drifted into more debate of what was supposed to be the now-closed topic of procedures. Bill smiled at Jack's persistence but felt it best to let him have his say.

"Bill," Jack said, "all that you said concerning procedures makes good sense and I have no quarrel with it at all. What I need to do now is give you some of my views on this subject. It's basically the same as the list we just discussed although, in parts, with different emphasis. There are three points that I think are important."

1. *Restrictive Procedures*

"Bill, can you find and read one of my favorite quotes from Professor C. Northcote Parkinson of Parkinson's law fame?" Bill read:

> The man who is denied the opportunity of taking decisions of importance begins to regard as important the decisions he is allowed to take. He becomes fussy about filing, keen on seeing pencils are sharpened, eager to ensure that the windows are opened (or shut) . . .(3)

"Thanks, Bill. Where we make procedures so tight as to restrict human judgment, they turn us into bureaucrats, who simply process information to give a predetermined result. I used to be a procedures man where I thought everything should be set out in a big book that would constitute the rules. Some auditors are happy with this model as it promotes control by suggesting that management provide for set responses to set circumstances. There's little room left for decisions or responsibility.

"The other problem I found with procedures is that they were taken from the satellite model of control. Managers would feel happy that they'd prepared a comprehensive set of rules that act as a guard over their staff."

2. *Overly Detailed Procedures*

"But the more complete and detailed the procedures, the more likely it will be that they're ignored. At times, they're prepared as one-off matters by specially recruited consultants. Over time they become more of a hindrance than anything else and end up being abandoned. This situation is most frustrating for compliance teams and auditors who perform compliance checks. They find breaches and follow them up with official reports seeking to reimpose the proper control, but fail to understand that most people want to make things work in a way that makes most sense.

"People who draft procedures find it hard to cope with this. Let alone those that are meant to check on the application of procedures. We can use the shall-should-may model when drafting procedures. Here we make it clear what is mandatory (*Shall*), say an immediate evacuation of the building when a fire is detected. *Shoulds* have less severe an effect, say relating to staff keeping a watch for obstacles that may impede fire evacuations. *Mays* are discretionary and could for example appear where staff are invited to join, say a health and safety committee reviewing fire procedures."

3. *Procedural Expectations*

"We may need to talk about higher level procedures as standards or ideals where they relate to nontechnical matters. Here we ask staff to live up to certain expectations rather than go through a mechanical checklist of duties."

Bill had taken on a look of mild interest, nodding gently and smiling as Jack spoke. Noticing this, Jack said, "We have a bit of a drive back to Mo'Bay. Let me give you the additional areas that I feel should be covered to complete our discussion on procedures. You're right to suggest that they form a crucial part of the system of internal control. They describe and set standards about the way we should work in an organization. At the outset we need to distinguish between:

a. *Policies.* I see these as high-level frameworks that set ideals on important corporate issues. For example, each component of the managerial control system that we discussed yesterday should have its own general policy framework.

74

b. *Corporate procedures.* These are set arrangements that cover the organization and deal with key processes that tend to cut across sections and departments. Here it's difficult to allow excessive freedom, as local events may well affect other parts of the organization. The example I would use here is procedures on disciplinary action, where we need to establish some form of consistency to deal with what can be a sensitive matter. There may be a number of rules attached to these procedures that are firmer in their requirements, that is, they fall under the Shall category. This might relate to a rule where no one can be recruited without the involvement of Personnel. If Personnel are the only people who can authorize a new hire, then it would be hard to bypass this requirement. I can imagine many formal rules that would form the basis of a health and safety procedure.

c. *Technical procedures.* These I see as specialist manual-based arrangements where the normal rules for drafting procedures may not apply. As such they could become very detailed and contain long lists of technical material and activities. I'd imagine that great use of cross-referencing may be made. There's no way to shorten these procedures as in the final analysis they would be required to support the handling of, say, dangerous material or expensive equipment. A scientific research company may have many such manuals so that experiments can be documented, reviewed, and verified. A manufacturing environment may also make use of technical manuals where gadgets have to be produced to precise specifications.

d. *Operational/administrative procedures.* These manuals are real important. They're extra guidelines used in service or administrative areas where the line managers may decide whether to use them. The other procedures (a through c) will be prepared by experts and there are many standard documents that can be used for corporate procedures relating to purchasing, recruitment, staff selection, performance appraisal, information technology (IT) security, project management, staff grievances, equal opportunities, travel and expense claims, ordering, building security, health and safety, and other well-known corporate systems. The technical procedures would be used by people fully trained in the discipline in question. So a nuclear power station would have detailed technical manuals covering issues such as materials handling and maintenance practices.

"To my mind, corporate and technical procedures manuals would have to be in place as a basic control. If not, there's no real starting place. The fourth type, basic operational manuals that are applied by administrative or managerial staff, also provides scope for securing better control. These are normally inadequate. Where we see these procedures as control standards, it becomes clearer. Bill, do you remember the model of control called COSO (Figure 2.13) that we discussed yesterday?"

"Yes," Bill replied. "There were five parts to this model: risk assessment, control activities, communication and information, monitoring, and one other that escapes me right now."

FIVE MORE POINTS OF INTEREST

"The final one is control environment, that is the culture and values of the organization," Jack said. "Anyway, the risk assessment part means we need to work out key risks to the achievement of our objectives. Once we've got these down, we can work out what to do about it. The answer is found in the control activities, that is, procedures or to put it simply, control procedures. Control procedures need to be in your manual. Anyway, let me list the areas that we need to discuss to complete this part of our journey. We need to cover

- Role of procedures
- Risk assessment
- Models for drafting and implementing them
- The compliance issue
- Perhaps an example, say the complaints procedure that you use in your company.

"We'll have to leave the major issues of creativity and innovation and how these features can be integrated into the control frame for another day."

It dawned on Bill that Jack was relaying these ideas in such a matter-of-fact manner, that it could not be seen as a normal conversation between acquaintances. Bill frowned and he said slowly and quietly, "Jack! You really *are* going to use our discussions to write your book on controls, aren't you?"

Jack smiled and taking his hands off the steering wheel shrugged saying, "I've wasted a year doing nothing so far and if you don't mind . . . talking through the concepts helps me think things through. Your ideas have already been a tremendous help. You know, I've got to get into this and start writing things down. I mean, I've already signed the contract and I need to make a start."

Bill looked at Jack and could sense the frustration in his words. What stops a man from achieving his goal in life? Many things is probably the right answer. Anyway he was getting a lot from this journey through the world of control. In fact this was the scenic route to control, driving around such a beautiful island with good company as well.

"What are you going to call it, this book?" Bill asked.

"Well. I was going to call it the *Manager's Guide to Internal Control*. But this title sounds a bit boring. I may need to call it something like *The Diary of a Control Freak,* but then this title may put people off. I'll find a title, don't worry. It's just that I've got to write the thing first."

"So you see yourself as a control freak, Jack?"

"I was actually referring more to you, to be honest."

Bill settled back in the car and relaxed, not bothering to think of an answer. Could be worse, he thought. "What about calling it the *Scenic Route to Internal Control?*" he said, "or something about our *Journey Through Controls?* Anyway, I believe you were saying something more about procedures?"

Jack concentrated on negotiating a series of tight bends. After a few minutes he went on, "Right, let's get back to it. I've told you the ground that I want to cover, bearing in mind the material that we've already gone through. The role of procedures is a good place to start. I see procedures as important, because they set direction and standards, which is what internal control is all about. The problem we have is in deciding the form of these procedures. The typical audit reaction is to ask that they're formally documented. I did one audit and inquired about human resource management procedures that should have been issued by corporate personnel. They had a lovely package, but told me point blank that they had no budget to allow a set for each individual employee; that would have run into the tens of thousands of dollars. The practicalities of the situation were all consuming. I recall a quote from Thoreau who said:

Our life is frittered away by detail . . . Simplify, simplify.(4)

"And this leads me," Jack continued, "away from my previous enthusiasm for comprehensive administrative procedure manuals. Organizational life is too complicated to seek to capture in a rulebook."

"It seems that some things simply cannot be set out as a formal procedure because they tend to be overruled or simply ignored, for example, recording every phone call received in a day book. I would argue that procedures should only be documented where it's absolutely necessary and comprehensive written manuals shouldn't be the norm. We need to employ motivated people with basic common sense and personal responsibility who can work to high standards. My self-control, or internalized control model, means operations are performed in the right way by people committed to this task and not through a dense rulebook. We need to give people freedom to define things in a way that makes sense.

"A procedure then, is an accepted method of going about one's business and implicit in this method are standards of performance, quality, and accountability. It may or may not become a document but it's important that it's understood and forms an integrated part of organizational systems in order to be a valuable control."

"Interesting," remarked Bill. "What you're saying then is don't develop formal procedures for obvious things. An abundance of procedures indicates an abundance of stupid managers—common sense is a higher level thing that must rule in the end."

"What I'm saying, Bill, is that you needn't develop procedures in low-risk areas. Do your risk assessment and then develop procedures where you cannot leave things to chance. That brings us back to this idea of risk assessment. Risk is basically things that can go wrong and things that need to happen that affect your efforts to succeed. It's really the flip side of control. Controls are things that help you succeed whereas risks are things that get in the way. Controls, or what we can call control activities, help sort out these risks."

Bill looked thoughtful and mumbled, "Never a simple answer is there? We seem to be going around in circles: risk, control, success, and all the rest of it. Can't we stick to the basics: procedures and how to get them to work?"

Jack said, "Okay, Bill. Point taken. It's very simple. Let's stop at this gas station and I'll give you an example of what I mean."

At this, Jack pulled up at a gas station and both he and Bill got out of the car. One of the attendants working there filled up the tank while the two men watched.

Jack said, "Look at the two signs posted on each gas pump. What do they say?"

"One says 'Do not fill up until the gas requested has been paid for in full' and the other says 'Smoking is forbidden in the forecourt.'"

"Right. The first one is redundant because the risk of people filling up and running away is too small. The second one is enforced because there is a real danger of a fire if people are allowed to smoke near the pumps. The real procedure—how things are done—is not written down. You tell the attendant what you want; he fills up, you pay and tip the attendant, get back change and a receipt, and that's it. That's the procedure. If there were no attendants, then the up-front payment rule may be enforced because the risk of runners increases. You're given a receipt to counter the risk of disputes. You get the point. In designing this system you assess the risk areas and then set a procedure to counter them. Can you think of one risk that hasn't been addressed, Bill?"

"Let me think. I guess I could get charged less for the gas if the attendant is a friend. Or maybe we could arrange to split the difference."

"Good point. I assume the cashier would check the amount used with the payment due. This would be the procedure to cover that risk. What I'm saying, Bill, is that there's no point having a procedure where there's nothing that could go wrong. Now going back to your point about going around in circles. I'm afraid the standard risk concept does include a cycle of events that form the risk management process."

"Ah hah," shouted Bill, as they got back into the car, "Just as I thought. Things are going to get complex now, aren't they?"

"Not at all. The risk circle's in the file. It's down as Figure 3.2. You need to assess the risks in any operation. In the gas station, gas

Figure 3.2   Risk cycle.

needs to be supplied, stored, priced, given to customers, and then paid for. What could go wrong? And are there any ways that we could sharpen the operation? Having assessed the risks, we work out who should do what, that is, who's responsible for what, including the risks we've guessed at. Then we design control procedures to counter these risks and implement, monitor, and review them. If I owned that gas station, I'd want these procedures in place and more than that, I'd want to ensure that they were working properly. The gas station manager should report to the owner that this is the case. Thus we have control and accountability.

"There's more, Bill. Risk management goes further. Instead of just controlling things, we might use a range of measures to manage the risks. We could accept it, if it's no big thing or there's no other option. We could get someone else to assume it, that is transfer it. Or we may set up a backup plan if things really did go wrong. For the gas station, we may accept the risk of motorists resenting having to pay tips to attendants because all the local gas stations operate the same system. We may transfer the risk of driving off without paying by making the attendants responsible for this money and getting them to pay up if the driver skips. Contingency plans could cover, say, fire extinguishers in case of a gas fire. You see, Bill, we can cover all angles simply by planning and preparing. That's the good thing about risk assessment; getting people to take responsibility for managing potential problems. The key is to get people talking the same language. What does risk mean to you? Not easy. Take investments. There's a view that the level of risk we should take with our personal investments roughly comes out as 100 percent less your age. So the younger you are, the more risk you can accept and vice versa. Your level of tolerance to risk is called your comfort zone. We need to set the same thing for the organization. How much return on capital does it need to survive? What then is its tolerance to risk, and do its employees buy into it? Remember risk becomes crucial when we get to a decision point. When we have to weigh up and choose between options."

As Jack said this, they drove past a remote spot at the bottom of a hill where a large gas tanker was parked and people holding metal canisters and looking somewhat sheepish were milling around.

Much to Jack's embarrassment, Bill pointed at the small group, laughed, and as they swept past them, said, "As you are fond of saying, controls can never be 100 percent perfect, can they?"

USING MODELS

"Come on, Bill, let's try to be serious. And don't point at people—it's rude. Well, that's risk assessment done. Now turning to models for the way procedures may be used by an organization. You've already described the one where we find out what processes are happening and then draft and review the document, while constantly double-checking with the users. Look at Figure 3.3 from the file.

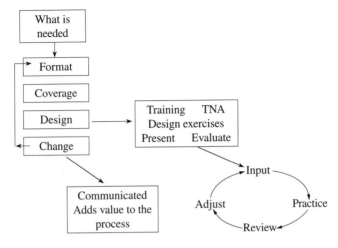

Figure 3.3   Designing procedures.

"When I drafted this figure I wanted to bring out the need to link procedures to the operational processes and the need to add value to the way it's carried out. Say, for example, we are granting car loans to staff. The procedure should act as a way of publicizing the service and ensuring it's carried out efficiently and effectively. It may also instill a degree of ethical transparency into the arrangements. The other point is the link between procedures and training where we design and execute training around the adopted operational practices. Staff may practice and review their progress in meeting these standards and get training where required. Oh, and TNA means training needs analysis, by the way.

"The next model most people use is designed to assess the adequacy of the resulting procedures. I believe that four key factors impact on this issue. First, the ability of the people using the procedure, which may imply a training requirement, or competency shortfall, if there are problems. The next is the competence of the writer, who would have researched the process and defined the underpinning practices that form the basis of the procedure. The extent to which the procedure supports and adds to the process, and other associated processes, is seen as an additional factor in the success or otherwise of the resulting document. Last, there must be a positive impact on risks to achieving business objectives. This won't happen where the procedure leads to poorly motivated staff. Each of these four forces in Figure 3.4 must be in balance before the procedure can be a valuable aspect of internal control.

"The final figure I put together relates to a nine-point process for developing and adopting the procedures and ensuring compliance. We can discuss this in some detail later. At this stage I would suggest the process flows I've jotted down in Figure 3.5 of the file." Bill screwed up his eyes and tried to study the diagram. He finally said, "Do you spend all your time inventing obscure diagrams?"

"Sort of. I'm a visual sort of person and I like playing around with models. Do you think it's clear enough?"

"In parts. But you better talk me through it . . . er . . . if you think it's important, that is."

Jack pursed his lips, "You mean, I can if I don't bore you to tears. Look, Bill, I've tried to use simple examples so far but my diagrams are important. It's worth going through them. I just hope that they don't seem too boring when they appear in the book."

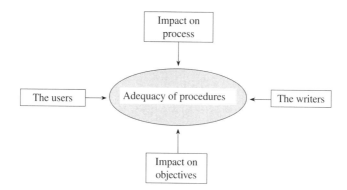

Figure 3.4   Adequacy of procedure.

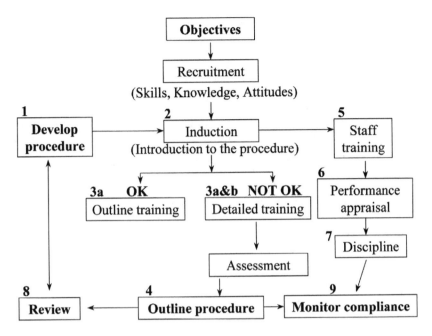

Figure 3.5 Compliance model.

Bill replied, "That's the first time I've heard you talk about your book as though you really mean to get it done. Things are looking up."

It was Jack's turn to look embarrassed as pleasant thoughts of writing the book and finally getting it done flashed through his mind. Smiling at this daydream and keeping his eyes on the road ahead, he continued,

"Okay. If you're ready we can go through the stages of my model.

1. *Development.* Development involves reviewing the underlying processes, simplifying them, and working with users, then drafting an agreed document that reflects the required activities.

2. *Induction.* It's important to introduce the procedure to new starters and show existing staff a new or improved procedure.
3. *The training manual.* The manual may be broken down into two levels. Where staff are assessed as able to apply procedures, an outline manual (a) can be provided. Where this isn't the case, a more comprehensive package (a&b) with exercises can be given to them to work through.
4. *Outline.* After the training or induction period, we turn to a shortcut outline document with key tasks and processes summarized for use thereafter.
5. *Training.* We've argued that the skills of staff affect the degree to which procedures are successful. The training on procedures is mainly about knowledge, and to supplement this we should also seek to develop the underlying skills and the appropriate attitudes as a parallel training initiative.
6. *Appraisal.* We would want to link the way staff are using procedures in their performance appraisal framework. In this way, it's seen to have some meaning to the work people do and their individual development programs.
7. *Discipline.* This position is a fall-back, where if all else fails we may need to discipline staff for breach of procedure.
8. *Review.* The review process should be straightforward in that it entails keeping the procedure relevant, vibrant, and up-to-date.
9. *Compliance.* It's the line manager's responsibility to ensure staff comply with procedure. This is best done by getting staff to understand how they can monitor themselves and supporting them in this task.

"Sounds good," exclaimed Bill, "but, you better not put that one in the book—it's too intense."

"Not at all," Jack responded, "you need to give readers some credit. There's nothing wrong with a bit of detail. Anyway to continue. We can argue that the skills of staff is one key factor in assessing whether procedures will work as an important control. I suggest that if we employ sensible and professional staff, they will not actually need an inch-thick procedures book.

"We defined procedures earlier to bring out the view that they help management deal with risks and give some direction, which is a fundamental component of control. At the same time, we need to admit to the growing view that if control is about achieving success, organizations cannot be successful if they install too much order and too much direction. This order stagnates systems and stops them from being at the cutting edge. Procedures are particularly prone to this criticism. If they seek to maintain order and the status quo, they may actually promote a lack of dynamic progress, which will eventually lead to disaster. We have arrived once again at the Jekyll and Hyde dilemma—two conflicting forces that are both present at the same time. I guess we'll need to find a solution to this dilemma before your vacation ends."

WHAT ABOUT COMPLIANCE?

"We've looked at the role of procedures as setting standards for control activities and mentioned a few models. Let's move on to the next stage—compliance. This subject should be interesting to you, Bill, where your search for control is based around a new compliance team. The normal audit position is simple: If there's a procedure or a control process, such as signing for portable PCs, we would wish to see that it's being adhered to. The audit view is to assess the degree of compliance before working out whether this control works. If there's poor compliance, we would report this and look for the impact (i.e., consequential problems). So if staff aren't signing for notebook computers that they take home, we may try to find out whether we can account for these machines and whether any are in fact missing. The procedure's there, it's not being used, and PCs may go missing as a result. This equation is quite straightforward and a compliance team may be used to undertake this kind of work.

"There must be something more than just setting procedures and ensuring staff use them in their work. Professor C. Northcote Parkinson reinforces this view:

> The person who is devoted to paperwork has lost the initiative. He is dealing with things that are brought to his notice, having ceased to notice anything for himself. He has been essentially defeated in his job.(5)

"We all have views on whether blind adherence to a comprehensive rule book is seen as defeating rather than promoting good control. Before we go on, we must also work out why compliance is important. You know, I argue that control can be a life or death matter—it's important. I also feel that noncompliance, or a failure to observe basic standards of monitoring and review, can also lead to dire consequences.

"By the same token an 'obey all orders' mentality may not always be the right answer. We've said that the art of control provides a greater challenge than the science of control. So here Art rules! We should recognize the reality of nonconformity and disorder as well as the importance of conformity and order. There's a spiritual element of procedures that impacts on the soul. I really do believe that self-control starts with the soul.

"To assess compliance with procedures we need to examine the role of conformity in organizations. Building compliance around this principle then has built-in dangers. Simply getting staff to action predetermined routines leads to what I call senseless consistency and all this entails . . ."

Bill looked at Jack in full flow. He was totally animated, his gestures and voice conveyed a real enthusiasm. Yes, that's it, control is so important and when you get too excited, you lose control. Bill tried to concentrate on Jack's words and said, "Sorry, Jack, I drifted off a bit. What were you saying? Or, perhaps preaching would have been a better description," he said dryly.

Jack said, "Okay, point taken. What I mean is procedures can dampen the spirits. McGregor(6) has developed a model that views management as having the power to create lively, creative staff who want to achieve (theory Y) or lazy, inhibited people who must be pushed into work (theory X). The attitudes are created by the way people are treated by their managers. If you treat your people as stupid they will tend to assume this role and vice versa.

"We needn't go further as it's got to lead in one basic direction, where a compliance-based organization is developed. In fact, enlightened management has been through this debate many times and one solution is to encourage the use of coaching to manage staff, as a supplement to the compliance-with-procedure model. Coaching is about developing people and not just getting them to action procedures.

"Coaching uses encouragement for securing improvements, which is based on giving staff responsibility for their goals, actions, and results. We can relate this to the control procedures environment. Instead of using downward control and command, can we use procedures as part of the learning process and link these to the three key staff components? Remember the three components of competencies?

1. *Knowledge.* Understand the procedures and how they feed into other sections and organizational goals generally.
2. *Skills.* Right techniques applied—we can use procedures as a way of focusing these skills to the task in hand.
3. *Attitudes.* Use procedures in a creative way that adds value to the organization and its customers.

"We're moving further and further away from the compliance model of management. Now coaches put in their skills and get employees to respond positively. Paul Kalinauckas and Helen King(7) explain this well. They illustrate in Figure 3.6 that future opportunities, in the top right-hand section, are targeted as the key to success.

"It would be wrong to suggest that we can simply ignore problems, mistakes, and breach of procedure. Corporate governance is about taking responsibility for all that goes on, including the downside of organizational life. We cannot talk about compliance without discussing noncompliance. Coaching and bottom upward (or theory Y) management doesn't depend on ignoring staff who blatantly breach important procedures and place the organization at risk. It's just that a positive environment is seen as better than a punitive one. Your organization is facing many legal actions for unfair dismissal and this is worrying. An organization with a strong disciplinary procedure generally indicates poor human resource procedures, because discipline is a last ditch effort where management has failed.

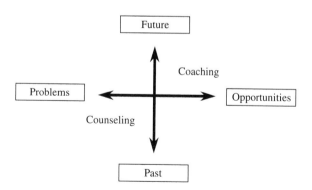

Figure 3.6 Coaching orientation. (Reproduced with kind permission of the Institute of Personnel and Development.)

"Breach of procedure may be caused by poor procedures that make little or no sense. Or, where the procedures are sound, nonadherence should be treated as an indication of failings in staff competencies that should be put right (i.e., training, development, and coaching). This retains a positive environment. It may also indicate that procedures have been badly taught and passed on.

"The idea of constant development means procedures can be internalized and compliance isn't an issue. It's simply a question of how well the internalization of learning has been adopted. There's a well-known process involving unconscious incompetence, conscious incompetence, conscious competence, and then unconscious competence. We move from not realizing we are incompetent (unconscious incompetence) right through to being competent without even trying (unconscious competence). It's embedded in the way we work. But, we must still be able to deal with, and put right, problems. Whatever our adopted theories, we cannot achieve good systems of internal control if our procedures allow an abundance of mistakes and uncorrected problems—that leads to unmitigated risk. There are times a manager must reprimand staff.

"We need to go back into management theory and use the work of Maslow to assess the impact of mistakes or breach of procedure. Maslow's(8) hierarchy of needs, starts with physiological needs where a person wants to secure the basics before being in a position to turn toward higher social and self-esteem needs. Organizations that meet these higher needs can be successful because staff tend to be self-motivated at work. Employees who're highly motivated initiate their own procedures where this makes systems more efficient or adds value to customers. Consider an example I've seen happen at work:

> An accounts officer noticed that she received customers' comments concerning a new product. After a few weeks, she approached her boss and suggested that she develop a tracking procedure. This

system became so successful that marketing took it over and received useful feedback from customers for the design programs.

"This staff member must have been high up on Maslow's hierarchy of needs to view procedures as something that was the responsibility of everyone to initiate and develop. This could be in the form of a formal document or simply an agreed arrangement that may or may not have been confirmed in writing. It really doesn't matter. Now let's get back to breach of procedure and how this can be dealt with by an organization. If we adopt the enforced compliance approach, we may instill such fear into staff that they revert to the lower aspects of Maslow's motivational drives in that they fear for their security (i.e., their jobs). Self-preservation becomes the keyword and all designs on development, initiative, and self-control fall by the wayside. Punishment-based organizations have this problem. They think the control and command model is most effective. In terms of controls promoting the achievement of objectives, a robotlike workforce, working to fixed procedures, with a compliance team looking over their shoulders, may not bring out the best in staff. It certainly flies in the face of the current support for coaching and empowerment as the way forward.

"The growing trend to use compliance teams as the solution to control problems has some support. But it must be set against the need to maintain self-esteem and basic business etiquette. I've said that control is about self-control and that it starts with one's soul. The soul is protected by self-esteem (i.e., a regard for oneself). We have to be comfortable with ourselves as a basis for self-control. From there, we move forward. If you develop a punitive organization where self-esteem suffers, self-control will not be achieved. We can have problems where compliance with procedure is incorrectly used as a key control.

"How are we going to encourage people to take responsibility for procedures and develop them in a blame-based culture? I've been on audits where people have admitted, in confidence, that they don't document their work procedure because they feel it would make a rod for their back. One person felt sure he would be made redundant if his job were documented in such a way that it could be done by someone new to the section. There's something wrong with this environment; it's not a well-controlled environment. The greater the externally imposed compliance controls, the more this situation is likely to arise.

"Compliance can be dealt with positively. First and foremost, we must be able to deal with noncompliance with procedures properly, bearing in mind the importance of the employee's self-esteem. We've mentioned the way that procedures may be breached, because they don't make sense in the first place. We've also dealt with the impact of skills, knowledge, and attitudes on procedures; any shortfalls in these aspects of competencies will lead to problems. What we've not yet discussed is the out-and-out mistake. Breaches may occur because of simple mistakes. You mentioned salary overpayments as one problem in your company, and I have seen this happen where a salary tape was run twice and $1 million overpaid in the month-end run. History records many examples of mistakes:

> On 14th April 1912, 1,513 men, women, and children died when the 'unsinkable' ship, the *Titanic,* hit an iceberg on its maiden voyage. There was a lack of lifeboats as the number provided was in those days based on tonnage and not number of passengers. Reports are that the ship was run at full speed although icebergs were spotted . . . There were also problems making radio contact with other ships in the area. These weaknesses were reported in a full inquiry after the accident and procedures introduced to tackle each of the above points.(9)

"The shipping industry is now safer due, unfortunately, to this major disaster. People learn from mistakes and there's no procedure that's fail-safe. They're organic and must be adapted to keep pace with the demands of the workplace.

"There's great power in the theory of mistakes that shakes people's fixed position and moves them onward and forward. I've read many writers who see the positive side of such problems and I won't bore you with my complete list of these comments. There are a few, however, that fit this discussion and there is no harm in repeating them. Like all good auditors, I started from the classical school of management where authority, structure, planning, and exception reporting were the keys to control. Since then, I've discovered the human resource approach and thereafter moved into a systems view of management before a brief return to psychology as the best answer. From here, I've moved on and considered complexity and creativity while superimposing over these disciplines what I can only describe as a spiritual view of management control."

"You're going off again, Jack," Bill remarked, shaking his head slowly.

"Okay. I'll slow down. Your compliance team will have a major task in achieving adherence and not creating an environment of fear and oppression. There's a fine line to tread on reporting back on what staff are doing and providing advice and support in their efforts to secure control through good procedures. The former is based on the use of punishers where people are 'found out' and reprimanded as they breach procedure.

"When a manager has identified a breach of procedure, there must be scope to take a course of action that reflects the severity of the situation and the implications of the breach. We need to be flexible in our approach to this subject. One well-known model involves a range of options for dealing with conflict:

- *Avoidance.* Look the other way or withdraw.
- *Hesitation.* Delaying tactics dealing with minor issues only.

- *Confrontation.* Power, physical force, bribery, punishment as a win-lose position or negotiation which seeks a win-win result by resolving the conflict with compromises.

"This brings out the multidimensional view of management action that may not be as straightforward as it seems at first sight. There's no point making a mountain out of a molehill. But where the breach is serious, then it must be recognized. We'll deal with the question of internal discipline when we get to discussing fraud. Best to leave this for another day, I think.

"I have to get through more material on the topic of procedures before the day is over. Before we leave the compliance issue, let me introduce what I call the *'It must never be allowed to happen again'* model of control procedures. I've noticed over the years that society tolerates many situations where there's a complete absence of sound procedures that mean when the inevitable disaster happens, the consequences are dire. This situation could relate to not bothering to license security staff at nightclubs; not stopping visitors from passing drugs to prison inmates; employing childcare workers without checking whether they have committed sexual offenses; allowing public workers to retire on medical grounds when they're not really sick; releasing from secure care units mentally ill people who have expressed dangerously violent tendencies; allowing politicians to accept cash to represent business interests; and so on. Basic controls are lacking but action is only taken when a disaster happens and the general public makes calls for improvement. Extensive inquiries that could take many years to complete, result in long-winded reports that go on to recommend *'It must never be allowed to happen again.'*

"No one asks why we didn't get sound procedures working before these disasters proved that proper procedures should have been established to support control activities. It may be better to ask whether the people responsible for these areas have other responsibilities that are as badly administered. Bill, sorry to go on so much. But it's really important. To recap, we've dealt with the role of procedures as a key aspect of the system of internal control. We've prepared a few models to assist this task. Some time was spent on compliance as an issue. I promised to provide an example of a procedure. Let's stop for a cold drink at a bar I know nearby and then get into an example of an administrative procedure."

AN EXAMPLE OF A NEW
PROCEDURE—COMPLAINTS

Bill drank a Red Stripe beer and looked around the bar. Four people in the corner were playing dominoes with zest, banging down each domino with such force that the table shook. The night air was cool and a refreshing breeze lightly blew through the barroom windows, making the leaves of a nearby palm tree sway. Vibrant energy and tranquility. Bill finally said, "You do realize that you go on and on like someone obsessed. Your argument rambles and twists and turns in all directions."

"Well, Bill, I did say we would take a journey through the world of controls, which I see as much the same as the rambling, winding roads that we've been driving on over the last few days. I hope it's been an enjoyable journey without too much technical stuff. Maybe this is the scenic route to this topic, taking the coastal road."

Bill understood. That wasn't a bad analogy—winding roads and colorful sights, rambling words, and simple examples and quotations. He took refuge in his drink, asking hesitantly, "How much further to go before we get back to Mo'Bay?"

Jack laughed, "You mean how much more discussion is left today. Less than an hour, you'll be pleased to hear. Bill, when I give you my views on control, you can add your thoughts."

"No, that's okay. You just carry on and I'll speak when I think I need to."

With that, the two men wished the domino players good night and continued their journey.

With the tape recorder once more switched on, Jack carried on almost as if he were giving a lecture, "I was going to give you an example of the way procedures can contribute to the system of internal control. Before I do, let me tell you about a problem I came across with a large cashiering function accounting for millions of dollars of income each week. When working for this organization, I received a phone call from the chief financial officer who explained that one of six cash bags, containing some $30,000 was missing. He asked me to interview the staff and prepare a report for the local police who had been informed of this theft. During the course of these interviews, I discovered that there was no procedure to cover the most important control over cash (i.e., relating to the physical movement of cash). Many people had had contact with the six cash bags before they were handed over to the security firm who collected only five of them. While the police pursued a criminal investigation, I recommended comprehensive procedures for making sure someone was responsible for the cash at all stages from bagging to handing over and that this responsibility was properly supervised and documented. Cash bags were left unattended on desks and this was one of those '*it must never be allowed to happen again*' systems. Breach of procedure in these types of systems leads to much risk. I still stick to my guns in saying that people want good procedures and they will devise and improve them if given half a chance. In fact, during the interviews, staff expressed a wish to be able to track cash within the cashiering office as they felt this would protect them if something went wrong. As it stood, they all fell under suspicion.

"Going back to an example of good procedures. Let's take a situation where we want to allow customers to complain if they wish to. We must start with a sound policy statement that sets the tone for the actual procedure. This policy may say that we actively seek views from customers and that all employees are responsible for securing and responding to any problems brought to their attention. Most companies go wrong where their staff view complaints as a major threat to be avoided. They also try to duck this problem by making sure they're not responsible for what they see as a negative aspect of business life. What they fail to see is that complainants simply stop using the product or service and tell their friends and relatives to do the same, unless they can get a positive response to their problem from the company. If they get this response they may go on to give even greater support to the company in the future.

"Let's go back to risk assessment. What could go wrong where customers or potential customers aren't able to express their concerns about the company? This is the risk that's being countered. Poor reputations, loss of customers, sales, and profits—it goes on and on. The risks are great and the possible impact quite severe. The likelihood of these problems depends on whether we have a good complaints procedure. Much can be gained from designing and implementing a procedure that makes sense and works. Figure 3.7 shows a framework for getting procedures up and running that I made up.

"If you don't mind, Bill, since the tape's running, let's go through each of the aspects of the complaints procedure:

"**1.** *Objectives.* We need to decide just what the procedure is meant to cover and what its goals are. This is important, as it sets a frame within which the procedure will operate and link back to corporate objectives. There's only so much a procedure can do and if a complaints procedure is meant to obtain feedback from customers and deal with any problems they may experience with the product, then it demands an attitude from all staff that promotes this view. Words written in a formal document have no value at all

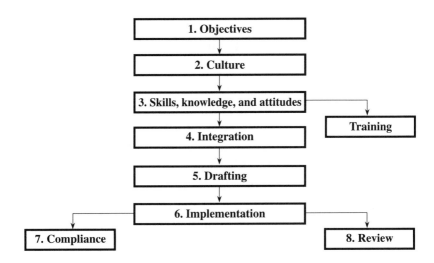

Figure 3.7   Complaints procedure.

unless they lead to this change in attitude. The goal shouldn't be to draft a formal procedure, it should be expressed more in terms of ensuring that customers' concerns are identified and addressed.

"**2.** *Culture.* We can support the type of culture we want to see by using appropriate procedures. Not forms and documents, but the approach the organization has toward its customers. A procedure can go some way toward creating a positive culture, but in one sense if the right culture isn't in place, the procedure will fail.

"**3.** *Skills, Knowledge, and Attitudes (Training).* It's a good idea to think about the types of skills, knowledge, and attitudes that should be in place to live up to the adopted standards, which is what a procedure should be anyway. We should think about the way staff currently deal with problems experienced by actual and potential customers. Any new procedure will probably cause a training need to be identified as we think about how staff will handle the new initiative. It may indicate a need for training in communication skills, listening skills, awareness of conflict management, and negotiation skills. It may require some investigative skills in working out what problems are being relayed and how they arose. My view is that training staff in procedures is probably the most effective way that a training budget can be applied, so long as training is geared toward knowledge, skills, and attitudes and effort is directed at understanding the procedure. It's better to train staff on the implications of new procedures than to simply issue them a rulebook. We used an earlier model to illustrate how a comprehensive training procedure may be condensed into a short reminder for staff once they have been trained in the new arrangements. The coaching approach to management can be used to get the message across.

"The empowerment concept is here to stay and relies on the manager assuming a different role by encouraging performance by one-to-one input into the employee's own development at work. We concentrate on knowledge, skills, and attitudes but know that these can only be changed by the person. It's more than training, counseling, or simply setting targets and monitoring. We can maintain control by getting people to recognize the areas they need to develop and deal with. Again, this isn't the old command framework based on past performance but a futuristic model where we seek to get employees to reach for their competencies (i.e., in this case, by the effective use of procedures).

"**4.** *Integration.* We need to make sure the complaints procedure fits with other organizational standards. It should reinforce roles and responsibilities. Most staff will assume some role but others may need to organize returns, compile statistics, send out formal letters, and assess whether the company has dealt with a problem that the customer insists should be taken to the top. What I'm saying is that it's got to fit with our overall corporate strategy.

"One of the most interesting aspects of organizational control is the fragmentation that many companies experience whereby each section has a different view of the business. Internal conflicts and power struggles are the norm. Top management has a completely different view of success from its more junior staff. Executives may lay off hundreds of employees and this streamlining is used to turn the company around to profitability. As a result, they earn bonuses and their contracts are extended.

"Meanwhile middle management must deal with the fallout from redundancies and perceives the entire exercise as a complete failure. When the company employs inexperienced people the following year as a result of an upturn, it reinforces the latter negative view. Peter F. Drucker takes the view that:

> Each level needs its particular vision, it could not do its job without it. Yet, these visions are so different that people on different levels talking about the same thing often do not realize it . . .(10)

"Corporate procedures tend to magnify this problem if care isn't taken to ensure they fit with other systems.

"**5.** *Drafting.* I still think that procedures should form the basis of staff training programs and should be documented with this aim in mind. Having said this, we don't have to write everything down. In fact, the rule should be to document something only if it's absolutely necessary. Otherwise simply leave it as the exercise of good common sense. We'll explain how customers' problems should be addressed, but we needn't detail every possible activity related to listening to customers and responding in a positive way to their concerns.

"We also need to ensure that commonsense rules become part of the procedure may simply say employees should use their judgment. This may be the case when deciding whether to refer a case to the section that handles unresolved complaints or seek to sort them out at the time and place they are identified. The procedure may simply say that the latter should be attempted unless it isn't possible. We must leave some room for intuition. I won't go on about this any further, Bill, just use your common sense. An army of form fillers is of no use in a dynamic organization.

"**6.** *Implementation.* The key to implementing the procedure is to start before a word is written. Introduce the concept of setting this procedure and ask staff to get involved in the process. Get them to view the drafts, test them, discuss them at team meetings, and solve any problems that result. If there's mutual trust, a caring organization, a culture of responsibility without blame assignment, and people are self-motivated and self-controlled, then there'll be no problems. If any of these attributes are missing, then it may fail. All else to do with implementation has been dealt with in staff training, mentioned under skills, knowledge, and attitudes. An example of what happened to me many years ago in the States may help here:

> I remember one occasion when I went to my doctor's for a prebooked appointment. After an hour of watching patients come and go, it suddenly dawned on me that something was wrong and I asked the receptionist why I was still waiting. He checked his system and said the doctor would see me in a few minutes. I said I would still like to know why I had waited an hour. He insisted that my turn would be next. I repeated that I wanted an explanation for the delay. He said that he forgot to log me as waiting on the system. I asked why he hadn't told me that in the first place. I asked for a complaints form and after much fussing around, he pushed a soiled form in my direction. I explained what had happened to my doctor, who shrugged her shoulders and said, "Nothing to do with me."

"If people who work for an organization accept that they represent it and are prepared to listen and simply apologize to customers where necessary, most people wouldn't bother to take complaints further. Unfortunately, this isn't always the case.

"**7.** *Compliance.* We've already spent some time discussing compliance. Nonetheless we need to make sure that staff understand

and are using the complaints procedure. They need to comply with it. The problem is where we hold the complaint's database centrally and start a disciplinary investigation every time a complaint is received. The data is used to police employees. You can imagine, instead of encouraging complaints as important feedback from customers, managers will want to suppress the information. Or, try to get the 'blame' assigned elsewhere. An informal 'nothing to do with me!' policy then operates and our original objective of actively seeking feedback from customers and ensuring any problems are dealt with, fails. We'll have the very opposite. We end up encouraging managers to hide problems and stop customers from lodging formal complaints, maybe by not making it clear that they can and should be encouraged to submit their views.

"Again, there's some danger in setting up compliance teams and using them to discharge this policing role. It adds up to the same problem in the long run. We need to discuss controls that impact on success. Poor controls stifle initiative and using theory X, creates friction and poor performance. Theory Y can be used to build positive relationships and self-control as the right climate where we develop good performance, while a policing state using people like your compliance team takes away this responsibility on the basis that staff are theory X in profile. This may become a trap and excessive central control can mean managers fall into the trap of making the compliance checks more important than the operations they are designed to control. There're no absolutes and each depends on the situation; what works in one place may not work elsewhere. Spying on staff through their routine returns may lead to a 'beat the system' climate, whereas if we work to the same goals, the manager's job may simply be to empower staff to get and use the information and advice that they need to unblock blockages. There's great scope for progress here and this fits with the coaching view. We still need to develop procedures but maybe we should use policies more as a framework and let work teams devise their own procedures.

"**8.** *Review.* Procedures will never be perfect. They shouldn't be designed with this aim in mind. They're based on a representation of reality and the types of decisions that may be made by members of an organization. As representations they are models and, as such, have all the faults and flaws that such models have. Constant review and updating is a way of life, which is why it's best to set the procedure in outline and not in fine detail.

"We may believe we can provide for most occurrences but in the end we must review our procedures to allow people to think. If they don't, then the procedure will not work. Rationing our procedures in line with these arguments is a good idea. If not, they will not be a control but simply a hindrance.

"Any review must be done with users of the system and in our case this is both employees and customers. Employees deal with, or refer the complaints, while customers are frontline users of the system. Most major complaints stem from perceived failings in the complaints procedure itself. In the final analysis, the arrangements we have for dealing with complaints may be causing the complaints that are pursued through the system as they fail to be resolved at each stage. If, for example, there's no provision in the current procedure to simply apologize to the customer (or tell them about progress of their complaint, or allow their comments to be recorded, or allow lessons to be learned by the company), then it will most likely fail. If our training program hasn't taught staff how to manage someone's heated emotions as they explain their problem, then again, the complaints procedure will fail.

"This eight-stage model is a system in its own right. The system has to be in place before we can use the concept of procedures as part of the overall internal control system. While we're on the subject, I'd like to describe one other model in Figure 3.8. I designed it to bring out the importance of training and developing staff using internal procedures as the cornerstone.

"Instead of the procedure being just another detailed document given out to staff on their first day at work, it becomes a dynamic process. We've already dealt with preparing and implementing the procedure (the eight-stage plan). Here, we need to ensure that staff understand and are able to use the procedure. The start is induction training for new staff or for newly introduced procedures. Next comes short awareness training courses (perhaps for half a day), so that all existing employees know about the procedure. The more extensive training workshop is for staff who need a detailed understanding of the procedure, say a dedicated team that investigate more complex complaints. This workshop requires a comprehensive document along with exercises and explanations that employees can work through over, say, two or three days with a professional facilitator. I've shown a refresher course in the diagram to tell staff about changes and remind them of the procedure.

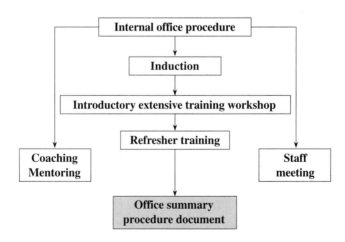

Figure 3.8 Outline complaints procedure.

This course is also available for those experiencing problems with implementing the procedure. Superimposed over this process are two important mechanisms where procedures are fine-tuned, communicated, and discussed. One is staff meetings where operational realities are discussed and work teams can ensure there's good interface with current practices. The second is the coaching and mentoring initiatives where managers simply talk to their people and help them come to grips with work practices. At the very bottom of Figure 3.8 sits the short (summary) office document, which sets out the role of the procedure, the policy framework, bullet points of key matters, and examples of any documentation that's used. Any comprehensive document, if there must be one, will have been given out as part of the training courses and referred to only infrequently. If staff need constantly to delve into the comprehensive document, there's something wrong with the procedure. It's too complicated, technical manuals excepted.

"That's it, Bill. That's what I wanted to say about the use of procedure as a key aspect of control."

Bill realized that he was meant to say something having drifted off into a light sleep some time ago while listening to this speech.

Finally his brain clicked and shifted into gear and the words followed: "Well then, what's the answer?"

"It's still seven squared," Jack said as he launched into an enormous laugh. "I could've said this at the outset and saved myself a lot of hot air."

Bill saw the funny side. "Can we sum up then?" he asked.

"Absolutely," Jack replied. "We're pretty close to home." How do we sum up thought Jack, harboring a strong suspicion that Bill had not been listening to all that had been said over the last hour or so. "How about some quotations?" he asked.

Bill's reply indicated some disquiet. "You use a lot of these and some are pretty much out-of-date now. Is that because you can only get hold of older textbooks here?"

"Not at all," came Jack's reply. "I use references that I think are important. I don't believe we should throw away good material simply because it was written some time ago. If what has been said is important, then it's important. What I say is that procedures should be simple and not demand complicated techniques. In the end, we may not need to express the basic activities. All procedures must make sense. Moreover, procedures cannot be perfect, they must leave room for getting one's hands dirty. I've got a good quote that fits here, from Ts' Ai Ken T'an:

Water which is too pure has no fish.(11)

"Procedures are about making things better, not sterile, because a sterile environment allows no real growth. For the worker, the team, the company, the organization, key stakeholders, and society in general, making better is about being comfortable with one's work and the organization. Having peace of mind, nothing more. Whatever we've said, well-written procedures have an important role in an organization. Well, that's about it on the subject of procedures. We've got a few more miles to go before we get back into Mo'Bay. Why don't we relax and leave any further discussions for tomorrow?"

Much to Jack's surprise, Bill was wide awake and actually wanted to continue the debate. Being the control freak that he was, Bill demanded a conclusion.

"We still need a bottom line on this," he said. "You've gone on and on, dropping a few quotes now and then. But your views have no real conclusion. Sorry, that didn't sound right. What I mean is . . . I've er . . . not been given . . . well . . . the answer."

"Okay," Jack was forced to backtrack. "I wanted to discuss topics related to control so as to create more awareness. I don't see that there are definitive answers as such. If you really insist, I'll give you what I think are the key points. The tape's still running so let's list them:

1. My model of the management control system includes procedures as a vital component. Procedures outline how an organization wishes its activities to be conducted. If staff understand and apply them, we are getting closer to good internal control.

2. The task of preparing and using procedures is a system that is part of the risk management process where we set standards for things that cannot be left to chance. We must move away from viewing procedures as simply documents. It's how they are developed and used to tackle known risks that's important.

3. We can end up with a very brief document or no document at all. The process behind understanding and applying the procedure entails getting involved in them. If a manager is unable to produce a detailed procedures document on request, it isn't necessarily a bad thing. If staff know what they are doing and have had their competencies assessed (knowledge, skills, and attitudes), then we have a starting place for good risk management.

4. Procedures should be owned by the users. They should develop and amend them whenever necessary. They should set up ways of checking their own compliance. When a management by fear regime is in place it can cause poor performance where people refuse to take responsibility or refuse to make decisions.

5. We cannot aim at perfection. That isn't the point. A commonsense approach whereby we move toward organizational goals and customer satisfaction is good enough. Procedures that don't reflect this approach should be discarded unless legally required.

6. Each manager and member of staff must ask themselves, 'Am I happy with the adopted procedure? Does it need to be documented? Do staff use them properly? Do they fit with the models we've discussed earlier (i.e., are all key aspects of these models properly addressed)? What else

could go wrong and am I, my team, and my section in control?

7. A review of procedures necessarily entails a review of the operational processes that underpin them. This is a most useful spin-off benefit. Again, we don't need to wait for consultants or auditors to tell us how best to work. It is the province of each and every employee.

8. Breach of procedure needs to be dealt with. It may be that the procedure is lacking, or the breach is trivial, or departure is right because of the special circumstances. If not, we need to take firm action, and if this involves a reprimand, then so be it. We needn't wait for a compliance team to tell us whether things are being done properly. This is ridiculous. If staff cannot tell whether procedures are working, then it shows there's a training need. Centralized policing because our people cannot be trusted implies a failing organization. Its energies are directed toward discipline, to the detriment of any hope of achieving excellence.

9. If procedures don't work, fix them. They're only useful to the extent that they make it easier to deal with potential problems. People shouldn't moan about cumbersome bureaucracy when they're not prepared to suggest improvements.

10. Since ten is a nice round number, we should make procedures part and parcel of everyday management practices. They should be discussed at team meetings, staff appraisals, coaching events, induction, and other training courses and staff development programs."

Bill recognized that this was a fair conclusion to the topic of the day and noticed that Jack was starting to run out of steam. Refreshed by his intermittent dozing, Bill felt like pushing Jack to the limit. "Jack, I appreciate all that you've said. But I would like to explore your philosophical approach to control and procedures."

Jack could not be sure whether Bill was being serious. Having spoken for two hours nonstop, he felt that the day should now be drawing to a natural close. To start a fresh conversation would be very tiring. Jack noticed a smirk on Bill's face and asked himself silently if this was an endurance test. However, he took up the challenge and said, "Returning to the organizational dimension. A common perception is that everyone knows the overall mission of the business and their own role. Self-control is important as again it's not top-down but part of one's role. Information, reports, and procedures are seen as belonging to employees to help them do and measure their work and not for managers to spy on them. If this happens, a game results, where we doctor the reports to suit top management and energies are used solely in this task and not for the benefit of the business. For example, procedures are only useful if they help us, not to create the notion of top managers looking down.

"Having said that, we have a problem when we see the organization as simple machine parts. We also tend to sort things out through a series of quick fixes that maintain the status quo. This isn't progress, since we need to adapt and change to keep up with our environment. We need an integrated approach that sees systems as consisting of much that is unseen. But can these intangibles (i.e., psyche, culture, and assumptions) really be controlled and if so, how? We recognize these issues, understand how they fit into the overall business systems, and we seek to manage them as well as possible. The biggest single problem is dealing with the child in all of us where we shun responsibility and risk for fear of failure. If we're also charged with dealing with things that we cannot control, it becomes worse. We must build processes that incorporate risk and uncertainty and the human psyche that is wholly unpredictable. Quite a challenge? But we need to explore this point further. We can ask people to understand and address their motives and ensure we can use procedures in a constructive manner that will keep them coming back with ideas. Perfection isn't the answer as it assumes a zero-risk/no-change position that in the end leads to frustration. If we view organizations as a mass of personalities, we get closer to the truth. How to set standards is another matter.

"Many feel that human energies are crucial to organizational success and systems on paper are just that, paper systems and procedures. They achieve nothing. They only have the potential to unleash and direct energies. If they cannot do this, then we will probably fail. The classical post-holder concept has given way to the change agent concept where making good things happen is our main goal. This in turn impacts the status quo with many repercussions. Controls that seek to maintain the status quo through an aversion to deviance do not promote a growth culture. The control chart becomes a blinker that restricts organizational growth. What can replace our friend, the control chart? Look at Figure 3.9.

"Maybe we should be linking our effort to the underpinning skills, knowledge, and attitudes. The task then is to equip people with the necessary tools and ensure their competencies are energized toward their goals. It's a vision of what we would like to be in the future. As we move closer to it, we refocus this vision. In this way we recognize the need to achieve goals by motivating people to move toward them while ensuring barriers to success are removed. For example, we may need to balance our corporate image with

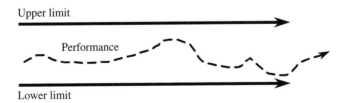

Figure 3.9   Control chart.
(See also Figures 2.1 and 6.13)

various cost-cutting exercises. How can we preserve our image and become leaner?

"Observing control isn't believing in control. It's blind obedience and normally the main reason why good people leave companies (i.e., excessive procedures, no freedom, being treated like children, no mutual trust). Shared control depends on self-control and should equate to organizational control and success. Where staff can't ride the wave of success the organization feels, then there's no control, only discipline and rigidity. You know, Bill, I've written a paper on ensuring compliance with procedures for organizations where this is an issue."

"What do you mean by that?" asked Bill.

"Well, you know, banks, insurance companies, investment bodies, and businesses that are highly regulated, and for things like health and safety. Here compliance routines are pretty much mandatory. There's no way around that. Anyway, my paper. I've called it *Three Strikes and You're Out.* You can have a copy of it, if you like, and I think I'll make it an appendix, say Appendix B to the new book. I'm not sure I can talk about it now. It's getting late and I don't know about you, Bill, but I've run out of steam.

"Ah, we're back at Mo'Bay. See those lights ahead of us. Those are the houses set up on the hills outside of Mo'Bay town."

Thousands of twinkling lights shone down at them through the dark skies as the stars also competed for their attention. Trying to hide his fatigue, Jack continued down the hill toward the hotel.

Bill turned to Jack and mumbled, "You mean you've finally run out of quotes? Thank goodness. This must be the first time ever."

Jack parked outside the hotel and Bill moved a weary body out of the car and into the grey shadows of the parking lot. Jack laughed.

"Bill, don't forget what Peggy Walker said," he shouted.

"And just what was that?"

"Something that we cannot provide for in procedures. It goes:

When faced with a decision, I always ask, "What would be most fun?" (12)

As Bill disappeared into the night on his way toward the hotel lobby, Jack heard him say, "Good night, Jack. Sleep well and see you tomorrow for the next leg of our journey through controls."

A weary Bill strolled into the hotel lounge area with Jack's words floating around his mind. He thought through ways to unwind for the evening. His favorite pastime was reading detective novels and he considered the stock he had brought with him sitting idly in his suitcase in his room. Never a social animal, Bill nonetheless decided to go to the bar, resigning himself to a quiet evening by himself, as usual. Sitting at the bar he asked Bigga for a cold Red Stripe and sat staring into space, while the barman was busy serving a small group of tourists at the other end of the bar.

"Penny for them?"

Ruth appeared at his side as if from nowhere and smiled at him. As Bill's social skills were a little rusty, he simply smiled back as she walked on toward her office.

"Will you join me for a drink, Ruth?" he finally asked. "That is . . . if you aren't busy."

Ruth answered by returning and sitting on the stool beside him. "A glass of red wine then," she said, "if you insist. How was your day, Bill? Did you see any good sights?"

"Well, yes, I did thanks."

"Where did you go?

"You know, I really can't remember. I saw a lot of the coast road. Very pretty. But we, that is Jack and I got to talking about procedures. Part of the control framework, you see."

Ruth looked at Bill with a mock frown, saying, "Are you trying to hint that you want me to leave? I can't believe that you have flown all this way to our beautiful island just to talk about office procedures. Don't you ever wonder if there's more to life than work?"

"Ruth. Please don't misunderstand me. I'm helping Jack with his book, and we have to discuss bits of it. I actually enjoy it. You know I'm not really very good at having fun. At least not lately."

Ruth relaxed visibly as though she understood. "What did you decide then," she asked, shrugging her shoulders and getting into the spirit of things, "about procedures or whatever it was you discussed?"

"I'm in the middle of rewriting the procedures manual. It's more or less done. We have a massive manual that we'll use to judge staff against. Compliance reviews that is. Now Jack tells me that it's all about risk assessment and control standards. It's annoying. I need to get the manual done and now I'm really not sure. I mean, what procedures do you use here at the hotel?"

"I choose my staff very carefully and define their overall role. Also, I set our polices, such as my favorite one: 'Give our guests tranquility.' After that it's up to them. They work out how best to get things done. Some things are written down. Checking in and out is documented. Head Office has written rules for the security box at reception, payments, the minibar, and where guests report an illness. I tend to draft value statements and get my people to buy into the spirit of these. It seems to work."

"So," Bill said, "if I can get my organization to understand risk assessment and then let teams set up their own procedures, I might be better off?"

"I guess so. As long as you set standards for any key corporate matters like security then that would work."

Bill looked at his glass and visualized the new-look manual.

"Is that all?" whispered Ruth "Can I go now?"

"No, Ruth," replied Bill, "Could you get Jack on the phone please? I need to talk this idea through before I hit the sack."

Ruth frowned and thought that Bill must be a complete workaholic, and shy too. An amazing combination.

After half an hour on the phone to Jack, Bill looked in at Ruth's office and said, "I just thought you'd like to know, Ruth, Jack's agreed to prepare a workshop pack for my staff covering the use of procedures and how people and teams can develop their standards. Great news, eh?"

"Wonderful," laughed Ruth as she locked the office for the evening and walked with Bill back to the bar.

"Yu nah go to yu bed, Bill?" shouted Bigga and then started as he saw Ruth walk in behind him, quickly adding, "Only joking."

"Ruth, I think I'll retire for the night," said Bill, "And thanks for all the help. You've been great. You know Jack's dream in life is to write his book and I think he's finally getting started."

"What's your dream in life, Bill?" inquired Ruth as she frowned again and looked him in the eye.

"I'm really not sure I've got one anymore. I used to think it was about making things happen at work. But how can that be a dream? I mean it can't provide happiness, only success. Anyway, goodnight, Ruth."

Ruth looked at Bill as he turned and headed for his room. That's one lonely man, she thought as she asked Bigga to lock up the bar for the night and headed upstairs to her room.

FOUR

Fishing, Witches, and Support Systems

*Discussed here are the other components of the control frame-
work and how they fit in. Standards that cover three important
aspects of organizational control are explained and presented
in a refreshing way using illustrations from Bill's journey
through controls.*

JACK DROVE INTO the hotel parking lot and was surprised that
Bill was not sitting in his usual place on the veranda. He
parked the car under the shade of a large banana tree and walked
into the hotel lobby. He saw Bill leaning over the front desk engaged in conversation with Ruth.

Jack smiled and opened the conversation, "Morning, Ruth.
Sharon sends her regards. You ready then, Bill?"

"Absolutely."

"We don't have far to drive. There are regular tours of the great
house, Rose Hall, just a few miles outside of Mo'Bay town. We can

take a slow drive up there and get some fishing done after lunch. Sound good?"

"Can't wait to get started. Tell me, Jack. I didn't quite get what you said yesterday about today's topic of conversation."

"I didn't really say as it's a difficult one. I want to get into three more big subjects—fraud, creativity, and the whole idea of a corporate internalized control facility. But before we get there, I need to sort out some lesser issues that relate to internal control. I really think that the managerial control system or what I call the MCS, addresses all important issues. Let's go back over my diagram in Figure 4.1."

"If all staff understand and apply all relevant aspects of this system, we can kinda say that we're in control. Or more rightly, we have established comprehensive systems of internal controls. It will not guarantee success, but it will put you in a good position to achieve this success. My problem is that, although the MCS comes

Figure 4.1 Managerial control system.
(See also Figures 2.12, A.4, and D.1)

118

to our aid in dealing with control, which is essentially about good management, there are still other important matters to be addressed. This is why I want to cover various additional items today. Let's get them out of the way."

Bill waved goodbye to Ruth, and the two men walked toward the car. "When are we going to talk about the corporate internalized control facility?" Bill asked. "You know this is what I'm really interested in."

"Okay. The internal control facility will take on board everything we need to deal with on the topic of internal control. It's right that we leave it to the last. Something like the best wine—leave it to last. We'll get there and as Bob Marley says, 'Don't worry about a thing . . .'"

Bill was now starting to recognize the road out of Montego Bay and looked for landmarks along the way. The trip lasted less than fifteen minutes and they arrived at a large expanse of land with the words "Rose Hall" marked in huge stones on the small hill which led to the great house above. A few drinks at the bar and payment of an appropriate fee to a young lady at the bookings office who complained of feeling unwell and the tour began. There was not much opportunity to discuss control issues in the group of a dozen tourists who gathered around the tour guide, listening intently to the exploits of Annie Palmer, known as the white witch of Rose Hall. After a brief reign of terror as mistress of the house, during which she murdered three husbands, she herself was murdered. Annie is said to haunt the great house and comes out to play after 6 each evening. Bill became quite engrossed in these stories from the past and even bought the book on Rose Hall. It brought home the hardship that was experienced in the Caribbean in those days and helped explain why people from these lands fight so hard against their current hardships.

"Right. That's the Rose Hall tour out of the way. Quite spooky, eh? Come on, Bill, let's get some fishing done," Jack suggested.

This proved to be rather a mixed blessing. They arrived at the spot advertised for fishing, and were greeted by several young men who showed them around the long river. The crystal clear waters flowed gently between two grassy banks flanked by trees and color-ful plants on either side. The river flowed past several large boul-ders before it disappeared around a bend toward the sea several miles away.

They were disappointed to see groups of tourists catching fish from a small part of the river that had been sectioned off. As soon as the line touched the water the fish took a bite and were hooked. They were being whipped out at an alarming rate. The attendants were nonetheless pleased, as customers had to purchase any fish that were hooked.

"What's the objective of fishing?" asked Jack, eager to start the philosophical debate.

"Er . . . to catch fish?" Bill was sure this was a trick question.

"For us, it's to enjoy a few pleasant hours by the river and catch the occasional fish, if we can. Picking them out of a barrel is a little pointless."

"Yes, I see what you mean."

Jack caused quite a stir when he insisted on fishing in the main part of the river, despite being told he might not catch a fish, as they had more room to avoid the trap set for them in the form of line and bait. Nevertheless, he spotted a middle-aged man with dreadlocks flowing down his back who was fishing under a shaded spot beneath a large star-apple tree. Bill and Jack joined him.

"Greetings," said the man as he welcomed them. "It's a fine day for fishing."

"Yes," replied Jack, "I'm showing my friend here the island. He's on vacation."

The three men set about the task of enjoying the scenery and catching a fish or two, in that order. Just perfect for good conversa-tion. Turning on the tape, Jack said, "I want to deal with three key aspects of internal control: information systems, financial management, and value for money. Do you remember we said that control objectives were based around compliance with procedure, protecting assets, sound information, and value for money (VFM) . . . you know economy, efficiency, and effectiveness? We've discussed the first one, procedures, and we'll deal with fraud tomorrow. Today we'll tackle the last two, information and VFM. I want to include financial systems because they tend to be high risk."

INFORMATION SYSTEMS

"Let's make a start, " Jack continued, checking the recorder. "I've met many people who suggest that control is all about information. We need information to be in control and so long as we have the right information, then everything will be fine. I believe information is an important part of control, in fact it's included in my managerial control system. But it's not control period. Figure 4.2 helps here."

"Data is any form of raw facts in no particular order. These facts need to be made into information in order to be of any use. Information comes together to form the wider concept of knowledge that has meaning, which enables us to act and move forward.

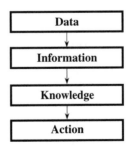

Figure 4.2   Control information.

121

It's the final part of the model that causes most problems. I believe that the real end-product is action. That is, a decision to do or not to do something based on the information available. If I pick up a train timetable and read parts of it, it has no real value unless it can help me make a particular decision. So control isn't based on information or even knowledge. It's based on action, supported by good knowledge. This is a key point because many information systems bouncing around an organization have little or no use to managers or their staff.

"Most basic control models suggest that we set targets, get staff to perform, monitor whether these targets have been achieved, and then take action. Monitoring is based on exception reports that indicate the extent to which targets have been achieved. Again, information is used as a key aspect of this control model. Our control chart does much the same. You know, it's based on setting an upper and lower limit and then measuring actual performance and assessing whether performance falls within the two limits. Movement toward one upper or lower level inspires action to adjust performance. Information is the way we measure performance.

"The performance management scheme is an extension of this basic principle. The line manager sets the performance targets based on a defined standard. Or better still, the staff set and then get their manager to agree to their performance targets. Actual performance is then measured and checked against this standard, again based on suitable information systems.

"The other side to information relates to communications. Internal control depends on good communications. We set objectives, get staff to rally round them, and then measure and control progress toward meeting our goals. Throughout this process, we depend on good communications to make it all happen. One-off information systems are giving way to general communications systems. So we may have e-mail, phones, faxes, video conferencing, and electronic diaries that form our communications infrastructure. Meetings, events, gatherings, and so on allow face-to-face contact to supplement the infrastructure. We use the corporate network to dip into specific applications as and when necessary. Work isn't so much based on working on these applications (say payroll, payments, or the customer databases). We're more interested in corporate communications that are able to call upon relevant bits of these applications as and when required.

"So individual databases are used as action mechanisms, and communications generally to form part of our control environment. I think people should view information systems in this way. This comes home when we develop a new computerized system. The focus is on the information technology (IT) and whether it will work. Energies then move toward project management on the basis that the project must succeed and all systems objectives should be met. We arrive at a great focus on project planning, data flow techniques, methodologies, and time management with reports to the project boards and quality team. The plan is sacrosanct. There's nothing wrong with this, as it all promotes good control over the project and the project plan. But beyond this, we need to think about other things. My diagram in Figure 4.3 explains effective information systems. If all four issues are taken care of, we can truly say that our information systems promote good control over the achievement of corporate objectives. Let's take them in turn.

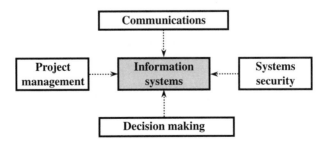

Figure 4.3   Effective information systems.

"**1.** *Project management.* Most people know about good project management and all that it entails for computerized systems and business projects. Systems profiling, user driven systems, rapid application developments, planning, monitoring reports, extensive testing, contract management in terms of bought-in software, staff training, steering groups, the project manager role, capacity planning, and all these things are pretty standard. What's also pretty standard is the high failure rate for new computer systems. They're normally late, expensive, and incomplete. In fact, these three factors—timing, cost, and quality—are always in conflict. They cannot all be achieved; there must be some give. We're now developing 'get-something-worthwhile-going' systems. Developed quickly and incremental in term of functions, so long as they're better than the old systems and deal with known snags. The aim isn't about perfection because people realize this simply causes frustration all around. The key point is that the principles of good project management should be in place for there to be control. Not necessarily formal project management methodologies as these projects sometimes fail because there's too much paperwork and reporting back. Creative people get bored and the administrators and auditors take over. Moreover, end-user computing is now seen as the way forward and this fits snugly into the self-control concept. People decide what information they need and then get the systems to provide this information. The technology is a side issue. So long as the organization has a corporate network that's driven by high-speed servers, we'll be okay. The technology is a barrier. It's there simply to enable applications to run. We only need to make sure that the network is powerful enough to support our applications. Control isn't about technology, it's about achieving our goals.

"**2.** *Systems security.* We can't discuss control in information systems without mentioning systems security. There are numerous dangers ranging from false invoices, ghost employees, altered stock figures to hide theft of stock, theft of credit card details, and so on. Our information needs to be protected against these threats.

"We need to ensure our systems are secure from unauthorized access and are only used for their intended purpose. Most people understand the importance of IT security better these days as they use the Internet to buy things and pass on their credit card details. It's also about managing the database, which means it's updated properly, protected, and complies with any regulations for holding personal data. I don't really want to go into great detail on this matter, because it's pretty basic. IT security is normally managed by someone in an organization who sets standards, checks that they're being adhered to, and looks out for problems. There's nothing wrong with this but you know my view of control—it's about self-control. Giving people more responsibility for IS (information systems)/IT security is my preferred solution. Show them why it's important and how they may live up to their responsibilities. Getting good data onto a system and ensuring it makes sense is part of IT security. Having rules for using this data is so important. Rather than forcing people into these rules, we should explain and help them use them. We should make sure that laws are adhered to by writing our own procedures on their requirements. We also need to ask about backup arrangements that ensure if something happens to our data we have copies that can be used to restart the system. Most networks have automatic backups, and most of our individual efforts should relate to the use of floppy diskettes, CDs, and data held on PC hard drives. If, when you open your desk door, dozens of diskettes fall out, there's a problem. You need to think about maintaining them, cataloging them, backing them up, and making sure access to confidential information is restricted. We may also need to be involved in contingency planning if we have a role in high-risk databases. Perhaps we may have to restrict the use of floppy disks and write-to CDs. One control that has a main role in IT security is related to the use of passwords. While passwords are being replaced by more dynamic controls such as retina scans, they're still important. Organizations and the people employed by these organizations should adopt a set of rules that form the cornerstone of IT security (i.e., password control). Bill, how many rules for passwords can you think up right now?"

"Not many," Bill replied. "Apart from trying to remember it."

"Okay. I guess quite a few examples of rules for passwords may be listed for your standards manual. Passwords should be:

- Known only to the individual and kept secret.
- Changed regularly. The system can prompt the user to change the password after x number of weeks.
- Not changed to a password used during the last x number of occasions.
- Not written down anywhere. Most people write down their passwords in a way that they feel won't be recognized. Some enter it in their diaries with no heading or write it in an unusual place at work.
- Not easily guessable, such as first name, child's name, middle name, house name, and so on.
- Linked to an ID that locates all systems movements and transactions to a known employee. The password shouldn't work unless linked to a specific and known ID.
- Gives defined user privileges: access to certain defined files, rights within these files, and parts of the database. Make sure these rights are registered with Personnel and write to the person telling them what their defined privileges are and that they're not authorized to use systems outside this framework. Make clear the implications of unauthorized access such as dismissal.
- Withdrawn as soon as the person leaves, or better still, when the employee gives notice of resignation.

- Forms part of the disciplinary code on use of systems. That staff shouldn't divulge their password to anyone and they should take all reasonable steps to protect them. They should also report instances where they become aware of another person's password.

- Respected as important. For example, you shouldn't enter the password when someone is looking over your shoulder.

- Encrypted so that it doesn't appear on screens and is held in an inaccessible file.

- Not excessive. Employees should not have to remember many different passwords for many different systems. They'll write them in their diaries and spend much time telling IS support that they've forgotten them. This means new passwords bounce around the organization in desk diaries and phone conversations.

- Protection seen as a corporate issue. A company may issue a standard password to new employees (say their surname) and ask them to alter it at the first opportunity, to a password that only they know. This may be used in conjunction with their initials as an ID linked to the password. We need only know the name of the new employee and start date to access the system under their password, before they've changed it to an unknown one. Also, if IS support accepts unverified phone calls from people who claim they've forgotten their password, it could lead to problems. The really committed criminal will try to form a relationship with an employee and work at getting her password from her.

- Have rules on leaving screens unattended. Where the organization has established a complicated procedure for getting through screens, staff will be very reluctant to log out fully. Screen savers can be used but the password protection on screen savers makes the use of PCs by anyone, say through hot-desking, difficult. We can also time staff out after the system has been unused for a defined time period.

- Train staff in the importance of password control. I've seen staff swap passwords where they have accessed a system at one desk and have answered the phone at another desk, and want to get back into the system. Good systems don't let staff access them from two locations.
- Allow the system to report inconsistent access patterns. Say starting at 7 A.M. and continuing at 10 P.M. the same day (unless this is remote access from outside the office). Or accessing unusual files or repeating or canceling many transactions.
- Don't allow repeated attempts to access systems. Lock out all attempts over a defined number, for example, three. We can also commission special reports on these instances.
- Ensure that remote access requests are subject to callback so that the terminal address can be verified before we accept the password.
- Be careful about establishing password patterns. Some networks don't allow the user to change passwords to one used before (or say on the last x occasions). The systems manager may be able to view a list of the previous passwords used. There may be an established pattern that means the current one may be anticipated. Where we demand alpha-numeric passwords, the user may use the name say, of a son along with an alpha, say James1, then James2, James3, and so on. The systems managers, or for that matter the IT staff in general, would be able to guess which one is next on the list.
- Make sure we can tell which terminal is being used for which transactions. We need to be able to pinpoint systems breaches and locate the offending access device.

"These rules should underpin the culture of the organization. The self-control concept means that violations should go to the user and line manager. The IT security manager should then make sure each one is dealt with by the line manager. To try to report dozens of minor irregularities to an IT security office, simply means bulky reports are left on someone's desk and ignored.

"**3.** *Decision making.* My model says that data become information, become knowledge, and become action. It's the action that's important at the end of the day. If the information system is developed without regard to decision making, it'll be inefficient.

"We need to ensure that people who build information systems understand the type of decisions that are made and how they happen. There's normally some conflict between accuracy and speed in reporting. The more detail required, the longer it takes to get a decent report up and running. Different levels of management require different degrees of detail. So the trend is for systems users to design, develop, and install their own information systems based around the corporate IS strategy. Figure 4.4 fits in quite nicely here.

"Business unit managers will want to know about the performance of business applications, such as the overall payroll figures and the performance of their staff. They'll want standard reports

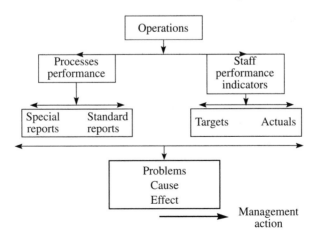

Figure 4.4 Decision-making information.

on items such as the number of people paid in the last run, total paid, tax, and so on. Meanwhile, managers may want special reports on, say, the total overtime paid in section X by grade of staff for the last three months. They'll likewise need information on individual staff to support an employee performance management system, to measure performance per targets that have been set.

"Thus we may identify potential problems (or opportunities), diagnose them, and then take effective action. It's the action that's important. So the information system needs to be based around the need to make logical decisions.

"Most system engineers design and build systems, then tell users what information they can get from it. What's starting to happen, and what's needed for information to really be part of internal control, is for managers and staff to work out what information they need to support decisions they have to make and then design systems around this. There're many information systems around today that don't do this.

"Also, the way we feed information into the decision-making process is important as we can see in Figure 4.5. My model suggests

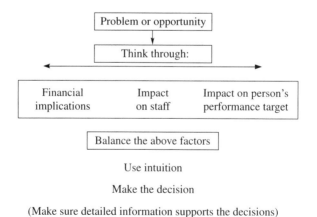

Figure 4.5 Corporate information systems.

130

that we need general information that's held in corporate databases. It includes policy documents, strategic intentions, performance targets, company trends, and so on. If we have to make 20 relevant budget cuts in our department, we need general information on this matter. Our decision is made having reference to financial data, the staffing implications, and how it will reflect on us personally (i.e., our performance targets). The decision on where and how to make these cuts is then made mainly by balancing these factors along with what many managers describe as a gut feeling. You know, intuition. We then look for detailed information that supports, or doesn't rule out, our decision. Control here is about having the right information on hand, but also recognizing how it fits into the overall scenario.

"One further point is that information isn't action. Information alone, even if relevant and useful, doesn't mean people take effective action. Giving staff responsibility for the managerial control system is one way of ensuring that there's responsibility, empowerment, and action. To my mind, information is part, but not all of this process.

"**4.** *Communications.* The last part of the information model, from an internal control viewpoint, is communications. New information adds to the overall state of communications, which is affected by the existing culture. The reports and screens that flow from an information system are affected by the way people view and use them. We've already said that information is about taking action, or seeing that no action is required. This information is part of what you are told and what you tell others, that is, communications. The way an organization communicates, be it via e-mail, phone, meetings, conferences, gossip, correspondence, and so on affects its culture. One key concern is which information is accessible by which people. We can promote an open communications culture by giving all information to everyone. Or we can use the need-to-know basis in deciding who gets what. The latter means that managers and specialist staff have the power to inform others on request or otherwise. The former tends to support an empowerment approach where people have the power to extract (e.g., download) whatever information they think is important. Communications will therefore turn more to exchanging ideas than simply passing on information. I'll give you a standard model of communicating information in Figure 4.6.

"Communicating information is quite straightforward, where we simply tell people something. It may be by memo, report, staff letter, notice board, computer screen, E-mail, open meeting, private meetings, and so on. The information speaks for itself. The next model deals with the act of conveying ideas and reflects a more involved approach in Figure 4.7.

"Here we turn ideas into action, where communication is about getting some kind of response from the receiver with information that conveys ideas and leads to action, which in turn tends to add more value to the organization than just standard reports. Information systems that don't do this won't add much value to an organization. They certainly will not assist the process of conveying ideas and making things happen as a result.

"To sum up, I view information systems as one key to internal control. But only insofar as they're effective and add value to the

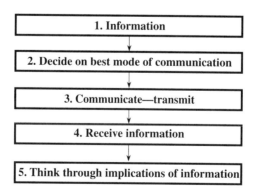

Figure 4.6 Communicating information.

132

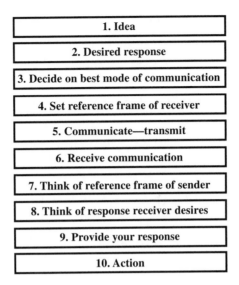

1. Idea

2. Desired response

3. Decide on best mode of communication

4. Set reference frame of receiver

5. Communicate—transmit

6. Receive communication

7. Think of reference frame of sender

8. Think of response receiver desires

9. Provide your response

10. Action

Figure 4.7 Conveying ideas.

organization. This control is based on recognizing four factors: communications infrastructures, sound project management, systems security standards, and a culture of positive decision making. The key to the successful development of new information systems is to use a project manager who recognizes and understands their importance."

At this, Bill jumped up and flicked his line as he felt something tug at it. With great effort and skill he worked his line around and coaxed his catch toward the surface of the water. Unfortunately after much effort, he pulled an old bicycle tire out of the water.

"That's a good start," the stranger said with a laugh, "I think you'd better carry on with your lecture," he said jokingly. "By the way, my name's Daniel. People call me Danny-Dread."

After the usual handshakes Danny-Dread continued, "I couldn't help hearing you guys. What's this about? I mean, your discussions?"

Jack was eyeing the tire and unsuccessfully trying to stifle his laughter as he said, "I'm not sure we can get this tire into a frying pan. You'd better put it back. To answer your question Danny-Dread, we, that is Bill here and I, are doing some research into business control and we've been going over the material for several days now."

"Okay," said Danny-Dread as he looked obviously concerned at this answer, "If that's what you do on your day off, so be it." He then turned back to his line with a frown on his face.

FINANCIAL SYSTEMS

Jack stared thoughtfully up toward the blue sky for a few seconds, then continued just as enthusiastically as before, "I need to talk about financial systems as a special subject when dealing with internal control, because they tend to attract a high-risk rating when assessing whether things are well controlled. Here, compliance with procedures becomes a key issue where there's less room for personal discretion. Fraud is also high up on the agenda, because if these systems can be penetrated, people will have access to our finances. The other key point is that these systems feed into the accountability requirements, where managers account to the organization's owners. There's a legal requirement where financial accounts have to be prepared, audited, and filed for public record.

"Going back to risk. One version of this is the amount of assets and interest at risk, times the likelihood that they will be eroded or lost. The resulting dollar figure indicates whether the organization needs to target specific controls such as internal checks, reconciliations, or defined authorization limits. These controls seek to reduce the likelihood of loss and provide a degree of assurance that finances are protected.

"We cannot simply rely on auditors to check financial systems and provide reports back to management on them. Audit can only comment on the existing arrangements provided by management.

There must be a start, in that systems of internal control are established to protect them. Where these are in place, they can be audited. Even here audit will look at matters that it believes are high risk, but only to the extent that resources allow. External audit looks at systems but only as a shortcut to verifying transactions that underpin the annual financial statements. Internal auditors look at systems subject to resources and within each audit. But they only comment on what they've been able to review during the assigned time. There's no shortcut to management assessing its financial systems, understanding the inherent risks, and establishing suitable arrangements for managing these risks.

"There are several things to consider when setting standards for financial systems for your manual. I'll list them.

- *Ownership.* Management must accept that it and not the auditors are responsible for these systems. I remember one external audit where on arrival I was presented with a trial balance that didn't balance. The debits didn't equal the credits due to an unidentified error. The Chief Financial Officer had happily left this problem for more than six months on the basis that the auditors would sort it out when they turned up. The finance officer didn't feel responsible for dealing with this problem.
- *Corporate procedures.* The organization should set procedures for dealing with finances. There should be rules on receiving income, paying invoices, making payments to members of staff or people employed on temporary contracts, operating cash offices, reimbursing expenses, and storing documentation and data in support of financial transactions. We need procedures covering systems that feed into the corporate financial system, that in turn is used to prepare the annual accounts. Also there should be provision for the operation of budgets and management accounts. One set of rules would

135

cover safeguarding assets and interests and proper accounting for liabilities. Further rules should cover the way transactions are recorded for the purpose of preparing accounts for a period gone (i.e., financial accounting). Another set of principles should cover management accounting where we assess the financial implications of decisions that we need to make now and in the future. The point I'm trying to make is that all staff members need to ask whether they're aware of and fully understand corporate financial procedures. If not, they should take it upon themselves to put this right. If there're no such procedures around, then we need to find out why.

- *Competence.* Building on what I've just said, all staff members need to assess whether they have a good understanding of financial systems, financial accounting, and management accounting. This cannot be left up to accounting staff and people who work for the Chief Financial Officer. All staff need to appreciate how accounts are prepared and how they rely on feeder systems such as debtors, creditors, and payroll, to strip off information for the accounts. They need to know about journal entries, reconciling accounts, and dealing with suspense account items. They also need knowledge of the key principles of management accounting and how costs move in line with activity levels and other related costs. They need to be able to assess the financial effect of their decisions. The self-control idea means that staff have a basic competence in everything that makes for the right control environment including finances. Most breaches of financial procedures are the result of ignorance rather than malicious acts. So, financial management should be firmly on the staff training agenda. It should really be part of the performance management scheme and something that's positively looked for at recruitment stage.

- *Budgetary control.* The empowerment concept means giving people freedom to manage in the best way they think fit. But this way will be within a given budget, a budget being a plan expressed in financial terms. It gives a delegated level of freedom, where the person in question is authorized to spend to defined levels and allocations. It acts as a control by setting actuals against budget (or standard) and seeking explanation of variances. Remember our control chart—standards, actuals, and variances? One interesting feature of budgets is the use of what's called flexible standards. Here the set budget is flexed to reflect the actual rather than planned level of activity. So we may spend more or less but this amount is adjusted by the level of output before we compare actuals to budgets."

Looking at the rippling water Bill mumbled, "This is getting very technical, Jack. I'm finding it hard to come to grips with some of these ideas."

Much to Jack's surprise Danny-Dread joined in and added, "I agree. You're going off into the deep end with this one my friend."

Jack said, "Well, I can't help it if there's a lot to get through. I can't talk in nursery rhymes all the time, can I?"

"Look, Jack. Just give a simple example and cut out the jargon. What do you say Danny-Dread?"

"Agreed," Danny-Dread replied, looking animated as he entered the debate again.

"Good grief," Jack said, "there's no pleasing you guys. An example might do the trick. Okay, look at this fishing lake. Suppose we made the fishing rods that are sold here. We need materials to make the rods—that is, wood and glue (direct materials)—people to make them (direct labor) and power (direct overheads). Say we also pay rent for a workshop (fixed overheads). And we sell each rod for $100 Jamaican. Our budget and actual results may well resemble Figure 4.8.

"Our sales have increased and so have our costs. The budget shows adverse costs of $24,000 because we have simply done more, which has cost us more. The variances are misleading as overall, we've made $26,000 more profit than planned.

"What we need to do is adjust those items of income and costs that move with the increased level of activity. The activity has increased 50 percent more than planned (from 1,000 to 1,500 rods), so we increase or flex the budget for all direct sales and direct costs. The fixed costs are left because, in the short term, they tend to stay the same, regardless of the level of activity. The revised figures for the fishing rods appear as Figure 4.9.

"An analysis of variances between the flexed budget and actual results makes more sense and we can now target materials for greater scrutiny as there is a large adverse variance. It may be that we are employing less well-trained staff that cost less, but lead to greater levels of wastages and therefore higher material costs.

	Original Budget	Actuals	Variances (B-A)
Activity levels	1,000	1,500	500
Sales	100,000	150,000	50,000
Direct material	30,000	50,000	(20,000)
Direct wages	10,000	12,000	(2,000)
Direct overheads	5,000	6,000	(1,000)
Fixed overheads	20,000	21,000	(1,000)
Total costs	$ 65,000	89,000	(24,000)
Gross profits	$ 35,000	61,000	26,000

Figure 4.8   Fixed budgets.

	Original Budget	Flexed Budget	Actuals	Variances (B-A)
Activity levels	1,000	1,500	1,500	0
Sales	100,000	150,000	150,000	0
Direct material	30,000	45,000	50,000	(5,000)
Direct wages	10,000	15,000	12,000	3,000
Direct overheads	5,000	7,500	6,000	1,500
Fixed overheads	20,000	20,000	21,000	(1,000)
Total costs	$ 65,000	87,500	89,000	(1,500)
Gross profits	$ 35,000	62,500	61,000	1,500

Figure 4.9   Flexible budgets.

"This example is simple but it holds many good principles that can be widely applied. If our budgets don't reflect our actual activities, then they will make little sense. Instead of being a control that sets standards and motivates us to reach these standards, they become a source of conflict and frustration. They demotivate and therefore lower performance. The more we do and the more we achieve, the greater our variance on costs and therefore the greater the scrutiny and pressure to hold costs. This equation may stifle productivity and make comparison of variances meaningless.

"Furthermore, if the budget is a tool used by accountants and auditors to keep a check on managers and their staff, it becomes an instrument of oppression. This tactic is useful if the main objective of an organization is to police variances from budgets assigned to employees. It gets worse when the budget becomes a cat and mouse game where managers spend or lose it next year, or they hide their spending by using vague terminology. If, on the other hand, the budget is seen as an important technique used by managers and staff to help them utilize their resources, target their efforts, and make good decisions, then it becomes an important control. This fits best with an organization whose main objective is the provision of value to its customers, through the best use of resources. The internalized control concept is obviously located with this latter view of the budget and the budgeting process.

"Financial management is important and each staff member should ask whether they are happy with their comfort levels when dealing with this topic. Likewise, a detailed analysis of a budget can address only part of the key issues facing management. It cannot answer all questions and global figures should be further analyzed before we get closer to the right answers.

"Also, financial management shouldn't be used to constrain the creativity that drives an organization forward. There are financial limits to be observed, but we must be careful that they are balanced with the demands of reality.

"Let's deal with the final part of today's topic after lunch," Jack said. Lunch consisted of curry goat and rice at a small restaurant near the fishing venue. Bill ordered a milky drink called Supligen and before they could drink them Danny-Dread appeared at the bar and added two shots of white rum and three blocks of ice to their drinks to ensure it hit the spot. Bill and Jack were both grateful for this added boost and thanked Danny-Dread heartily.

"Why do you fish?" Danny-Dread asked quietly. "For me, I enjoy the view by the water and the feeling of tranquility. How do you guys see things?"

"Well," replied Bill, "I think the peace and quiet is important, but I really need to think about hooking a few fish. To be honest guys, I mentioned the fishing trip to Ruth and she said I'd probably talk so much that I'd come back empty-handed. You know, I'd love to prove her wrong."   .

Jack could only raise his eyebrows and smile. "Don't worry," he finally said, "I'm sure we'll bag a few fish today and get some more work done on the manual."

The two men walked back to their fishing spot, since Danny-Dread had told them he would come along later.

With their lines gently swaying in the water Bill took up the conversation, "I guess we can add another objective of fishing to Danny-Dread's point. That is, to impress Ruth with a fine catch."

"Yes," Jack said, "we can start to develop this list of objectives. It may be to discuss control, to view the scenery, to catch a few fish and throw some back as long as no one sees us, to have something to eat tonight, to find out what type of fish live in these waters, it goes on and on. That's why we sometimes have difficulty in establishing systems objectives, because each person has a different interpretation of them. Controls are in place to make sure that objectives are achieved, as best we can. Where these objectives are unclear, it's hard to work out the type of controls that we should establish. This point is often overlooked. Mission statements and clear policies and strategies are some ways that help us envision our goals and ensure staff understand them. It is important to understand that the managerial control system starts with objectives."

VALUE FOR MONEY AND QUALITY

"Why do you want to deal with value for money as part of controls?" asked Bill.

"Good question. You remember the key roles of internal control we discussed a few days ago. They should aim at:

- Sound information systems
- Compliance with procedures
- Protection of assets and interests while minimizing losses
- Economy, efficiency, and effectiveness

"If these things are properly in place, we can be said to be in control. Systems of internal control must deal with each of the items in the foregoing list. We've already dealt with all but the last two of these items. Economy, efficiency, and effectiveness equates to value for money, which is where we are now.

"Unfortunately, I get a bit lost when it comes to this concept of value for money or VFM. In my dictionary, value can mean *benefit, desirability, help, importance, merit, profit, use, worth,* or even *advantage.* It's all these things for the least outlay (i.e., least cost). Quality is seen as a parallel concept and is defined as *aspect, attribute, condition, feature, mark, property,* or *trait.* That is, what the thing is, or looks like, or feels like.

"Quality as a process is about doing things well, getting good results, delivering the right thing, and achieving success. More than anything else, it's about setting high standards and a culture where these standards are the norm. Quality in action is about having the type of procedures that promote quality products and services. The problem with accreditation schemes is that, although we can show that we have these procedures in place, it can simply become a paper exercise. Going back to the concept of value for money, it consists of three main components as you can see in Figure 4.10.

"It's based around a simple system of inputs, a transformation process, and resulting outputs. Economy means getting inputs that can do the job at the best price (i.e., shopping around and negotiating well). Remember our fishing rods? Well, the inputs include the material, the workers, and power. Efficiency means getting the best results from these inputs (i.e., being productive and using resources well), making the rods in the most productive way possible. It also means fine-tuning the process so that it works well and is up

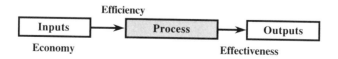

Figure 4.10   Value for money.

142

to date. Effectiveness means getting the right results, achieving systems objectives whatever they are. It's easy to see how making rods has a clear objective, but we also saw how it's difficult to set clear objectives for fishing from the customers' viewpoint. Let's move away from making rods to fishing itself as an activity. For you and I our inputs to fishing are the rod, line, bait, our time, and the fee we paid to use the river. Economy is about asking whether we have the best deal here. Efficiency is about the way we set about the task of fishing—the way we used the equipment, our position on the river, technique, and the way we land the fish. How well is this done? Effectiveness is in one sense about how many fish we landed. But we know that we have to pay for each fish so we don't want too many. But we do want some, particularly you my friend. At the end of the day have we met our objective in going fishing? That is, how effective have we been. If we wrote procedures to cover the best way to undertake the task of fishing, we could call these quality procedures. A recognized fishing body could come along, approve these procedures, and we could refer to the fact that we have achieved this accreditation.

"However, our goal may be to have a stress-free day out fishing among the natural beauty of the river, and to free the mind of all problems and worries. Negotiating a low fee, observing all published fishing procedures, and documenting the catches for the record may induce much stress and paperwork. This may, in effect, mean that the original goals aren't achieved at all. In this way fishing will have become a major hassle.

"Having completed numerous VFM audits, my view is that VFM is nothing more than employing good managers and using good staff. If they establish clear procedures, you will have quality systems. It's as simple as that.

"I recall the days before organizations felt uncomfortable about laying off their people. They used to rely on VFM initiatives to make savings and audit carried out many high-level projects in this respect. I carried out such an audit of two major transport functions.

My recommendations included merging the two functions and getting rid of excess stocks of vehicles, as well as using the vehicles more flexibly. These changes led to more than a million dollars worth of savings. At the end of the day, any sensible transport manager could have achieved these savings (i.e., efficiencies through basic good transport management). It's wrong to have auditors doing this job for them. All my VFM reviews have had the same flavor. In contrast, basic good management and talented and motivated staff provide VFM in its purest sense. It also goes hand in hand with the self-control concept. There may be some facilitation required to get staff to use their skills and show them how to get projects through the organization's review and approval process. But again, we can address these issues through the corporate internalized control facility.

"We can see instances where things have been done badly. Management decisions having led to poor VFM. But VFM is about seeking improvement and making progress as well as sorting out problems, which again, I see as basic good management.

"Auditors review systems and then form suppositions that certain areas need improving. They may use comparison with norms, national standards, or similar operations. We look for evidence that supports our original suppositions and then identify these problems, underlying causes, and recommended solutions. An action plan then takes the solutions to management for their attention and action. Formal presentations and close working with management are hallmarks of a good VFM project. I still argue that the alternative and more effective approach is to ensure management have the skills and techniques to review and secure good VFM as part of their everyday responsibilities. Ensuring that they have established the managerial control system is one way of doing this. The old-fashioned review should give way to a new approach of providing facilitation and advice where required.

"Operational managers are best placed to assess the situation and seek improvement; the review and audit people sometimes simply go around in circles talking in generalities. As usual, I have been able to think up a basic model for our work on VFM and quality as in Figure 4.11.

"Remember, I use these diagrams to represent systems in the sense that each component feeds into and is dependent on the other components. Together they form a system whereby each needs to be in place for the system to work. Okay, back to the components of Figure 4.11.

- *Services.* We need to define at the outset what we're responsible for. This sets the parameters within which we seek efficiencies and service delivery. It may be contained in a mission statement or charter that spells out this role. It's important because we cannot be responsible for efficiencies

Figure 4.11 VFM and quality.

145

that are located elsewhere. In this scenario, we would need to work as a team to deal with cross section problems.

- *Define Quality.* Setting out exactly what you want in terms of defined standards is also an important aspect of VFM and quality. We need to define quality standards. This definition says what we expect to see in terms of the final product and creates a reference frame for staff to rally round. It's a bit like the control chart we've used before, a model within which our activities should fall. Some will be subjective and relate to the impression customers receive when they use the service, what they experience, how they're treated, and whether they feel happy with their treatment. A simple matter such as handling phone calls can be quite an important aspect of quality standards.

  If you walk into Burger King, McDonalds, KFC, or Pizza Hut, you'll find a different atmosphere and staff culture. The questions to ask are, Is this what we want and how do customers feel about it?

- *Quality Management Systems.* I see this item as all those systems and processes that contribute to the delivery of products and services. If these work, then the service will work. The managerial control system is one way of viewing these underpinning processes. Another way is to view those systems that relate to managing, training, and developing staff as key to quality and value for money. The list we have covers:

  - Rewards
  - Training
  - Coaching
  - Motivation
  - Empowerment
  - Mentoring
  - Teambuilding

If we can get these right at the outset, we're well on the way to an excellent organization. Excellent here means VFM is built into the way the organization works.

Consider an example of the staff performance management scheme. We need to set standards and ensure that staff have the competencies to meet these standards. A version of the control chart can be used to define high and low performance levels. Good performers are further developed as having great potential, while poor performance means staff may fall into the area where counseling may have to be considered as in Figure 4.12.

- *Develop Systems.* This stage is about ensuring the systems are in place and that they're reviewed, assessed, and kept up-to-date. There's also the important concept of change management that needs to be addressed. Here, we ensure that change is built into these systems and we're able to deal with the implications of asking staff to rally around change after change as the norm and not something unusual. Change management is about communicating with staff and getting them fully involved in the change process. Bottom-up communication and empowerment are two initiatives that'll

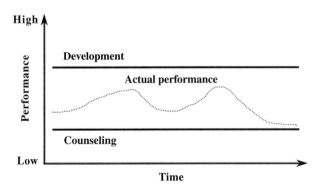

Figure 4.12 Performance chart.

drive successful change strategies. Change only works where all employees are pulling in the same direction. Commitment, motivation, and enthusiasm are all prerequisites.

- *Focus Energies.* Having developed our systems, we need to ensure the people working for us can drive them. Organization charts, documented strategies, a room full of consultants, and speeches from the chief executive are all very well. What's more important is the release of energies to make things happen. VFM is about a constant search for better ways of performing and delivering services. Constant probing only happens where there's an energy to support this force. Where this energy is focused, we'll achieve VFM—no doubt about it. But we need to balance accountability with creativity. Accountability is important and relates to what was done in the past. Creativity focuses on what we intend to do in the future. To achieve this balance—to be creative but accountable for one's actions—is a goal that should be aimed at. Figure 4.13 shows how accountability features as important for past periods where we justify what we have done, while creativity has a high profile for activities that are happening now and in the future.

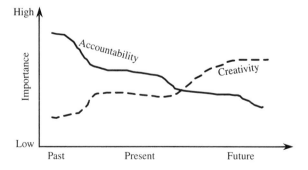

Figure 4.13   Accountability and creativity.

148

- *Measure Product.* We have defined quality and efficiency at the outset. This is fine as it sets the right environment within which staff work. But we must also measure the extent to which these standards have been achieved. We must be able to tell whether we've been successful and the degree of any shortfall. One useful way of doing this is to establish feedback mechanisms so that we can tell what impact the service or product has had on our customers. A complaints procedure also helps. More formal measuring devices can be used where the outputs are physical in nature, like the fishing rods we used in our example of flexible budgets. Do the fishing rods pass our quality standards in terms of appearance, measurement, and use? If our inspections show there's a problem, this must be fed back into a review of underlying processes and the causes diagnosed. Most people accept that quality and VFM aren't about inspection but about good processes. Effort concentrated on these processes reduces the resource we need to dedicate to inspection. This argument also applies to compliance. Instead of sending in armies of checkers, we may wish to establish processes through which compliance happens by training people in the best way of using their section's procedures.
- *Deliver Quality Services.* The final result of all the factors we've mentioned so far is the provision of quality services. There's nothing more than this to say although, this doesn't always work out. You know, all organizations need to know when things aren't quite working out.

"Okay, we've discussed information systems, financial systems, and the importance of quality and value for money. They're all key aspects of the system of internal control. I want to close this part of our discussions by referring to a quote that makes an important point much better than I could. Let's repeat a warning from Daniel

149

Meacham who asks that we don't get obsessed with the worries and problems of life but maintain a sense of perspective in all things:

> Maintain a sense of perspective and proportion in all your endeavors . . . A simple rule of thumb: Whatever you're looking at is not as big a deal as you think it is.(1)

"Where we're looking for the perfect business process and will accept nothing less, we'll always be disappointed. There is no perfection, only what's best at this point in time in comparison with other options. My final point relates to the other obsession that grips control freaks—the need for everything to be planned and organized. This cannot always be so and the natural flow of things often takes precedence."

Bill looked deeply into the river scanning it for fish.

"Jack," he said, "I told Ruth I'd catch some fish and I'm starting to get desperate. I think I'll try over there," pointing to the sectioned-off part of the river where dozens of fish were crammed into a small area. After dipping his line into this pond three times and coming out after a few minutes, each time with a large fish flapping helplessly, Bill looked more relaxed.

"This may be cheating, but so be it. I wanted three big fish and now I've got them," Bill said, looking at Jack in a way that meant he expected him to join the conspiracy.

Danny-Dread returned to the group carrying three ice-cold Cokes, and gave them one each.

"I thought you guys were fishing from the main river," he said.

Bill raised his eyebrows, smiled and suggested, "I guess we changed our minds. We know when we're beaten."

"Good," Danny-Dread replied, "and just what *are* you discussing?"

"To cut a long story short," Jack said, "I'm writing a book and Bill here is redoing his company manual."

Danny-Dread said, "You really mean, you spend your vacation labrishing about controls? I still don't believe it. You can't think of a better way to relax?"

"What does labrishing mean?" asked Bill.

"I tell you what Danny-Dread," said Jack taking up the challenge before Bill could get an answer to his question. "You can't run a business without setting up standards. What if this fishing venture were run with no written standards. How would that work, eh?

"Simple," the slim long-haired man replied, his locks swaying as he moved his head vigorously to reinforce the points he made. He sat next to them on a wooden stool. "If," he continued, "you and your people know what they're doing, then it all works out easily."

Bill smirked and winked at Jack. "Don't worry yourself buddy," he said loudly. "Things don't really work like that. How can you know that there aren't loads of procedures in operation here?"

Danny-Dread turned his head slowly to face the river and as Bill looked at the long and twisted dreadlocks going down his back, said in a quiet voice, "Because I've been the manager here for the last seven years and we've had an annual growth of around 20 percent per annum since I took over."

As he said this he flicked his rod and pulled a large fish from the river and placed it into his net.

"You see," he went on, "you have to trust yourself and your staff. I spend most days fishing and keeping an eye on things. Making sure the tourists are okay and everything's going smoothly. You think control is something you write down on a piece of paper and that's it. Control is about getting your people to deliver. They will make sure things are done right. Every morning I meet with the people you see working hard around you and we talk about what's good and what's not so good. After that I get them coffee and they're off. Simple. The rest of the day I fish, deal with any problems, and think about what's good and what's not and then talk this through with the staff next morning. Simple city. Anyway, enjoy the drinks. I've got to get back. I'm meeting two new members of staff and I need to get them into my system. You know, build on what's right and sort out what's not. Once staff have that, they're fine."

At that Danny-Dread shook hands with them, wished them well, and Bill and Jack watched him walk casually toward the main office greeting people enthusiastically as he went.

"Wow!" said Jack. "Maybe he's got a point, you know. I think Danny-Dread's just blown some of my theories out of the water. Anyway Bill, we've really got a lot of work on internal control out of the way. We've discussed definitions, procedures, information systems, financial systems, quality, and value for money. These are important parts of the big picture. Managing these issues means we achieve corporate control. And then I want to explain the final subject—how all these things can be put together in a corporate internalized control facility. But before we get there, I need to go over the topics of fraud and creativity. I'm interested in reconciling the need for control with the need to promote creativity within organizations. This dilemma has perplexed me for some time now. Talking it through with you may help. My other concern is about getting fraud under control and I think we should talk about that tomorrow. How about I pick you up and we can get some work done on the subject of fraud?"

As the two men headed back to the car, the feeling of achieving a good and enjoyable day's work swept over both of them.

"What does labrishing mean?" asked Bill again.

"Oh. It's just talking, gossiping about nothing much. I guess what we've been doing most times."

"Right," Bill mumbled as Jack laughed loudly.

"Don't forget your fish," Jack said as he got into the car. "You don't want to disappoint a certain young lady, do you?"

FIVE

Fraud, Corruption, and Lots of Rain

Many organizational scandals relate to fraud and irregularity. Ways of using the most important techniques of fraud prevention, detection, and correction are explained along with many practical examples.

"**G**OOD MORNING, JACK," Bill shouted his greeting as Jack drove into the hotel forecourt and parked in his usual place under the banana tree.

"Morning, Bill." Jack looked upward as soon as he got out of the car. It was overcast and there were huge dark clouds rolling around the sky. A loud drumming sound echoed the distant thunder that heralded the coming storms.

"I think we're in for storms today," announced Jack as he walked across to where Bill was sitting on the veranda facing the parking lot.

"Hmm," Bill murmured, "Does that mean it's not a good idea to tour the island today?"

"Well, the rains can come and go very quickly this time of the year, or they can be very heavy and fall for some time. We really need a weather forecast."

A few minutes discussing this point with Ruth made it clear that storms were expected all day along the North Coast. She suggested that they could always retire to the bar or the games room. A satellite TV was also available in the games room.

Bill secretly thought a day lounging around the hotel would be quite pleasant. "Why don't I invite you to spend today here, Jack?" he said. "We could continue our discussions."

"Sounds good enough to me."

The two men gravitated toward the pool table in the games room, whose large windows allowed in a light breeze. Bill picked up a cue, which seemed to indicate what they would be doing for the next few hours.

Sinking a striped ball, Bill clicked on the recorder and wondered how much they would be able to cover during the day's conversation. He asked, "So today's work is on the subject of fraud?"

"Yes, absolutely. What do you know about fraud?" Jack inquired, playing a safety shot much to Bill's annoyance.

"Exactly nothing," came the reply.

"I've got a lot to say on this, if you don't mind that is," said Jack, feeling a little embarrassed about his lengthy speeches the day before.

"Fine," Bill said. "Our consultant's initial report has suggested that fraud could arise because of our lack of controls. It also appears that our chief purchasing manager has been involved in underhanded practices. The police have enough to arrest him and I'll have to help deal with the consequences when I get back to work. Fraud and corruption are unpleasant subjects. There's nothing positive about them; they're just human greed. But what I'd like to know is, why is fraud not part of the managerial control system that you keep referring to? Surely it's an important component of control?" Bill then missed what should have been an easy shot and cursed softly.

"Well," Jack took up the question, "the managerial control system consists of key processes that should be dealt with for good control. But, there are also key control objectives (i.e., what promotes good control). Remember them:

- Compliance with procedure. We discussed this subject already.
- Sound management information.
- Value for money, that is, economy, efficiency, and effectiveness. We discussed this subject and information systems yesterday.
- The protection of assets and interests that may be subject to fraud and abuse, which is our subject for today.

Our assets are protected by good procedures and accountability as well as physical security. If we're not careful, they can be depleted by dishonest people.

Bill sank three balls in a row, and said, "I guess if we employ good people, we'll be okay. The problem with employee fraud and corruption is that it flies in the face of current management practice. Most organizations have reached an enlightened view of management, where we get staff to take full responsibility for their activities. Instead of giving them a long-winded job description, we now say you're responsible for this area and leave the rest up to their good judgment, within the bounds of our standards and procedures. This practice is great in getting commitment from people and allowing them to release their energies. But, once fraud is on the agenda we return to policing, checking, supervising, and documenting everything. We go back to the view that people cannot be trusted. You just cannot discuss controls without addressing the issue of fraud. It's impossible."

Bill continued, "I suppose we go back to the *'it must never be allowed to happen again'* model every time a scandal happens. I guess this will be the case when the problem with my purchasing manager breaks. Another problem is internal discipline when employee fraud occurs. Here procedures, instructions, investigations, reports, reprimands, and all the negative aspects of management come back to the foreground. You can't win. Management must come down heavily on staff where they are implicated in fraud. And we'd also need to carry out a detailed investigation."

"Right, let's push on then?" Jack asked as Bill lined up a shot. Jack winced as the last red stripe spun into a side pocket, leaving the white ball positioned nicely on the black, which Bill then missed. Jack said, "I'll tell you the areas I want to cover today.

- Definitions
- Responsibilities
- Dealing with allegations
- Detecting fraud
- Carrying out investigations
- Internal discipline
- The ethical dimension
- Whistleblowing
- Prevention

How about that as a start?"

"Sounds good enough to me, Jack. How about some of your famous quotes. I understand you now take a spiritual view of life?" Bill sighed as Jack's safety shot meant that he had lost his chance of winning the game quickly.

"I'm pragmatic, Bill. I use standard material where it fits the circumstances. I use poetry when it better expresses a view. It all depends on what I'm looking at and how I'm feeling at the time."

"Ha!" said Bill, as he failed to sink the black ball again.

"Right," continued Jack. "Back to the things we need to cover."

DEFINING FRAUD

"Corporate fraud can take many different forms. It can be perpetrated against the organization, as happens when a gang intercepts your checks in the mail and diverts them. It can be perpetrated by an entire organization, where it fabricates its accounts to secure bank loans. It can be carried out at random through a smash and grab incident where someone walks into a payroll office and robs it. It can be a common fraud that is programmed into the figures, such as minor theft. It can be perpetrated by people who don't work for an organization, perhaps someone submitting false invoices to the payments section. Where this happens one would call in the police to investigate. An organization wouldn't have authority to access third party information and there's not much we could do outside of cooperating with the authorities. The type I'm most interested in is employee fraud where we take on people who do, or try to defraud us, because of their special position in the organization. Fraud isn't set out as a particular criminal offense. One definition argues that fraud involves the use of deception to obtain an unjust or illegal advantage. This advantage may be financial or simply a defined personal benefit or advantage. It may be secured for the perpetrator or on behalf of someone else. Fraud covers offenses such as:

- Theft—simple or conspiracies
- Forgery
- Bribery
- Corruption—accepting large gifts from a preferred supplier

157

- Misrepresentation
- False accounting
- Extortion through the use of blackmail
- Other acts that fall under the banner of deception and illegal acts.

"A feature of many frauds is concealment, sometimes associated with false accounting, where the fraud remains undiscovered and the person responsible is not found out, in contrast to the smash and grab frauds, where the problem is immediately obvious. Frauds come in numerous forms and formats. At times, when it all becomes too complicated, we may only be able to prove false accounting. This is important, because we can only say someone has committed a fraud when it can be proved in a court of law (i.e., beyond all reasonable doubt). The key in this respect is the existence of relevant and sufficient evidence. That's the big problem with fraud, Bill. If there's a lack of relevant evidence, we have no crime. Even if we're sure someone is guilty. That's the frustration.

"Some argue that fraud depends on motive, means, and opportunity. That is, a person has a motive for committing the fraud; they may have financial difficulties or feel the company owes them. In fact, I have a theory that all fraudsters justify their actions. Their excuse may be warped or it may simply not add up to acceptable standards of behavior. Nonetheless, they still have some kind of excuse that satisfies them. Means is a bit more obscure as a concept. Some argue that the criminal must have the intellectual capacity or be streetwise enough to plan and get away with it. It may also require the ability to lie or conjure up a convincing excuse and so require the type of personality that can pull off these acts. Finally, the criminal must also be able to perpetrate the fraud, that is, they have the opportunity. This opportunity may entail the use of passwords to computerized systems or physical security devices such as keys or keypad numbers. They may be in a position of trust that gives them some privileges. The point is that motive and means isn't enough, without being given a chance to defeat the systems. A more cynical view of the three-component model is that if all these attributes are in place (motive, means, and opportunity), then there's likely to be a fraud—not a very comforting thought. The upside is that a little research may isolate the types of areas at risk and some of the signals that there could be problems, for example, a payments clerk who can process payments unsupervised, and who has just been told he will be laid off in a month's time.

"I don't need to go on. Fraud is big business and if you allow your organization to become vulnerable, someone, somewhere, sometime will probably take advantage and defraud you. Your systems of internal control are there to act as a safeguard against this risk. In fact, a typical manager will probably link the goal of internal controls to the problem of fraud more than anything else. Certainly the press and politicians take this view. They also feel that formal regulation by external-type agencies is the only answer.

"That's why I need to include fraud in any discussion of controls. My view is that fraud as something done by crazed criminal gangs or unbalanced employees is gradually being replaced by the growth of sleaze as the major concern of society because of a general 'get as much as you can' attitude that permeates the corporate world, the public sector, and the political arena. It has more to do with a lack of morals or standards generally.

"This broad concept involves social issues. Sleaze is about an unwritten rule where all parties to a situation benefit. It forms a wide conspiracy where people take turns skimming the cream off the milk. No one loses and all walk away happy. Most people know what is going on, but it suits them to maintain the status quo. It's useful to list some of the areas where fraud can occur. These areas will obviously vary, depending on the organization, but they can include:

- Income
- Expenditure
- Petty cash
- Sales
- Payroll
- Travel and expense claims
- Overtime
- Bonuses
- Free gifts
- Purchases and contracts
- Attractive and portable items
- Automated information, e.g., customers database
- Credit cards
- Mortgages
- Insurance policies
- Capital contracts
- Government grants and loans
- Internet transactions"

RESPONSIBILITIES

"Talking about employee fraud is one thing. Getting people interested is quite another. Most people who work for an organization won't be bothered about getting involved in this subject. It's something for the chief financial officer, the head of Human Resources, or the chief executive officer. Well, I've got some bad news. Fraud—understanding it, finding it, investigating it, and making sure there are controls to prevent it—is everyone's responsibility.

"Organizations that establish a fraud team need to be careful. If you suggest that it's not a concern of anyone but the specialist fraud team, you've introduced a basic flaw in your systems of internal control. We come back time and time again to the view that self-control is the only way forward. Taking away responsibility for control from staff and managers is wrong. We'll get back to this point later.

"Stewardship is about holding something on behalf of others. The stewardship role isn't discharged by relying on a mature, long-serving employee who is loved and trusted by everyone in the company. It isn't discharged by ignoring fraud on the basis that it really doesn't matter. It's certainly not discharged by leaving it all to a central fraud team or internal audit. I really don't want to be prescriptive, Bill, but we can define the roles of specific parties in respect to fraud. In fact, Bill, it may be better if you had a go at this," concluded Jack realizing that excessive talking was affecting his performance at the pool table, having lost three games in a row. As if to reinforce this point, Bill missed an easy shot as he thought through his list in response to Jack's challenge.

"Certainly," Bill replied, chalking his pool cue. He wondered whether they could stop talking and just play the game, but he felt a little guilty about not concentrating on their discussion, as at that particular moment, he could not remember any material relating to fraud. It didn't matter; he could hazard a guess. He said, "The chief executive must take steps to ensure the company is protected against fraud and if it does occur, ensure it's properly investigated and resolved.

"The board should ensure there's a fraud policy in place and it's working.

"The external auditors will be concerned about any fraud that affects the accounts and their responsibilities to give an opinion as to whether they show a true and fair view or not. They may also refer less material problems to management. Moreover, they may express any concerns they have regarding a company's steps to guard against fraud.

"The chief financial officer may be the nominated person responsible for investigating allegations of fraud.

"There may be an internal audit set up to discharge the finance officer's responsibilities.

"Individual managers have a duty to ensure fraud is dealt with via the appropriate organizational policies, having reference to the parties I've just mentioned.

"The head of Human Resources must ensure any staffing implication of fraud is dealt with properly, and in line with internal procedures relating to staff discipline.

"We may also have a compliance team actively looking for problems of this nature.

"How about that?" For Bill, the enthusiastic debate was actually improving his game. Jack applauded his friend and muttered, "Bravo, bravo . . . well done."

DEALING WITH ALLEGATIONS

Jack had resigned himself to losing badly to Bill as the black ball trickled into an end pocket of the pool table. Bill suggested in the most innocent manner that they record the number of wins, while Jack sought solace in the day's topic of conversation, and continued, "The fact that the company has an established procedure for dealing with allegations of employee fraud and subsequently launching an investigation is a control in its own right. This is why we need to ensure managers, staff, stakeholders, and all those who affect an organization, understand what fraud is about and know the company's policies and procedures on this matter."

"Yes," Bill remarked, "a company may encourage people to give tip-offs where they have reason to believe an employee is involved in fraud. If we use whistleblowers, many frauds can be detected."

"That's not really whistleblowing," Jack said thoughtfully. "We can deal with this subject later. It's number eight on our list I think. Anyway where were we? Right . . . allegations. In my experience, many frauds come to light because someone mentions their concerns. People stumble across a fraud or the perpetrator confides in them, and they decide to bring the information to someone who can deal with it. Some make anonymous phone calls, some write letters, either signed or anonymous. Others will tell you, but ask that their name is kept out of it. There aren't many people who will want to be involved in an inquiry, but they still feel it's their duty to inform. This isn't to say that fraud won't come to light through other means such as exception reports, discrepancies from information given by a customer on payments they've made, or someone may simply make a full confession. Going back to allegations. Managers may experience fraud as an issue for the first time when they're told that a staff member is up to something. Most will panic. The right response is to go through the following process and ask:

- What is the organization's policy on dealing with allegations?
- What do I say to the person making these allegations?
- Who can I turn to for advice?
- What initial steps should I take?
- Can I document the allegation and make sure I can contact the source of the information?
- Could it be true?
- What kind of evidence may exist to support the allegations?
- Do I need to inform the police at this stage?
- How do I launch an investigation?
- Are there control weaknesses that should be dealt with?
- Do I need to take urgent action to stop further losses?
- Should I confront the subject of the allegation?

"Let's spend a brief moment on each of these points. But before we do, I want to emphasize that being able to answer these questions is an important part of internal control. If a manager or staff member for that matter isn't able to deal with these questions, then the system may fail. Okay, back to the list."

Jack was feeling more relaxed, having abandoned the pool table to Ruth, who was on a lunch break, and Bill who was also playing. Bill nodded at opportune moments, suggesting he was paying close attention to Jack's remarks while still managing to keep up with Ruth who was an accomplished pool player. Jack, feeling able to concentrate fully on his material continued, "Right, the list of questions."

"Before we go on," Bill said, "we're looking at a list of questions about allegations, within the points you are covering on fraud, er . . . points one through nine, and we're on number three, dealing with allegations."

"Correct," replied Jack, trying hard to remember if this was actually where he was in the debate. He frowned at Bill who had just sunk a ball and thought, so he is paying attention, not realizing that Bill was thinking that this guess at where they were would keep Jack quiet for a while, so he could get on with the game.

"Now, back to the questions when you receive an allegation." Hesitating for a minute, Jack added, "We won't spend long on each one."

"*What is the organization's policy on dealing with allegations?* People within an organization shouldn't be left in the dark on the question of fraud. There should be a formal statement on this matter that indicates roles and responsibilities and what people should do when they discover a fraud or when it's brought to their attention. In fact, going back to our discussion on procedures, we would want a clear policy on the whole topic of fraud and its implications. It would at least cover these twelve questions. We should also provide staff training based around this policy document.

"*What do I say to the person making these suggestions?* This situation can be difficult. Most informers ask to be kept out of things. They want assurances that this will happen and may well refuse to talk unless these promises are given. Unfortunately, you cannot do this. The local police or an internal disciplinary panel may need to hear from the informant. You can say that their name will be held in a confidential file and tell them exactly who will be given access to it, which will be restricted on a need-to-know basis. You'd then need to reinforce their public and corporate duty, if they work there, to give full information and that it is appreciated. You cannot force someone to talk if they don't want to. If you're not careful, they may come out worse off for talking in the first place and this will discourage others.

"*Who can I turn to for advice?* The company should make this clear. We argue that everyone who works for an organization is responsible for dealing with fraud, but they do not carry this responsibility alone. There must be someone responsible to advise on fraud where it happens. It may be the chief financial officer, head of human resources, chief internal auditor, chief policy officer, chief executive, a specialist frauds advisor, an outside consultant, a security officer, compliance officer, legal counsel, or anyone who has the knowledge and position to assume this role. If this is worked out beforehand it helps.

"*What initial steps should I take?* This is quite important. It sets the tone for the rest of the inquiry. You need to work out how serious the allegations are. If they indicate a minor issue such as private phone calls, then it may simply confirm that staff need to be reminded that there are rules on this. If however it's more serious, then a full inquiry may be necessary. In fact, private calls can be serious as I've seen a company phone used for frequent overseas calls running into thousands of dollars. What appears to be a minor problem may also be the tip of the iceberg. I've also seen many allegations that were based on limited knowledge and incomplete facts. The real picture was much more serious and implicated many people in wide scale abuse. Good judgment is the keyword and again this is something managers can work on in a training environment.

"Can I document the allegation and make sure I can contact the source of the information later on?" These two points are crucial. By documenting the allegation you are in effect opening up a 'file.' This is the first thing that the police or other investigating officers will want as the work is started. You never get the full facts from the first contact with an informant and it's important that they can be traced for further information.

"Could it be true?" There are people who spread malicious rumors. They tend to want to remain anonymous and give inconsistent information that doesn't stand up to detailed probing. The question then to ask is, could it be true? If the claim is that Fred Jones is up to no good, then ask, does Fred exist and could he carry out the alleged acts? If the answers are no, there's little work to be done on this matter. Again, informants may only be aware of some of the facts and we need to take this point on board. However, it must pass the *common sense* test, which is best posed by the manager for the area in question. If it could be true we need to take it further.

"What kind of evidence may exist to support the allegations?" We agreed earlier that there's no fraud without evidence. This is still true. When receiving allegations we need to think through the type of evidence that would support the allegation. One obvious source is the information provided and it may be well to capture it in a formally signed and witnessed statement from the informant. This is known as a witness statement, which is taken down in the words of the statement giver. It's best to go through the material first before recapping and writing it down as a statement. This statement goes in the file and it should be in a format that could be submitted to a criminal court if need be. The person giving the statement should be told that he may be required to give evidence based on this statement in a court of law, investigations panel, or internal disciplinary hearing. The other point with evidence is to ask whether there are documents that need to be secured as a result. They may

be in the possession of the suspect and we need to think about keeping the matter secret and confiscating the documents. At an early stage the inquiries must be kept secret for fear of destroying or tampering with evidence. This is where most people go wrong. They immediately confront the suspect who then interferes with the evidence.

"Do I need to inform the police at this stage? The organization should have a nominated person who will contact the police. It may be best to refer all cases to the police for investigation; we may make further inquiries and keep them advised on progress or we may simply seek general advice on how best to deal with the problem. For example, in the case of large fraudulent overtime claims, the local police may ask the company to investigate, open a file, analyze the documentation, carry out interviews, and then pass the file over to them for a decision on police involvement. It may be well for the company to install a policy whereby all allegations of fraud are given to the police immediately, as any delays will lead to awkward questions later on.

"How do I launch an investigation? The company will launch an investigation if needed and this will involve the manager in some way. It shouldn't be a unilateral decision and advice should be taken before too much work is done, referring back to my earlier point.

"Are there control weaknesses that should be dealt with? This is important and may entail quick fixes and a longer term review of what went wrong and why. Most frauds are the result of failings in control, and we need to put these right. Quick fixes such as replacing locks where people have unauthorized access to secure areas are important to stop this type of abuse.

"Do I need to take urgent action to stop further losses? Unlike the previous point, this question has to do with stopping the fraudsters in their tracks. There's a responsibility to protect organizational assets and if we're told abuse is happening, while we may want to carry out an undercover inquiry, we may need to stop further

abuse. If we let them continue we may get good evidence for prosecution, or discipline, but we must be careful. Allowing the abuse to continue once you are aware of it may be seen to be condoning it.

"*Should I confront the subject of the allegation?* The answer should be no, not without advice. If the confrontation isn't handled properly, the person in question may hide evidence, go off sick with stress, and sue the company for causing undue suffering through unfounded accusations. The person would also claim victimization and would probably be able to show that the company had not acted reasonably and had breached its own procedures for carrying out proper investigations, which would be grounds for a legal claim. A decision on whether to suspend the person pending the outcome of the investigation also has to be made, but accusing them out of hand will lead to problems."

"I still don't understand why people commit these frauds. What drives someone to crime?" Bill asked, while sipping a Red Stripe beer. He and Ruth had taken a few minutes off from the pool table before resuming the talks.

"Good question," replied Jack. "I've thought about the type of people who commit fraud and I can't find any common denominator. I know that if the organization doesn't care about sleaze, then the justification I mentioned earlier is more likely to be found. If everyone's up to something, then why not me? may be one favorite motto. It can come back to the corporate culture more than anything else, particularly where a whole group of workers are involved in what can only be described as regular scams. A *concern for people* manager (remember Blake and Moulton's grid?) can lead to *looking the other way*. Where we cannot give pay raises or where promotion isn't possible, due to the economic climate, perks, authorized and unauthorized, may be seen as a way of life. This doesn't excuse anyone or provide for the hardened criminal who joins a company with the sole objective of defrauding it. It does, though, give us a clue as to why some companies are seen as easy pickings. I believe if you allow yourself to be vulnerable, someone will penetrate your controls, or more accurately exploit gaps in these controls. If you pay invoices willy-nilly, with no supporting documentation, it's only a matter of time before unauthorized payments get through. Now, let's move on to detection."

DETECTION

"Relying on allegations is one thing and I still argue that this is an important source of information. A further approach is to actively look for fraud and irregularity. Again, each member of staff should be aware of this possibility and be vigilant. It's a bit like the neighborhood watch scheme. We all need to keep our eyes open and take responsibility for finding fraud. That isn't to say we encourage an organization of people spying on each other, it's more a view that things can go wrong and we need to be aware of this.

"I give you an example of one fraud I've seen. A junior accounts clerk had been processing petty cash claims for many years. This ran into thousands of dollars a week. When a claim had been made the clerk would often include a $100 after any claims of less than $100 and insert a couple of lines to account for this disbursement. The employee even made up what appeared to be receipts from local stores to support the claims. So a typical claim might start out as in Figure 5.1. After being doctored it was turned into Figure 5.2. The extra $100 would be pocketed and the claim, with supporting vouchers for the additional lines, would be filed for later review by the auditors. The clerk's line manager checked a selection of filed claims and felt there was a pattern, that something was wrong. We were called in and after an investigation going over two years worth of claims, the suspect was interviewed and eventually admitted it. Apparently it was done mainly out of boredom. The records looked sound and were supported by vouchers, but something was wrong.

Petty Cash

Officer .... Section .... Date ....

Expenditure code ....

	$	$
Supplies for mailshot	34	
Travel from a to b	16	
	-----	50

Total		$ 50

Signed ... *A Brown* .... Authorized *H. Rules*

Figure 5.1   Original claim.

Petty Cash

Officer .... Section .... Date ....

Expenditure code ....

	$	$
Supplies for mailshot	34	
Travel from a to b	16	
	-----	50
mailshot folders		100

Total		$ 150

Signed ... *A Brown* .... Authorized *H. Rules*

Figure 5.2   Amended claim.

It's notoriously difficult to work out detection routines. There are times when you have to sit down and think about the way systems can be penetrated and abuse can occur.

"I once thought through how fraud could be detected and ended up launching a project whereby we ran the pensioners on our pensions database against the names and references on a national deaths database. We found that we were paying pensions to dead people; some of the annual declarations had been fabricated to suggest that the people in question were still alive.

"One word of warning—check with the legal people about data protection before embarking on this type of fishing expedition. Also, it tends to be corrupt and incompetent organizations that end up in this position (i.e., allowing fraud to happen). So asking yourself how you got into this mess in the first place is as important as doing the detecting. An organization that needs to employ a huge fraud detection unit who generate a policelike state with vast sweeps and surveillance exercises suggests an organization run by a bunch of incompetents. This is a pretty standard equation.

"For the local manager and staff, it's simply a question of understanding the risks, keeping in mind signs that not all is well and being able to take action and seek advice where necessary. Assuming responsibility for fraud is the starting place, which is why I don't always like the idea of a large dedicated frauds unit. We simply need an internalized control facilitation unit."

Bill looked up from his cue stick at these familiar words.

"Patience, my friend, patience," Jack was forced to add. "Before we leave the question of detection let me give you a word of warning. I had one fraud case where income was being systematically diverted and I informed the manager. The response was to show me the statistical analysis of this income that implied all was present and correct; what they thought they should receive was being received, at least in round figures. What they hadn't realized was that the fraud had been going on for so long that the figures had always been artificially deflated. The investigation eventually lead to arrests and criminal convictions as well as dismissal."

CARRYING OUT INVESTIGATIONS

"I could go on and on about investigations and investigative techniques such as analytical review, data mining, and surveillance. This would be a little over the top because the average employee needn't get involved in this level of detail. Anyone may be roped onto an investigations panel or team, and my view is that the manager for the area where the fraud is alleged to have occurred should have a role in the investigation, to reinforce the management's ongoing responsibilities. It isn't good practice to simply refer a problem to the investigators and leave it up to them. The manager must ask, What do we do about this problem? Do we have enough evidence to conclude it? Where do we go from here? If the investigating team disappears with the file and leaves the manager out of it, then the manager must complain. This is only acceptable where the manager may also be implicated or cannot be ruled out at this stage. The fact that the manager is friendly with the suspect doesn't matter; there's a professional duty to discharge nonetheless. So don't let the investigators disappear with the case. They work for you and you must demand action and you must make the executive decisions in the case.

"You may have to action immediate suspension or bring disciplinary charges. Suspension is done to aid the progress of the investigation and should in no way indicate guilt. You don't suspend someone so that you can investigate before bringing disciplinary charges; you suspend them so that you can investigate properly and then make a decision as to whether to bring these charges. This is an important point that's sometimes missed. It also applies to interviews. If you are going to charge someone, then do it. If you wish to interview them, it's only to enable you to decide whether to pursue the investigation and not to catch them out once you have already decided to charge them. Some employees simply allow an organization to make these mistakes then sue them after the investigation is messed up. It's only because companies settle out of court that it's hushed up and everyone goes away thinking they've won. In my view these payments are hush money to cover up mistakes by the organization, part of the sleaze we've talked about. An organization that spends its time making such payments is basically corrupt. So is one that suspends people out of hand, sometimes for years and them pays them off in the end because it cannot find a case to bring against them.

"For an organization, the purpose of an investigation into employee fraud is twofold: It's to assist the police in their efforts to tackle crime and make society a better place for all and also to ensure that people who cannot meet the required standards of conduct are removed from the organization as soon as possible. These two points are obviously linked, but we must deal with the fraud in the context of dismissal if the circumstances and evidence warrants it. The key is to dismiss for breach of procedure and not a criminal offense; you can only prove a crime in a court of law. We will deal with this later in the discussion on internal discipline.

"For our purpose it's enough to go through a brief model of an investigative process, bearing in mind that each one will be different in practice. My first model's in Figure 5.3. In this model we work within a policy of fraud awareness so that if and when a problem of this nature arises, people know how to deal with it. At least they know about organizational policies and contact names. We've already dealt with allegation, where the problem came to our attention.

"The next point, which I've called 'flowchart,' describes the task of documenting the process at risk and who does what, in order to gain an understanding of how the work and information flows operate and how the fraud has happened.

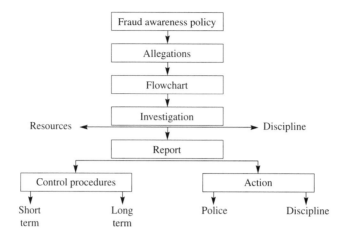

Figure 5.3 Fraud process.

"We then have a three-stage mechanism, where we have a defined resource to advise on fraud, an investigations procedure, and a clear link into the staff disciplinary procedure.

"The diagram suggests a two-way split—one dealing with the implications for the system of control involving immediate action, then longer term improvements. The other side is the criminal prosecution and the internal discipline.

"My other model, Figure 5.4, gets down to some more detail and deals with the investigation proper:

"Most of Figure 5.4 is self-explanatory, but we could go through it in outline.

"Allegations and the adopted policy have been discussed.

"We can suspend the employee, which will bring the thing out in the open. An inquiry panel may be used to investigate, with the line manager playing a key role. If the police have arrested employee X for diverting company checks, we may suspend him pending further information on the case. One can only suspend without

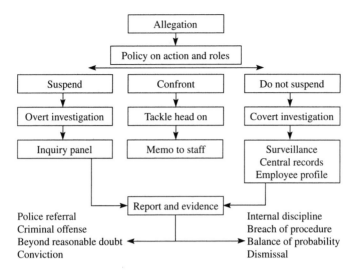

Figure 5.4 Fraud investigations.

full pay where this proviso is built into the contract of employment. Otherwise the salary will continue to be paid, which reinforces the view of innocent until proven guilty.

"We can confront the culprit, say for an obvious problem or minor offense. If someone tells us that a cashier X was convicted of shoplifting in court last week, we may simply call in the employee to clarify this point.

"We can keep the problem secret and carry out background work in a covert investigation. This may entail accessing central records that relate to the offense or the employee. An employee profile may be put together giving us all the information we want on the suspect, employee Z. Moreover, we may carry out a surveillance exercise and seek evidence to support the allegations. If someone tells us that a supply clerk is selling our inventory at a local flea market, we may care to visit this market as well as retrieve all the supply records that may support our case.

"A police referral puts the case into the hands of the authorities and seeks a conviction for a criminal offense that must be proved beyond all reasonable doubt.

"The parallel route means we must try not to wait on the outcome of a court case that may collapse, take a year to conclude, or be won, and then lost on appeal. We will seek charges for breach of procedure, say unauthorized disposal of company stock at the flea market, rather than theft, which is what the police will be looking into. The strength of evidence isn't as demanding as a court of law as we will seek to prove our case on the balance of probabilities.

"In one sense the investigation should seek to prove there's no case to answer, which is just as important as proving guilt. It all depends on the available evidence and what it suggests. Good cases depend on good evidence, which may take the form of:

- Witness statements
- Prime documents
- Analysis of figures
- Computerized audit logs
- Records made by the suspect

"The case shouldn't depend on extracting a confession, because this approach has been shown to be flawed. Using threats and psychological pressure to extract a confession has no place in proper investigating methods. We investigate to seek explanations."

Ruth decided to add her thoughts on the subject, "You're going on about evidence of the crime. Listen to this. A friend of mine witnessed a car accident. One evening in a country district a driver ran over a small child, who died on the spot. It couldn't have been avoided, as the boy just ran out into the road. This was seen by other witnesses to the accident. Anyway, the driver wasn't insured to drive the car. When the car stopped further down the road, the passenger got into the driving seat and pretended to be the driver, having all the right papers. Well, they were then questioned by the police. Witnesses described the driver but the police were convinced that it was the passenger who was driving after they examined the fingerprints on the driving wheel. They were obsessed with the forensic evidence and ignored what people told them."

She sighed and added, "I think you'd better be careful when gathering evidence. It doesn't always lead to the truth."

Jack looked thoughtful, and said, "Point taken. But there's no point discussing masses of material on investigations and procedures. I don't suggest that internalized control is about getting employees to be experts in investigating fraud. This isn't necessary. I would, though, recall one case I was involved in that required weeks of surveillance, five main suspects, the use of video recordings, a team of fifteen auditors, and extensive analysis of documents and witness statements. It was carefully planned and monitored, after which we passed huge files of evidence and formal witness statements over to the police. This case led to internal disciplines and dismissals for the five employees along with criminal proceedings. I wouldn't expect a manager to be able to handle such a case. Rather the line manager would support this investigation and help make decisions along the way.

"What I would say is that an important part of the investigation is based around interviewing people. They might be informants, people who have background information, key witnesses, senior managers on policy issues such as rules on accessing computer systems or taking home equipment that belongs to the company, and finally the suspect or suspects.

"You may think that policy matters have no place in a court of law, but I know of at least one case where a worker was found not guilty of stealing work tools as we had no clear policy on temporarily storing such items at home.

"So interviews are an important stage of an investigation. They can be done well or end up as disasters. Most employees dislike fraudsters and frown on their activity. They wish to see problems dealt with quickly and efficiently by managers. However, they also like to see fair play. The way people are interviewed and the kinds of explanations that are sought and provided can have a great impact on the perceived value of the investigation, particularly in the case of inquiry panels, where people present themselves to a formal hearing and give evidence. It must be done sympathetically, but with the best interests of the organization in mind. A firm but fair approach is best, using listening rather than interrogation skills. We need to encourage people to come forward with information. We want the interview to be controlled but not simply an interrogation. This is done mainly through clear explanations and addressing the witnesses' concerns throughout the interview. Control, here, means getting to the facts, but remaining pleasant, no matter how hard one has to work. In contrast, an interview with a suspect cannot really be pleasant, but it can still be fair and not intimidating.

"We must get to the bottom of things in an interview and the use of body language in assessing a response helps. We must try to see through lies and inconsistencies. Body language here is about using signs of discomfort to probe areas where the person is experiencing some tensions. We need to get these out in the open, not in an aggressive manner but simply in pursuit of the truth. Remember witnesses may be friends of the accused. If someone looks away, uses gestures, shortens answers, pauses, turns to negative phrases, taps a foot, changes position, or blinks a lot when facing certain questions, there may be a problem that needs to be probed, although this isn't necessarily the case in all interviews."

Lunch consisted of stew peas and rice, eaten on the veranda, just a few meters from the Caribbean Sea. Bill watched the surf drift in and out and felt a tingle through his spine. Drinking rum punch topped up with ice, and hearing the rhythmic beat of reggae music audible from a bar across the road, he felt so relaxed. This is the life; nothing to worry about, no sense of time. Meanwhile the words of a Bob Marley song being played in the bar drifted past them, 'Don't worry about a thing . . .'

"You guys have a wonderful life here, don't you?" Bill asked his newfound friend, Ruth, who had a few minutes to spare before her shift started.

"This island is a complete paradise," agreed Ruth, "but it's quite a struggle to survive. Many salaries are low and the cost of living is really high. It's one thing being on vacation and quite another when you have to live and work here. It's not easy for many of the poorer people here. In the words of Freddy McGregor, one of our most famous singers, 'to be poor is a crime.'"

Bill closed his eyes and thought about nothing. This is the first time in a long while he'd been able to do this. Just thinking of nothing.

Jack asked, "What do you feel like doing—pool or pool? That is, the hotel swimming pool or another game of pool."

Bill said, "The thunder has stopped and I feel like a swim. Have you got your swimming gear, Jack?"

"That's OK. I'll relax by the pool while you have your swim."

The rain had stopped, the sun was shining, and the swimming pool was inviting and cool. Bill returned in his trunks and jumped headfirst into the blue water. After Bill had done a few laps, Jack resumed the topic of the day.

INTERNAL DISCIPLINE

"We've gotten to item six, internal discipline. I think this is so important when employee fraud's on the agenda. To be honest, and I know this is sacrilege, but the organization should leave fraud investigations to the police and concentrate on the disciplinary side. The police won't really encourage you to carry out your own inquiry and put an internal case together. They normally feel that it would interfere with their criminal case. I don't agree. We need to retain our own set of documentation and create a file of evidence. As a rule, give the police copies of evidence and retain the originals. Only give these up if instructed to.

"Internal discipline is a prime example of the Jekyll and Hyde dilemma. This famous Robert Lewis Stevenson story involves Dr. Jekyll and Mr. Hyde. It describes what happens if we release the bad side of our personality, which is the hidden moral deviance existing within us, although the story suggests that we have problems controlling this side once released. I use this idea in a different way to describe the dual nature of management: To help develop staff to their full potential, but also to monitor, review, and take action if they fail, despite all your efforts. And to deal with unacceptable behavior; at one extreme, to action dismissal after the case has been heard by a disciplinary panel. It's sad, and unfortunate, that this must happen and it's so difficult to rebuild relationships after the process starts. This is why, if we're sure a staff member is involved in fraud, we really mustn't allow them to remain with us. A knee-jerk response may be to sack 'em regardless. Be careful. If the police reckon they've committed an offense and should be locked up, that's their view. The temptation to suspend the person and wait to sack them when the court case is heard causes many difficulties. You need to install a disciplinary procedure and ensure it is used.

"Furthermore, the problem is that once we start disciplinary action, relationships tend to break down. We adopt a win-lose stance and start to view the employee in question as the enemy.

"Let's consider some general points related to fraud:

- Make sure you make breach of procedure a dismissable offense. Normally a first breach should result in a warning. But, if the offense is related to fraud, the employee should be dismissed. Unfortunately, we play a subtle game whereby we don't suggest that the charges relate to fraud, but we deal with them as serious breaches because they involve crime. This is a moot point. All correspondence relating to the charges should state breach of procedure, say unauthorized removal of xyz. But make it clear to the panel that this incident is serious (i.e., a theft).

- Put together a disciplinary file as well as a file to hand over to the police for prosecution. For example, in the case involving our petty cash fraudster, we put together a file of forged claims and interviewed our friend on these unauthorized claims. We then convened a disciplinary panel who heard about these breaches. Meanwhile, the police interviewed him and started the prosecution. Our internal case was removed and not dependent on the court case. We pressed for dismissal because of the seriousness of the matter and the panel found the charges proven and dismissed him. If the police case were dropped or were unsuccessful, it wouldn't matter. Our work was done and we got rid of a bad apple. Following this line, you must convene an inquiry into what your purchasing manager has been getting up to. You must put together evidence of any breach of procedure and deal with it as such. There's no point sitting back and waiting for the police to take action. You must work with them on this.

- The line manager should present the charges to the panel based on a report and file of evidence prepared by the investigating officers (i.e., the persons who were assigned to investigate the case). The investigators would be called as witnesses to answer questions about the evidence.

- Make sure there's someone who represents the organization in terms of a judicial position. The role is to agree to suspension based on the circumstances; commission an investigation into the matter; decide whether this investigation should form the basis of an internal disciplinary hearing; hear recommendations from the panel on dismissal or other action resulting from the hearing and agree or not to this recommendation. It's important that the person, say the chief executive officer (CEO) or director for the area in question, is senior enough and has at heart fair play for all concerned—the interests of the organization, and the rights of the employee. The mistake that's normally made is for a senior figure in the organization to make ill-advised comments such as 'I want that person sacked now'; or 'Let's get an investigation done and get rid of the thief'; or 'Suspend now and sack when we can'; or 'I want a panel set up that has the guts to dismiss.' This isn't what we mean by assuming a judicial position.

• Interview the employee, who should be given a chance to explain. When fraud is involved and the person is taking part in police inquiries, that employee probably has engaged a lawyer. The lawyer will recommend that the employee doesn't attend a disciplinary interview to discuss matters that are now subject to a criminal investigation. The lawyer will argue that talking about matters that may go before a court of law will prejudice the case. The response to this is to simply point out that we're dealing with the person's role as an employee facing allegations of breach of procedure and that the criminal case is quite separate. If the employee refuses to attend such an interview, then you will assume there's no explanation that can be offered and proceed to the formal disciplinary stage. Make sure you request the interview as a means of seeking explanation before a decision on discipline is made. Get this right—the interview isn't to seek further evidence once you have decided to pursue charges. This would be an abuse of the rights of the employee. Furthermore, I believe reading suspects their rights should be done by the police, not all and sundry. When we interview an employee, it's as management to deal with organizational issues and procedures.

- Make sure the panel is there to get to the truth and isn't constrained by formal rules and regulations. The panel can ask questions and show concern if the employee isn't being represented properly or hasn't had a chance to state her case. I sat on an appeals panel where the employee hadn't attended a predisciplinary interview. He also refused to attend a subsequent formal disciplinary hearing that was held in his absence. He appealed against dismissal on the basis he hadn't been able to state his case. The appeals panel Chair wanted to turn down his appeal on the basis that he'd refused to attend his hearing. I felt the employee was simply preparing a civil case and asked him to state his case now in front of the appeals panel. We couldn't let him go away without ever having his side of the story heard. It turned out that he had no real defense, but we could safely say that he had told his side of the story.

- The rules of evidence applied at disciplinary hearings are far more flexible than a court of law. This is why many people who get lawyers to represent them at an internal disciplinary hearing find they fail. They look for technicalities, such as the rules on hearsay, and upset the panel during the process. The panel can look and listen to anything, so long as it helps them come to a fair decision. What I'm really saying is that members of disciplinary panels have a big responsibility and should be trained before being allowed to sit on the panel.

- Set the tone for the entire disciplinary hearing as a constructive search for the truth and pursuit of ethical standards of conduct. We will not accept fraud and corruption but we will defend our employees' rights at all times. Line managers, senior managers, witnesses, investigating teams, panel members, personnel advisors, and all others should adhere to these basic principles.

- Give Human Resources a key role in staff discipline. They should correspond with the employee and advise all parties about the proper operation of the disciplinary procedure. Better still, employ our internalized control concept and get Human Resources to put on workshops on internal discipline.
- Make sure your file of evidence is sound. This file is given to the panel and the employee in advance and it may be difficult to introduce new evidence during the hearing. There are basic rules on filing, presentation, and ensuring completeness that are well known by investigating officers. Also, place the investigator's report on top as this helps the panel understand the case, since some frauds can be quite complicated. Frame the charges carefully. Make them specific but not too detailed. If they are too tight, they could be thrown out if at all inaccurate, for example, if they're badly worded. If there are several charges rather than one main charge, then the fact that some may be dropped or not proven is unimportant. Never provide one general charge as this forces the panel into a one-issue debate. I remember one case where a senior manager was implicated in a fraud that was being investigated by the local police. For several years the manager had not bothered to provide a corporate service to the seven directors who were the main clients. I attended a meeting to review the case and discovered that we had employed a consultant who was covering the work that wasn't being done because the manager was by this stage on suspension. The consultant was going to prepare a short statement suggesting that the manager wasn't performing and should be dismissed. This would form the basis of a disciplinary hearing. I objected and said that a proper case should be prepared against him, keeping away from matters that

related to the fraud investigation. Opening my big mouth unfortunately meant that I got the job. I filed the manager's job description and strategic plans for the service in question. I obtained statements from the section staff about the work they had been assigned. I obtained statements from each internal client (i.e., the seven directors) on what they expected and what they received in terms of service delivery. I put together a comprehensive file of evidence along with a covering report supporting the various charges that had been devised to put to the disciplinary panel. This is the least that needs to happen to avoid losing an appeal case.

"Let's move on to the topic of interviews. Just to set the scene we can think about what could go wrong. The key point to tackle is resolving the Jekyll and Hyde dilemma. The manager is seen by some as turning into a monster, harassing a poor victimized employee. In reality, the manager sets a standard where fraud will not be tolerated and the strongest action will be taken. No one can criticize a manager who lives up to that responsibility but delivers it humanely and with humility. Managers who take action against their staff aren't at fault, it's the employee who tries to defraud the company who's in the wrong. My view is that a person who feels no shame for committing crimes against the employer deserves no such respect."

At this point Bill was floating on his back. Swimming and trying to make conversation was proving very difficult. So he was happy to leave it up to Jack to do the talking, pretty much as he had been doing since he first met him.

A short break for further drinks at the bar provided a refreshing diversion. Watching a couple of birds chipping away at a bird feeder hanging from a nearby mango tree proved very relaxing indeed. Bill put down his drink and returned to floating on his back, which appeared to signify a continuation of the main conversation by Jack.

THE ETHICAL DIMENSION

"We've arrived at the topic of ethics. This is part of the controls that ensures the risk of fraud is properly managed. I've seen many frauds in my time and as I've said before, although there's no common denominator that I can find, there are general features. Where, from the top, an organization sends out signals that it doesn't care, then this attitude spreads throughout the organization. The employee frauds that I've seen involve intelligent people who take part in careful planning and execution, exploiting all the system's weaknesses. One fraudster paid in a $100 refund at a cash office and then submitted a forged document for $5,000. Because he had paid in the $100 on an official form, he wasn't asked for ID as the cashier assumed he worked for the company. He spent $100 to gain $5,000. The energies of fraudsters are directed toward the task of defrauding the company and they take great pride in beating the system. I've sometimes tried to discover why they do it. I've also wondered if they don't feel that it is morally wrong to defraud, lie, cover up, and generally involve themselves in what can only be described as deceit. Some of them seem to take their cue from their managers and senior management. They complain that top people do worse and only care about themselves. This position can be reinforced where executives earn what seems to be huge pay raises, even when the company is obviously tightening its budgets. What I'm saying is that the moral climate is a key aspect of the system of internal control. In fact, in a hierarchy of controls over fraud, it comes at the very top.

"This view isn't accepted by everyone. If we suggest that an organization with a bad track record for fraud and irregularity probably has its top management to blame, we will not get much support from them. However, this doesn't detract from the truth of the matter. A corrupt company attracts corrupt staff who take part in corrupt activities either for the company or simply for themselves. A firm of financial consultants who sell investment schemes regardless of whether they suit their clients, will end up employing an army of wolves. It isn't easy to tell wolves which victims to attack—they work mainly on predatory animal instincts. This is the downside where there are no rules or standards."

Bill looked up at Jack and wondered how many rum punches he had drunk. Stopping for a sip of his drink at the small poolside bar, he hoped that the conversation wouldn't get progressively silly. He hadn't seen this philosophical side of Jack before.

"Anyway," continued Jack flapping his arms around to illustrate his points, "ethics is really about integrity, fairness, respecting people, and essentially doing your best to deliver quality products and services. We could go further and suggest that it's about safety, the way we market our products, and even whether we're bothered about security at all. It's the foundation of our control environment. How we see things. We also acknowledge the role of compliance, particularly laws that make the workplace better and fairer for staff and customers, which you may care to consider, bearing in mind your new compliance team."

At the words, "compliance team," Bill butted in and said, "Hey, are you going to say anything positive about my compliance team?"

"Oh, of course," replied Jack, "there's a lot to commend in your efforts to resource compliance and it does have a role. It's just that we need to give responsibility back to people, not take it away from them. Anyway, back to ethics. We need a system of ethical standards that can be used to form a framework for our antifraud stance. It's not just about getting people to smile and be nice to each other. It's a real system that seeks to manage this aspect of business life. In fact, one thing that deters people from abusing an organization's systems is a feeling of letting their colleagues down. If employees have an allegiance to the company and feel part of a team, they're less likely to sit in a corner and plan how to defraud it. The point being, if we treat people as important, they therefore feel important and are likely to respond in a positive manner. Some might still defraud us, but returning to our previous argument, it may be harder for them to justify it to themselves.

"An entire company can behave in an immoral way and spy on its competitors for design ideas. Again what kind of standards do we expect from our staff where we run our affairs in this manner? One concern I have isn't so much the corrupt company, but the one that simply doesn't care. People know something is wrong but no action is taken. Any allegations are covered up or just ignored. A form of stalemate is reached whereby corrupt employees are left alone, while at the same time they don't blow the whistle on their managers who may also be involved in sleaze, cover-ups, or be so incompetent that they would be blamed for allowing such a situation.

"Managers who are responsible for defined activities and who ignore problems are vulnerable. Any dishonest staff member can use their manager's failure to install controls for leverage. If the fraud (or scam) becomes public, the manager is likely to be embarrassed or even dismissed. So a truce is entered into whereby no questions are asked and the scam is kept within limits. Excessive overtime and expense claims tend to happen in this manner. The manager doesn't know, or care, what hours staff have worked and signs the claims on this basis. Managers may feel justified to do this, as long as their own claims aren't falsified. The organization and the manager have set no moral code that can help staff. The self-control concept depends on this moral code so that people can work within it, and go on to develop their own controls. Without this moral code, there's no starting place.

"Having inadequate systems of internal control that fail to protect the organization from abuse is morally unacceptable. The organization's assets and reputation are therefore at risk. To my mind, an organization that doesn't address this problem is suffering from impoverished morality.

"I remember the first job I took as an accounts clerk in a large manufacturing company. I spent many hours listening to my boss on the phone relaying lie after lie to irate suppliers who were pressing for their invoices to be paid. I found this somewhat amusing. In fact, I compiled a list of twenty excuses ranging from the chief financial officer being away and unable to sign the checks, through to the invoice being lost and a replacement required before we could release the payment. I'm not sure what kind of moral code I was learning as my frame of reference for working in business, but my manager certainly didn't help set good standards. In fact, one evening when I'd decided to work some overtime, he came over to me just before he went home for the day and handed me a pile of magazines, suggesting that I would be bored by myself and these would keep me company. What a way to start out in the corporate world!

"We need to manage the ethical dilemma or we'll be in trouble, as it affects the level of perception of fraud and sleaze and their justification. It impacts on the way we interpret legal requirements and sets the culture of the organization. A look-the-other-way view is difficult to defend, since we allow breach of procedure and sanction the wrong behavior. The catch-them-out route is also difficult as many feel that ethics should be integrated within the organization and is based on respecting oneself and others. We can install an ethics committee and controls such as exception reports, rules on accepting gifts, hospitality registers, punishment of offenders, inquiry panels into for example the effects of freemasons, but it's more about deciding where the company stands and then spreading this message through all systems. There're no short-cuts. My three strikes model (Appendix B) covers some of these issues.

"I recall one very senior manager who took it upon himself to coach other managers in the best way of securing retirement on the grounds of permanent ill health and so receive an early pension for life. Top managers took it in turn to take this lucrative route. Moreover, the less efficient their performance, the greater the chances that they were let go as being obsolete. Imagine whole groups of directors and top managers waiting for their turn, and knowing that if they performed well, it would lessen their chances. The fact that the organization had extraordinarily levels of high stress didn't help. It meant that people were desperate to leave and they could argue a strong stress-related case. One such highly paid individual, who got her lucrative retirement deal when she threatened to blow the whistle on what was happening, retired on the grounds of permanent ill-health (i.e., severe depression). Two months after she left she was being employed in a similar organization as an independent consultant. The coaching involved telling managers how to make a medical panel feel sorry for them by expressing how they cannot remember things, they don't sleep, and they can't face people. If the panel doesn't make an early decision, they claim this is increasing stress levels and they'll sue them if they continue to stall. Since the panel members are also waiting their turn to retire, cases are usually approved. One director using this route managed to stay home for weeks suffering from stress, locked in his room, refusing to see anyone until he got his retirement pension, after which he miraculously recovered.

"Early retirement was seen as compensation for the corporate stress that was caused over the years, as a tit-for-tat move. This culture leads to deep-seated problems in the long term. To compound this problem, top managers implicated in sleaze allegations tended to get the medical retirement they wanted as a way of getting rid of them. They would be suspended for many months, even years, and suffer stress as a result. Then instead of disciplining them and allowing them to blow the whistle, which they always threatened, they were retired with a lucrative dollar package. All sides ended up happy.

"An even more sinister development occurred in the public sector, when people were being promoted to more senior grades before

190

they were medically retired. The point being that their annual pension was based on their last salary level. A virtual merry-go-round of corruption. This is public sector sleaze of the worst kind. Control suffers because of the implications of Figure 5.5.

"We cannot escape this cycle that starts and stops with our ethical stance and drives and pushes our systems and controls. Where people are found out by controls, this is hypocritical, where they're actually working within an impoverished ethical code. People being paid off under threat of disciplinary action happens more as the norm than an exception these days, in companies where investigations are botched and controls are lacking anyway.

"Ask this one question, do you really care about your company apart from meeting the performance indicators? Do you really care, are you pursuing their goals with all your energies or do you just seek fun and relaxation at work? What about your employer, does he care about you at all? Are you a post or a person? There will always be problems in a wholly unsatisfactory ethical framework with high turnover, bottom line blinkers, and emotional sparring matches, compensating for a lack of good systems of internalized controls.

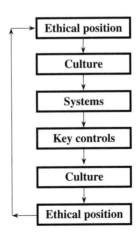

Figure 5.5   Ethical dimension.

191

"I see that training in ethics management is a key part of control facilitation. Having said this, we cannot teach morals, we can only make clear our expectations and available options. It's a wise organization that seeks to employ people who have verified references and work experience. We should also look for the right attitudes in new employees before they pass their probationary period. Right now let's turn to the topic of whistleblowing."

WHISTLEBLOWING

Now lounging in a poolside chair, Bill relayed his own view. "Whistleblowing is part of the frauds hot line that you have already mentioned, isn't it?" he asked.

"Well, not really," Jack replied. "A fraud hot line is a formal part of the organizational systems that support antifraud moves. Whistleblowing is more to do with unauthorized disclosure where all else has failed, including internal systems. Professor Gerald Vinten argues that whistleblowing is:

informing on illegal and unethical practices in the workplace.(1)

"Unfortunately, the concept of whistleblowing has many negative connotations. At school, you were told not to tell tales. Not informing on your friends has always been a feature of popular culture and is ingrained into our childhood and throughout our teens. When starting work, it's difficult to adopt a new mind-set and see it as okay. The history of whistleblowers is fraught with unhappy endings. Dismissal, resignation, persecution, and stress at work and at home are all possible results from going public.

"The first thing an organization should consider is the state of its internal procedures for dealing with people who need to talk. The main problem is that it tends to undermine the line management relationship where we encourage staff to go to a third party. There may still be situations where people go outside and disclose information that they aren't authorized to. Whistleblowing proper occurs when all internal procedures have been exhausted. It breaches the organization's contract of employment and the employee's duty to keep company affairs confidential. It also tends to breach the company's disciplinary procedures, which may lead to serious charges including dismissal.

"There are those that feel whistleblowing can be justified but only in certain circumstances where the matter is very important and all internal procedures have been exhausted. And there's a good chance that it'll lead to resolution of the problem. That is, if the whistleblower can prove there's a problem that can be sorted out. This is a really tight model that means going public only makes sense if it will really achieve something that the organization refuses to deal with and is based on a legitimate motive. There are many problems for the prospective whistleblower. I've designed Figure 5.6 to show them.

"The three points B on the right of Figure 5.6 equate to breaking the company's internal disciplinary rules on taking confidential files home and showing them to outsiders, which could lead to dismissal.

"We start at the top and ask not whether we agree or disagree with what the company is doing. We need to establish whether any real harm is being done. Is anyone being defrauded? Are any laws being broken? Are the best interests of society being jeopardized? If the answer to any of these questions is yes, then our case needs to be heard. A decision to go public at this stage will lead to disciplinary action. Using the internal procedures is the right approach, although the person may be seen by some as a troublemaker. However, if our motives are sound it shouldn't be a problem and the law gives us some protection. Resolution stops the process and all is well. If not, we move into dangerous grounds. The main problem

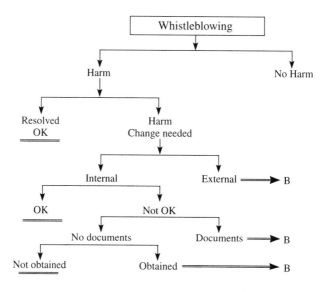

Figure 5.6 Whistleblowing options.

is that releasing or obtaining the necessary documentation to support the case (in order to secure reasonable grounds for successful resolution, point B) means we will again be breaking our internal disciplinary code. The reality then, is that we risk dismissal, which is normally enough to put most people off. It's very important that a diary of events is maintained in these circumstances. But imagine employing an army of people who spend their time spying on each other and keeping secret records. This environment is not very healthy for good performance.

"At some stage we must move away from the arguments that justify whistleblowing, if the person feels this is the right thing to do. Maybe we should be moving toward informing as more of a moral obligation to speak out. History records the many times that the excuse of 'just following orders' has been used. On one hand, the employee must decide the ethical position and how the organization deals with it. On the other hand, top management must have procedures to promote a clear ethical framework.

"Figure 5.7 sets out those things that I think are important in dealing with this topic based on four different interpretations of whistleblowing.

1. *Troublemaker.* The whistleblower is seen as a troublemaker who complains all the time and uses veiled threats to blow the whistle, mainly about the way he is being treated. This all feeds into the performance appraisal (PA) scheme, as the person is seen as an unbalanced individual who spreads disorder throughout the organization.
2. *Allegations.* This person is seen as having a suspicion that they secretly investigate and take whatever is found to an outsider. This may be a reporter, a special interest group, a

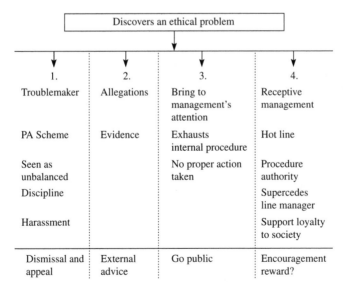

Discovers an ethical problem			
1.	**2.**	**3.**	**4.**
Troublemaker	Allegations	Bring to management's attention	Receptive management
PA Scheme	Evidence	Exhausts internal procedure	Hot line
Seen as unbalanced		No proper action taken	Procedure authority
Discipline			Supercedes line manager
Harassment			Support loyalty to society
Dismissal and appeal	External advice	Go public	Encouragement reward?

Figure 5.7 Whistleblowing stances.

group of friends, or a representative of the state authorities. Apart from them, no one knows about this activity and it therefore becomes an undercover operation.

3. *Brings to management's attention.* Here the person takes the problem to management and goes through the entire internal referral process, after which the person goes public, feeling that all internal routes have been exhausted.

4. *Receptive management.* Receptive management encourages people to come forward as part of an emphasis on personal initiative and a move away from the sacred line-management relationship. Hot lines, counseling, independent review teams, and others are used to get people to talk to them about perceived problems. The performance management scheme has scope to view this activity as a sign of good initiative. It averts the need for whistleblowing but, if not managed properly, the arrangements may turn into an extensive grievance procedure where staff complain about their managers and work conditions generally.

"Figure 5.7 can be used to decide on the most appropriate way of dealing with the issue and assessing where a case fits in terms of its validity.

At this stage the heavens opened up again and it rained and rained and rained. Buckets, no, it seemed more like bathtubs, full of water poured down on Montego Bay. A quick decision was made to resume the pool tournament in the games room.

PREVENTION

"We've dealt with fraud in general and the importance of detection. And we've considered how to deal with allegations," Jack continued. "We've also suggested a procedure for investigating frauds as and when they come to light and the implications for internal discipline. We finished by looking at ethics in business and the topic of whistleblowing. An organization that has installed comprehensive procedures for all these things still has a problem. A focus on investigations is backward looking. An abundance of resources applied to sorting out these messes is also inappropriate. What's needed is a culture where we don't encourage fraud, sleaze, and all that goes with it—a positive environment that gives people responsibility and support so that they feel committed to organizational goals. And not self-interest and greed. So let's look at the most important component of internal control as regards fraud, that of prevention.

"There are great pressures on organizations, which means systems may not necessarily restrain frauds. In one sense, our discussions on fraud prevention needn't take very long. Prevention consists of everything that we've already spoken of throughout this journey through controls. That is, the need for basic procedures, good organizational climate, and ethics management. The managerial control system that we've referred to several times already is also important. Many argue that good detection and investigative procedures provide a deterrent for would-be offenders, although we've criticized an excessive focus on these measures. What we need to do is discuss some of the key issues that set the scene for fraud prevention.

"A lot of prevention is implicit in security procedures—stopping people from unauthorized access to valuable items. I recall one external audit I carried out many years ago. The managing director of a small film production company insisted on leaving large sums of cash on his desk at work. We pointed out the risk in doing so, to which he replied, 'If I can't trust my staff, who can I trust?' We stuck to our view that it isn't fair to place unnecessary temptation in front of people. Going back to our motive, means, and opportunity criteria,

197

- *Motive.* Give people a reason to want to contribute at work and spend their energies on organization goals, not devising ways of beating the system.
- *Means.* I guess means is based on the need-to-know principle. People don't need to understand the access profiles of systems they don't work with. They don't need to be told about detailed security arrangements. Employees needn't discuss their systems with other staff who don't use them. Having the means is about understanding the systems and how they can be beaten.
- *Opportunity.* If we allow people the chance to abuse systems, then there's always the risk that they will. If they pass up these opportunities today, they may succumb tomorrow. Their circumstances may have changed.

"Society expects standards that govern what we do at work in both the private and public sectors. Society also wants to be able to govern almost everything we do, although this isn't always easy. Systems of internal control are designed to drive through good performance and stop bad things from happening. Simple. They should stop frauds from occurring and everything will go well. In reality this simplistic model will never work. Things can and will go wrong and people will be tempted to dip their fingers in the till. Staff collusion is still harder to control. I need to include allegations and investigations in my consideration of systems of control, since there are times when we need to sort things out. In fact, we can use a standard PDC model to reinforce this point, PDC standing for preventive, detective, and corrective controls. The idea being:

- *P.* To stop problems happening in the first place. So we seek to install strong control over assets at risk and ensure they're protected. For example, we may require checks over a certain value to be countersigned by a senior director to avoid large amounts going out under one signature only.

- *D.* If there are problems, we need controls that isolate them for our consideration. A bank reconciliation will tell us whether the amount paid on a check has been altered since it was drawn and dispatched. It won't agree with our record of that check and it could well be that the amount has been altered as part of a conspiracy to defraud the company. The point is that if wrong or irregular transactions get past our first line of defense—preventive controls—they will still be picked up early.

- *C.* Corrective controls seek to put right what went wrong. In respect to our check fraud, this may mean close contact with the local police, a hot line to the bank where funds can be frozen, where a check amount has been altered. These types of control seek to limit damage, correct errors or problems, and may even involve a snap review of what went wrong so that we can install better controls quickly, if necessary.

"Let's move away from background issues and try to develop an integrated seven-point model of fraud prevention. My version's in Figure 5.8.

"Take a quick look at each of these.

1. *Ethical Framework.* We've already dealt with the implications of a strong ethical framework. This model simply reemphasizes the view that fraud prevention starts with the management of ethical issues.

2. *Corporate Culture.* The type of culture an organization promotes is derived in part from the ethical framework. A turn-a-blind-eye policy encourages a don't care ethical stance. A scratch-my-back approach again stems from a view that fair play doesn't matter. We could go on.

199

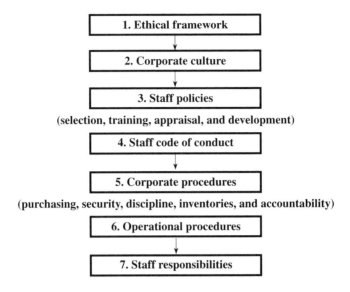

Figure 5.8   Fraud prevention.

3. *Staffing Policies.* This item covers selection, training, appraisal, and staff development. If we employ people who cannot do the required job, they'll eventually become disillusioned when they cannot meet set standards. If we employ people who are overqualified and we promise promotions that aren't forthcoming, again they will become disillusioned. If we don't bother to train staff or set standards and assess performance based around a development program, they may become disillusioned. Disillusioned staff concentrate their energies in ways that the employer may not have anticipated, normally not directed at organizational goals. One outlet is to research and probe key systems for weaknesses and then abuse these loopholes for personal gain. If we employ people who have falsified their work experiences and qualifications, we cannot expect them to live up to our standards of conduct. If they've no work permit or have an

undisclosed criminal record, we must ensure our systems can pick up these matters. Employee fraud prevention is based mainly around ensuring staff are competent, know what's expected of them, and are motivated to contribute to organizational goals. Where this isn't happening, we may find people defrauding the organization.

4. *Staff Code of Conduct.* It's one thing to get the right staff and develop them in a positive and team-building manner. Superimposed over this is the need to establish a clear code of conduct. This sets out our expectations of all employees whatever their grade—a moral reference frame that emphasizes honesty, fairness, diligence, and other such attributes.

5. *Corporate Procedures.* Having dealt with personal standards, that is, a staff code of conduct, we need to set standards for corporate systems that affect most staff, including purchasing, security, internal discipline, inventories, and general staff accountability. Most frauds stem from breach of procedure. If the organization hasn't bothered to set these standards, it will find it difficult to decide what's proper activity and what's unacceptable. Setting these standards implies formal guidance, responsibilities, resources, and good information flows. These all need to be in place to combat the threat of fraud.

6. *Operational Procedures.* We dealt with this subject yesterday. Procedures are important as they help define authorized and unauthorized activities. Remember though, procedures are affected by custom and practice.

7. *Staff Responsibilities.* The final aspect of the model relates to giving people responsibility for their actions. It goes hand in hand with the delayering and empowerment initiatives happening in most organizations. The word *responsibility* goes with the concept of accountability. You have much more power but you must account for what you do, how you do it,

and the results of these actions or decisions. One way of catering for this is to develop Accountability Boxes. These can be used to record those key decisions where there's some sensitivity. They may be used to deal with such things as staff promotions, risk ratings, supplier selection, assignment of resources, and so on. In this way everything can be kept above board. An example appears as Figure 5.9.

"We need to fight fraud as one would a battle that needs to be won: Install controls that protect assets and information, get rid of bad apples, make positive statements and stick to them, and, above all, set a good example from the top of the organization. We all have responsibility to fight this battle. It's all part of our systems of internalized control.

"Some argue that fraud is a concept, something that happens to other companies, not theirs. It's not a difficult moral issue or a set

```
┌──────────────────────────────────────────────────────┐
│                   RECORD OF DECISION                   │
│                                                        │
│   Subject ............................................ │
│   Background ......................................... │
│   ................................................... │
│   Decision made ..................................... │
│   ................................................... │
│   Reason ............................................ │
│   ................................................... │
│   Impact ............................................ │
│   ................................................... │
│   Signed .......................... Dated ........... │
└──────────────────────────────────────────────────────┘
```

Figure 5.9   Record of decision.

of principles. It's a real living thing where bored, disillusioned, or dishonest people toy with the thrill of danger and getting caught. Clear and firm controls need to be in place to combat the real risk of fraud.

"The internalized control concept is simple. It's about people taking responsibility for what goes on around them. Going back to the example of the cashiers who couldn't account for one cash bag. The staff should be ready to insist that all movement of cash is properly recorded and accounted for. During our review, we saw staff wandering around the office, some of whom didn't work in the cashiering section. We saw guards from the security firm sitting around on desks before taking away the bagged cash for banking. I remember asking the chief cashier for a specimen of a check to gauge the adequacy of the security features. She produced a blank, presigned check. I was amazed and asked whether she had signed out for this valuable item, to which she simply laughed. The manager, all staff, and all persons who use and visit cashiers should want to see adequate security measures. It's not something that you wait for the auditors to report. Self-control means that people insist on working with key controls that they install, review, discuss, and agree on an ongoing basis. Having an awareness of fraud and the damage it can cause, along with knowledge of the types of controls that should be in place, is something we should train our staff in. Self-control is the way forward. Give staff the tools and knowledge they need for this to happen and you'll never go wrong. Right now, controls and audit trails along with management directive don't really belong to staff and this lack of ownership makes control a foreign body, not something that people see as a key part of their everyday responsibilities. Well, that's about it on fraud."

The rain finally stopped and Jack realized he had lost almost every game of pool he had played with Bill so far. He made a mental note to avoid this game, if Bill suggested it in future.

"That fraud stuff is pretty heavy. Anyway it's all down on the tape. What happens tomorrow, Jack?" Bill's question signaled the end of the day's activities.

"How about lunch at my place? We'll have time to consider where creativity fits in. Ruth, could you walk me to my car? I've got something that Sharon sent for you."

As they walked toward the car, Ruth was very quiet. Jack handed over a small bag of plant cuttings.

"Ruth," Jack asked, "would you care to join us tomorrow? You wouldn't feel awkward having Bill along as well. Sharon would like to see you."

Ruth was not listening and looked very worried. In the fading light in the parking lot she frowned and assuming a conspiratorial tone, waved her hand softly inward to indicate that Jack should come closer.

"You know, Jack," she said, "I think I've got a fraud at the hotel but I've let it alone for some time now. I thought I was imagining it and it would just go away."

"Not really," Jack replied also whispering, "management sets the tone for their staff. And if you don't care, then neither will they. What's it all about anyway? Do you trust me enough to tell me?"

"Look, Jack, I really don't want to worry you with my problems. I know you're a consultant and that you've done fraud work before. I just need some basic advice, since you obviously know about this sort of thing. I don't really want to let Bill in on this. He's a guest on vacation."

Jack thought for a while and finally said, "Let's go back inside for a minute."

Jack and Ruth went back into the bar and hovered over Bill. Jack held up his hand saying to Bill, "Sorry. I forgot to tell you that I'll be late tomorrow. Say sometime after midday."

There was an embarrassed silence for several minutes before Bill suggested they have a final drink for the night. The three of them sat around the outside table overlooking the gently lapping ocean. The night lights gave their faces a soft glow.

"Well," Ruth asked, "what did you think of today's discussion, interesting at all?"

Bill answered, "As a matter of fact, yes. I've got all I need to deal with corporate fraud. How about that? Jack reckons we should all get into the fight against fraud. And I think he's right. I'm definitely going to write a standard for the manual about this."

After a further silence, Bill concluded that something was wrong and said, "You all look so serious. What's wrong, folks?"

Jack placed a finger over his lips to suggest some secrecy. Looking serious, he finally said, "Ruth here has a problem. How about it, Ruth?"

Looking worried Ruth placed a hand on Bill's arm and said, "Don't take it personally but it's just that I've got a problem that has to do with the hotel and as you're a guest, I shouldn't really burden you with it."

Bill reddened, stood up as if to leave and said, "I can take a hint, if you can't trust me."

"Okay, sit down. You can stay," Ruth said reluctantly and turning to Jack continued, "Lately, we've been short on the drink stocks. I really like Bigga and he's done so well here, but there are regular losses that really seem too large. If I accuse Bigga, and he's innocent, he'll never forgive me. And if he's guilty, then I've lost a man who I like and trust. I just can't win, which is why I've left things alone. I know it's wrong but I'll need to talk to the head office about this. But then they'll get rid of Bigga and he's got a wife and two kids."

The three sat around the table with their heads close together and in whispered tones Ruth relayed her concerns and how sorry she was that Bigga turned out to be a crook. At that precise instant Bigga appeared in front of them with a tray of glasses and a large bowl containing a dark red drink. He smiled and said, "Compliments from myself. It's my birthday today and I made up my special rum punch for you folks. Compliments!"

As he disappeared back toward the bar, Bill, whose eyes were wide open gasped, "Look at that!" He said, "He's stealing the stuff and then giving it to us. Man, this is a crazy world."

Ruth gave Bill a stern look and was about to say something when Jack interrupted. "Hold it down, Bill," Jack said. "You need to take a step back before jumping to conclusions. Ruth, let's sort out this situation. It can't be left like this."

"You know, Jack," suggested Bill, "you can use this case to show how all this hot-air and theory on fraud you've been going on with works in the real world. How about it or doesn't it work in practice, eh?"

The combined effect of the drinks they had been consuming all evening had made Bill a little aggressive, Jack unsure, and Ruth somewhat moody. After some minutes Jack broke the ice and turning to Ruth said, "It's up to you, Ruth. I don't mind giving it a go."

Ruth assumed a determined look and pursed her lips, "I've already said too much. You two should not be involved at all. Especially you, Bill. You're a guest."

"Only a guest, not a friend?" Bill asked, looking a little hurt.

Ruth mumbled, "Well, yes, of course. It's just that it's such a mess . . ." Her voice trailed off.

Jack continued, "Okay. But just for argument's sake, say you needed to deal with this now. What's the next step, Ruth?"

"I guess I need to talk to Bigga. You know, confront him and get him to admit it. Then I'd tell him to stop it and maybe warn him about it. Or maybe it's better to just let him go. I don't know. It depends if he realizes he's wrong."

"Bill, what about you. What would you do?"

"Easy. I'd report Bigga to security. The security guy who covers in the evening could keep an eye on Bigga and well, sort him out. I guess we could then get rid of him once security confirms he's up to no good."

"Okay," Jack pursed his lips and said, "The first thing you need to do is look at the hotel's antifraud policy and basically implement it. What does it say, Ruth?"

"Oh. I'm not sure. I have a copy somewhere. I'll be back."

Ruth eventually found a paper in her main office file that was headed *Dealing with Fraud*. She returned and said, "It says here that all suspicions should be reported to the head office internal auditor. But we don't have any. They got rid of our two auditors last year due to budget cuts."

Jack said, "Okay. This is why I say policies really have to make sense. If people don't know about them or they're out of date, they don't form part of the control framework. Let's take a new position. If we're going to launch an investigation, let's establish just what the objectives should be. What do you think, Bill?"

Bill replied, "This is good stuff for my manual. I'll have a go at listing them.

- Stop the problem.
- Identify the culprit—that is Bigga.
- Take action against him."

Ruth added, "And close the loophole that allowed the problem to happen in the first place."

Jack smiled and said, "Great. But I want to add two more. To protect the interests of the hotel, and, last but not least, to protect the innocent. Actually I guess it's also to secure enough evidence to establish the facts. Good. We're getting somewhere now. If you confront Bigga with no evidence then, if he's innocent, he'll never forgive you. If he's guilty, then he'll cover everything up and you may have promised him an amnesty. You're on a lose-lose. You need to follow a proper procedure. Okay, Ruth, now I need to get some facts together. Who has the key to the bar storeroom?"

Ruth said, "I have a set and so does Bigga. That's it. He gets supplies whenever we need them. Simple."

Jack was sipping his rum punch and getting into this problem. Rubbing his hands together, he proceeded to interrogate Ruth, "How much bar stock are you missing Ruth?"

"Quite a bit. I thought that we may be having spillages, but we're missing quite a few bottles of spirits each week. In fact, lately it seems like a few bottles each night."

"And how long has this been going on?"

"Actually, it's only been happening for the last three months. And only the last few weeks have seen an increase that's starting to worry me."

"Did anything unusual happen three months ago?"

"Not really. We refurbished the restaurant. And I remember a power cut one night and I was woken up so that it could be sorted out."

"Did Bigga have any problems around the time the thefts started?"

"Not really. Not that I can recall."

"Okay, Ruth. Let me deal with another important matter. That is evidence. Bigga looks as if he's pretty busy right now and he can only leave the bar if you take over right? Let's have a look at this storeroom."

At this, the three adventurers slipped out of the bar, around the corner and Ruth let them into a large room filled with bottles, crates, and an assortment of hard and soft drinks. There must have been dozens of boxes set out around the room in no particular order.

Bill stared and said, "This is an absolute treasure trove. How come you keep so much stuff in one place?"

"Head office," replied Ruth, "insists on bulk buying, and since they've nowhere to store it all, they split it between the hotels and it's stored locally."

Jack came in, "You know, this is what we call attractive, portable items that are at risk of theft. You shouldn't really keep so much at hand. It's such a temptation. You know what I said about evidence. I want us to make a record of the stock right now. And mark each bottle of spirits at the bottom with a marker. This will give us a precise record of these things that we can trace if necessary. Bill, go get your camera and take a photo of the crates. If Bigga takes any, we can track them back to him."

After twenty minutes or so they had completed their task. Jack suggested, "Right, that's done. Let's get back to the bar and you can tell me some more about our prime suspect."

With that they strolled back to the bar and avoided eye contact with Bigga who was busy talking to a customer. They returned to their outside table and resumed their deliberations. Ruth said, "I wish we could work out why Bigga started his games three months ago. He's so solid. Why should he do this?"

Jack butted in, "Temptation is a powerful force. But, Ruth, tell me about the power cut three months ago."

"No big thing. The main fuse blew and I was wakened from my sleep so that they could get to the keys for the fuse box. I gave them my office keys and they returned them after the box was sorted out. There's nothing more to say."

"So," asked Jack, "There are keys held in your office. Remind me what keys are held there?"

"This is getting very detailed. The fuse key is in my office and the master keys are in my cabinet. Jack, can we get back to the investigation? What to do about Bigga?"

"Ruth," Jack stood up and held his hands up for emphasis, "It's real important. You have a set of master keys in your office?"

"Yes. Sorry I forgot to tell you about them. But only I have a key to the cabinet."

"They're on a bunch yes? And you gave out your keys around three months ago. Who did you give them to, Ruth?"

"The night security. What's his name? Eh . . . Brown I think. Yes, Compton Brown."

Bill was trying hard to follow Jack's thinking and said, "I can't see where we're going."

"Look. Three months ago Ruth gave up her keys to this Brown and since then we've had a problem with the bar stocks. Come on, let's go for another walk."

Ruth and Bill wearily marched behind Jack toward the main office and once again Ruth let them in. Jack said, "Ruth, unlock the master key cabinet and find out what's there."

All three of them made a list of keys that were jumbled in the cabinet and finally Ruth declared, "The spare key for the bar storeroom is missing. It's been taken."

Jack clapped his hands and said, "Now we're getting somewhere. What time does security man Brown start?"

Bill lay slumped in the big leather chair and looked about to fall asleep. Ruth tapped him on the shoulder to wake him up and answered Jack, "He comes on duty around ten in the evening. He stays around all night and then leaves at around seven in the morning when the receptionist comes on duty. That's about it."

"Wake up, Bill," Jack said, "Let's get back to the bar. It's nine now and we need to get some planning done."

Once again the three sleuths marched back to the veranda and took their seats as before. With their heads so close that they were almost touching, Jack mumbled, "I've got a plan. It's all about evidence. We need to secure evidence that sorts out what's going on."

Bill, having completely lost the plot said, "Yes. Bigga must be drinking the stuff every night. So we need to examine his liver."

Ruth frowned at Bill and pushed his drink away, out of his reach and replaced it with a freshly poured glass of ice water. "That's your lot for tonight," she said sharply.

Jack continued, "I'm going to call a friend of mine, Sergeant Walker. He's a police officer who lives quite close by. As he's based in Runaway Bay, I doubt if anyone here knows him. I'll call him, then we'll get cracking on tonight's plan." Jack pulled out his mobile phone and made the arrangements.

Soon after, Ruth stood up and said in a quiet voice, "Guys. I appreciate all your help, but how would it look if I let you investigate this. It's not your responsibility and, in any case, it's not right for you to get involved in the hotel's business. It's unfair to you."

Jack countered her comments politely, "Ruth it's going to be okay. The sergeant's on his way over. You can report the matter to Walker and he'll investigate. We're just along for the ride. Trust me, Ruth, it'll be all right. And if you don't want to report it to Walker, it's up to you."

Ruth looked at Jack, whose eyes sparkled with anticipation, and then to Bill, who looked just about ready for bed and said, "Okay. Go for it. But I want it done by the police officer, not you two. Okay?"

"Fine," replied Jack. "It'll take Sergeant Walker some time to get here. Let's use this time to set standards covering fraud investigations. Bill, this is what you want for your manual, isn't it?"

Suddenly Bill said, "Great. If we can get some more of this stuff down, I can use it for my manual. You're right, Jack."

Jack leaned back and stared out at the moon. It was a bright night and visibility was quite good. He said, "We started off with a suspicion that something was wrong. The stock figures didn't add up. This is all about detection. Our fraud standard should say that staff should be on guard for inconsistencies and consider the possibility of fraud. That's a good start. After that, we felt that only Bigga could have done it because he has a key to the stores. This conclusion turned out to be incorrect. Therefore our standard should say that we must not jump to conclusions and accuse anyone without doing some research. Likewise we needed to use company procedure as a guide, although in this case it didn't help much. The key point is that procedures must be up-to-date and understood by staff. Some sort of training would probably help, so that they know what to do if a problem arises. Next, we considered the need for good evidence. You cannot accuse Bigga, or anyone for that matter, without good evidence. The task of setting objectives helped focus our efforts. You remember the one about protecting the innocent. It's good that you didn't sack Bigga, because I'm not convinced he's doing it. We've marked the bottles, taken a photo, and we know exactly what should be there. The problem is we cannot say who's taking the stuff. We need some more evidence. Bill, a standard covering evidence and its importance should be in your manual. I'm going to suggest to Walker that he do some surveillance tonight. This may give us a direct link between the culprit and the crimes. That's the key—getting the evidence to show you who's responsible. Not confessions, just good evidence. The final thing to sort out is prevention—less stock, better security, more control over keys, and regular checks on spare keys. Closed-circuit TVs dotted around the stockroom and the rest of the hotel can also help. Controls like work references for new staff should be in place. Make urgent changes now, like control over spare keys, and other measures as longer term improvements. Learn from your experiences. And learn quickly."

"This is great material for my manual," Bill said, "I tell you what Jack. It's better to see the process unfold for real than to listen to hours of theory about it. Er . . . not that your talks haven't been interesting. They, er . . . have, it's just . . ."

Ruth butted in, "You two are like little boys playing an exciting game. Someone's ripping off the hotel and I think that's really shameful. It's not an adventure."

"Point taken," Jack said, "But remember Ruth, you were all for confronting Bigga a few minutes ago. At least we can say a proper investigation is being carried out. And I agree. It's unpleasant and sad. But it's got to be done. Hey, here comes Sergeant Walker. Hi, Bobby. Let me introduce you to my friends."

Jack did the honors and, between the three of them, Walker got a full understanding of the problem, suspects, and evidence they had so far. After a while Walker asked Ruth to provide a map of the hotel as shown in Figure 5.10.

Walker was a tall young looking man with a small ferretlike face that was constantly looking around the room as if he were a special agent protecting the President. His habit of placing one hand inside his shirt reinforced this image. His wiry body was well toned and fitted well into his casual black slacks and grey shirt. He took charge of the small group and said, "I'm happy to do some work tonight, although my experience of surveillance is that most times nothing happens and it takes days if not weeks to get a result. We'll

Hotel Map

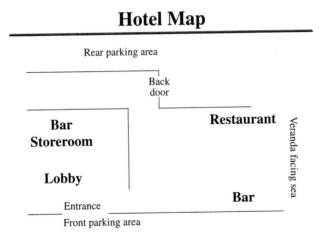

Figure 5.10   The map.

need to watch Bigga tomorrow and maybe set up a closed-circuit TV link. But let's give it a go for a couple of hours tonight. May as well, although I doubt if much will happen. We know what bottles are there and we know someone has the spare key and is taking them. The security guy comes on duty in twenty minutes from now. I want to set up observation points where we can see anything that happens. Jack, you park your car around the rear and stay inside watching the parking lot. Whatever happens, stay in your car. Just watch and tell me what's happening. If anything does happen, that is. Ruth, you stay out of sight in the restaurant and you can see the bar storeroom from there. I don't think you need to be around, Bill, since you're a guest and I can't be responsible for you. Okay so it's bed for you, Bill. I'll be upstairs in the room over the rear door. I can see the parking lot from there. Set your mobile phones on vibrate and we can keep in contact. The bar closes around eleven and Bigga normally leaves shortly after that. Let's continue our drinks and appear to leave for the night then get in position, say by eleven thirty. Ruth, you can go to your room after Bigga's gone and return when it's quiet. Any questions?"

"You know," Bill said puffing out his chest as far as it would go, "I'm going to stay with you, Ruth. I don't care what you say, I'm not budging."

Dozens of fireflies flashed around the veranda lights and the moon kept up its promise to brighten up the dark skies. A mild breeze blew refreshingly and made it an almost magical evening. Ruth turned to Bill and Jack and warned them, "You are so stubborn, Bill. Anyway, I don't want you getting up to anything dangerous, okay? Especially you, Bill. I still don't feel right about this."

Two sets of, "Yes, Ruth, promise," did little to comfort her.

The parties assumed their positions as planned, and listened to the guests moving around the hotel. The night security guard was now on duty, and dressed in khaki gear, walked around the hotel on his regular rounds.

It was very quiet for an hour or so but at around one in the morning, just as the night started to drag a bit, everything happened at once. Brown, the security guard, appeared outside the bar storeroom, quietly slipped his key into the lock, and disappeared inside. Ruth phoned Walker while Bill was flopped over the restaurant table fast asleep and only woke when Ruth stuck an elbow into his ribs.

"Not now, darling," Bill muttered dreamily and received a fierce glare from Ruth in return as she said, "Stop being silly and wake up. Something's happening outside, look."

As they watched, Brown came out with a box of gently clicking bottles and put them down, relocked the storeroom, and carried the box out of the back door to the poorly lit parking area toward his car.

As Brown placed the box inside his car boot, Jack stepped out of the shadows, approached him and demanded, "What are you up to?"

Brown swung round and growled out, "Move from me bwoy. Don't trouble me."

As Brown took out his car keys, Jack blocked his passage to the driver's seat and Brown said, "Move. Give me pass!"

Jack stood still and Brown pulled a large knife from his pocket and thrust it toward Jack. Jack parried the knife hand and stepped right past Brown slamming his heel into the back of Brown's knee. As Brown dropped to his knees, Jack turned, grabbed the back of his neck, pushed his chest to the ground, and grabbed the knife hand so that it was twisted behind his back, immobilizing him. Walker and Ruth came running toward them with Bill panting at the rear, and in a flash Sergeant Walker had the handcuffs on the security guard. A phone call to the local police station resulted in a patrol car arriving within ten minutes and as Walker jumped into the car with his prisoner, he called out, "Well done, people. I'll need statements from all three of you tomorrow. Well done, Jack."

Looking tired, Ruth led the way back into the hotel saying, "You're terrible. I told you to behave and stay back. Crazy macho men!" And seeing their guilty looks laughed and said, "You were both wonderful. My heroes."

Jack said, "What a night. Hey, Ruth, can you come with Bill to my place for lunch tomorrow?

Ruth replied, "I'll see what I can do. Now let's call it a night and I'll see you all tomorrow."

SIX

Controlled Creativity and Chaos

An understanding of controls is incomplete without discussing creativity. This chapter gives the reader a way of integrating control reporting standards with the need to promote innovative approaches to business. Inherent conflicts are isolated and tackled, again in a problem-solving manner.

"Good morning, Bill," Jack said as he got out of his car. "What a wonderful day," came the reply.

Jack looked at Bill and smiled. Bill had changed quite a lot during his vacation. His clothes, consisting of shorts, a loose T-shirt, and a baseball cap worn at a slight angle, reflected a more comfortable personality. This contrasted with his first few days, where trousers and tailored shirts were the norm. Interesting . . .

"Right," announced Jack. "A day at my place. Is Ruth ready?" This question required no answer as Ruth appeared in a most attractive peach-colored dress, which Bill thought suited her perfectly.

217

"Good morning, Ruth." Again Jack smiled as he thought how good these two looked together.

The drive to Jack's house did not take more than fifteen minutes. They went past Mo'Bay Town, and took the road heading toward Ocho Rios. A right-hand turn up into the hills took them into Ironshore and another picturesque residential area called Coral Gardens. They drove further up into the hills through more winding roads and eventually stopped at a beautiful house set right in the middle of an acre of land. A large mango tree stood at the left, bearing several different types of mango. Breadfruit trees were scattered around at the back of the house standing out from the landscaped lawns. Colorful plants, including white bougainvillea blooms added to the lush foliage that was most pleasing to the eye. A kidney-shaped swimming pool glistened with sparkling blue water and three small children swam and splashed around with occasional shrieks of laughter. Vibrant energy, tranquility.

"Meet my wife, Sharon," said Jack as his wife approached from the house and took part in the introductions. As the two women already knew each other they soon disappeared into the house leaving the men to their own devices.

After a few minutes spent introducing Bill to Jack's neighbor's children who were in the pool, the two men sat on a huge veranda overlooking the swimming pool. The breeze that blew in from the sea and across the veranda kept everything in its wake cool and comfortable.

"I'll show you around the house later," Jack said as he sank back into a reclining chair and offered Bill a glass from a large bowl of iced fruit punch.

"This is wonderful," Bill observed looking around the grounds, "and so cool up here on the hill."

"Yes. We chose this house carefully, and we don't really need to use the air-conditioning most of the time, it's so breezy here. By the way, I think you've lost Ruth for the day," Jack continued as he heard the two women inside talking and laughing loudly. "Shall we get into today's topic?"

"Yes. You wanted to deal with controls and creativity," Bill replied.

Jack switched the recorder on, looked toward the sky and sighed, "I'm really not sure what to do about this subject. I need to ensure controls take into account the impact of creativity. This is so important, but I'm not sure where to start."

Bill came to the rescue, "I've been thinking about this subject. In fact, throughout the last few days I've constantly thought about where this fits into some of the things you've been saying. I'm quite happy to talk about it if you like."

"Absolutely," Jack crossed his legs and sank further into his recliner chair as if to show that he was ready to listen.

"Right," Bill rubbed his hands together, leaned forward, switched on the tape, and started. "I'll give you my views on creativity and control. You use the out-of-bounds model to illustrate the way control frameworks confine things. Let's look at your Figure 6.1.

"We contain activity within the upper and lower limits so that staff stick to the right route and don't go over a cliff or bump into

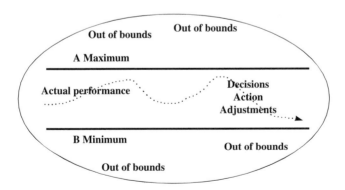

Figure 6.1   Out of bounds.
(See also Figures 2.3, 6.14, and 6.15)

219

something nasty. But having them march blindfolded along our chosen route means they'll miss what's outside. At some stage, we need to reconcile these forces and sort out this dilemma. But before we get there, I would like to think about the concept of creativity. It's less about being controlled and more about having the freedom to generate new ideas. You have an interesting reference from Jane Henry's work, *Making Sense of Creativity:*

> The suggestion is that creative ideas flow where new ideas and challenges are welcomed and where people are encouraged to play, rather than controlled and threatened.(1)

"So we start with the view that controls may inhibit creativity."

Jack put up his hand in a stop sign saying, "Bill, this is where I get stuck. We need controls and the auditor in me believes this is fundamental. There're no short cuts. However, creative people need the freedom to operate freely. As I said, this is where I get stuck."

"Okay," Bill took up the challenge. "We aren't suggesting that there's no control. You said that we need controls that recognize the importance of innovation and change. It's as simple as that. You need to start thinking more in terms of the art of control rather than the science of control. Art is subjective, organic, and free floating. It means different things to different people. This conflict between art and science is also seen in business as quality versus costs. The art of control recognizes the need for controls to attach to people, move with changes, and inspire energies and emotions. Moreover, it should encourage creativity in areas where this is important, in contrast to areas where we must be firmer and clearer. For example, there's no way we can suggest that a health and safety procedure that says you shouldn't try to fix PCs by removing their backs and playing with wires is optional.

"Having said this, we still need to ensure we cater for the creative freedom of thought. Reason and order are the cornerstones of control. But do they, at the same time, support progress? Creating unreasonable controls, now that's an idea."

Jack came into the conversation, "This is it. Order and reason must be paramount. How else can we prove that controls are in place, they're sound, and they work? I can't condone a form of anarchy where people move around the organization, dreaming up ideas, and just going ahead with them. Financial management, good structures with clear reporting lines, project management, information systems, and performance targets are all required. We must set standards within which our people should work. This is where I get stuck reconciling these things."

Bill looked at the children playing in the pool and wondered if he would ever be blessed with a family. What a lifestyle—living in your dream house, a wonderful wife, working as and when you wish, and, most of all, being your own boss. Bill took up where Jack had left off.

"People want to perform and achieve. Ask anyone what they want from life and they'll have a thousand ideas. Ask them whether they can achieve these at work and they'll tell you about the obstacles. Working for someone isn't easy. We have large organizations that employ excellent people who fail. They fail to have ideas, they fail to stay ahead of the opposition, and they fail to survive. I agree that managing is about setting up systems, such as your managerial control system, and ensuring they work. And it's then about solving the people problems caused by these very same systems. If these people problems aren't dealt with, the company will fail. Where these people problems are dealt with and employees feel committed and competent, then we've a much better chance of success. Getting people to release their creative energies isn't easy. At first it seems that controls work in conflict with these creative energies; they pin people down and lead to excessive paperwork. Rigid rules on accountability may mean people refuse to make decisions for fear of reprimand. Where these decisions are confined to a narrow frame in our out of bounds example, we lose accountability. The procedures make decisions and not people paid to take the occasional chance and manage corporate risk properly. In the end, we lose this accountability by enforcing it too rigidly. We take no chances but make no progress. All new computer developments involve gambles to get better performance through better information. To do nothing means there's no risk; we simply rely on our old legacy information systems. If our controls, say in this case project approval procedures, mean people won't come up with ideas on new systems, then this'll happen. We make no progress, don't keep up with competitors, and so fail."

"To be honest, Bill," interrupted Jack, looking excited, "I've carried out many investigations into why computer development projects fail and they all end up as witch hunts. At the end of the day, I've felt sorry for the project manager and team members who take on the tasks within this blame culture. They're always hard working and committed, but lack the insights and most importantly the top level support to make the projects work. I really cannot understand why anyone would take on these types of projects."

"Okay," said Bill, acknowledging Jack's view, "let's get back to the issue in hand. Getting people to release their creative talents is needed for organizational success. Take your comments over these last few days. Creativity is about freedom to act, to make decisions, a freedom to think. Control is about restraining activities within set parameters. We've said that control is about achieving objectives; if we refuse to empower people and allow them to think, they'll operate within our confines and nothing more. Objectives for any organization must involve creating change, innovating, improving, and energizing. There's no way around this point. So we restrict creativity, we make no progress, and we don't achieve our objectives. If this is the case, controls have failed. Controls are an important aspect of creativity; they must cater for it and promote new ideas, not hinder them. This isn't to say I'm encouraging anarchy. It's just that we need to start thinking about creative controls, or perhaps controlled creativity."

"We'll have to address the role of creative destruction at some stage. For the time being I'd like to quote from your file the words of the civil rights leader, Martin Luther King, on the importance of tensions:

> The Negro's great stumbling block in the stride toward freedom is not the White Citizens Councillor or the Klu Klux Klanner but the white moderate who is more devoted to order than to justice; who prefers a negative peace which is the absence of tension to a positive peace which is the presence of justice. (2)

"Maintaining the status quo can be more dangerous than building tensions that challenge it."

Bill managed to bend over the side of the pool and splash the children without falling in. In fact, he had become so relaxed since he first arrived on the island, he wouldn't have minded falling in and getting wet.

Bill continued talking, "Let's go back to this concept of creativity before we work out how it can be managed. Creativity is a disturbance of order; it means going off track from time to time.

"It's linked into change management. Not the change management where the organization's required to install new procedures resulting from government legislation, new automation standards, or basic adjustments. It's the kind of change that the organization creates simply because it wants to stay ahead. This latter change is so important to success that we should adopt procedures that promote it. That is, we can control the use of creativity. Taking a positive approach to creativity isn't new. Dynamic change is so important to organizational survival, but, we all agree, it must be done in a controlled environment. Controls mustn't lead the process, they must be organic and follow what the organization requires.

Your definition of controls means that they're part of the change drive. It all fits together. Since you like using diagrams, I'll sketch out a chart I've been thinking about in Figure 6.2.

- *Inertia.* No change, no controls, no one cares, managers assume a waiting-to-retire stance, incapable staff are employed.
- *Bureaucracy.* Overcontrol, control and command, forty forms to fill out for every decision made.
- *Chaos.* Change for change sake, no rules, no direction, no measurement, free-floating environment where we lose any sense of direction.
- *Structured Innovation.* Controls keep pace with change, driven by change, sets direction, there is measurement and review.

"We want to get to the top right-hand corner, that is, structured innovation. There we have change but also stay in control. Things happen as they are meant to happen. In this way, controls aren't

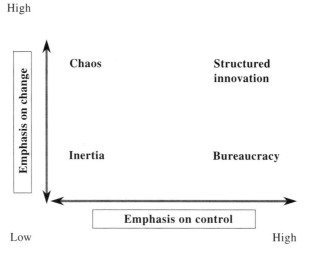

Figure 6.2 Control/Change model.

forgotten and we're still asking, are objectives clear and communicated? Do staff know what they're doing? Are they equipped? Can we measure performance? Can we adjust as we go along?"

"Yes," Jack came in, "My self-control format can still fit well with this idea. The traditional compliance model is linked to poor performance by attacking people's insecurities and fears. A better version uses self-control to inspire top performance, which is in Figure 6.3."

"But," Bill came in, "We can pursue the need to promote a self-control framework based on a positive view of the organization. But at the same time we need to adopt a three circles approach, where we cater for control, creativity, and chaos as in Figure 6.4.

- *Creativity.* Innovation, ideas, fresh thoughts, and lateral thinking.
- *Control.* Process through which lateral and random change can be focused by managing risks to achieving organizational goals.

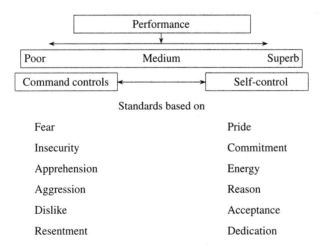

Figure 6.3 Self-control and performance.

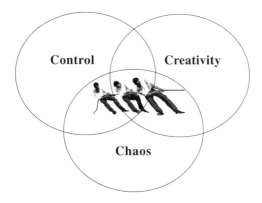

Figure 6.4   Three circles.

- *Chaos.* Conflicts and struggle where systems adapt to changing environments in a random manner."

"What do you mean by chaos?" Jack asked.

"Ah," Bill rubbed his chin. "I still say that your discussion of controls is incomplete. You've spoken about systems and how they're established and maintained. These are controlled so that they achieve their goals, that is, whatever they were meant to achieve. But we need to deal with the concept of chaos. Chaos is just as important to successful companies. And I'm afraid that it flies in the face of your steady-state view of controls. Your managerial control system argues that a set of parameters comprising all the key processes underpinning the management function should be in place. However, I suggest that these systems must be allowed to break down and regroup to be of any use. Chaos looks like Figure 6.5.

"It leads to changes, which lead to dynamic creativity, which in turn leads to improvement. The old systems become volatile, break down, and energize into systems that better respond to the changing environment. The stage where these systems have deteriorated and haven't yet been replaced is dangerous. If not managed and left

Figure 6.5 Systems patterning.

too late, we move into anarchy. As we approach chaos, we anticipate new successes but must have the nerve to allow success to happen. A performance appraisal scheme might start to break down or repattern because it doesn't work—it doesn't reflect the new ways that staff work. Managers start to use creative methods to compensate for this lack of proper performance appraisal. These organic systems should then be integrated into a new and improved corporate standard that replaces the old system. There's no point in auditors reporting noncompliance with a system that is breaking down. There's no point reporting we have chaos (i.e., no real system). We must manage this chaos as a natural search for a more realistic and usable system for establishing standards and assessing performance. Allow it to happen and allow a repatterning so that the new one grows naturally from the ashes of the old. Forcing the old system onto staff has no use. Inventing a new one is also dangerous. Allowing the growth of better arrangements and then consolidating them is much more sensible. Or setting an appraisal standard that simply says 'all managers must establish suitable means of setting targets, and measuring performance' is another alternative.

"You find the topic of creativity difficult because it requires judgment and balance. There's no finite answer. You used to tell me at the start of these discussions that control freaks like me need quick answers to all problems. There's a lot behind this, balancing freedom to act with direction from above.

"It comes down to contingency. Some aspects of work, some people, some situations, and some times, we need to set clear guidance and tell people what to do. We need to write formal memos and sign and date them. Other times we can simply give people freedom to act—they'll decide when they might seek advice and they will decide what controls should be in place. You used to be an auditor, do you accept this point?"

Jack took time to think before answering. He finally said, "I need some kind of standard. There must be a format that's defined by the organization and agreed and accepted. We anticipate adherence with these standards. I cannot accept an 'if I feel like it' attitude when dealing with specific control routines."

"Okay," Bill agreed, "But we must explore the need for creativity. Let's go back to your comments on motivation. What makes people tick? You made reference to Maslow's hierarchy of needs. Can control help one reach the top of this hierarchy, that is, self-actualization?"

"I don't accept that controls should necessarily stop people reaching this so-called state of self-fulfillment. They should encourage it. When I considered the standard material on motivation, I felt that the available research supports the view that people search for real value from work. I agree that a blame culture means they revert to protecting the lower needs of safety and security and they can't think about higher needs, where innovation sits. We may see some productivity where autocratic control is used, but over the years this'll decline where mistrust and resentment take over to lower motivation and performance. In fact, working within the rules means that little achievement will be made as people generally stick to the rules as the norm, which will always be below best performance. As long as they obey the rules this is accepted. For excellent performance we must move away from the rulebook and talk about creative progress. Expectancy means people will behave in a way that increases the chances of perceived rewards. Sticking to the rules may be the best strategy to preserve basic needs but the organization of tomorrow needs people who will take it from now to then, and doing so depends on innovation and commitment and not threat of discipline."

The morning's debate came to a natural conclusion as Jack announced that he would have to help prepare lunch. This gave Bill the chance to spend some time with Ruth who came out after talking with Jack's wife, Sharon. Bill and Ruth spent a happy hour playing with the children, who were still in the pool, and trying to keep dry—not too successfully.

A rather wet Bill sat back in his chair said, "Ruth, why is an attractive woman like you not married?"

"Some men are funny," she replied. "My last boyfriend didn't want me to live at the hotel. He wanted to control every aspect of my life. You see, Bill, I'm a very independent person and I can't stand being told what to do or someone trying to control my life. Anyway, we went our separate ways last year. You know people say that a caged bird never sings."

"So you want to be in control of your own life?"

"Exactly," Ruth shrugged. "If you try to hold on to someone too tightly, you'll eventually lose them. Okay. Your turn now, Bill. Why did your wife leave you?"

"Come to think of it," Bill looked up toward the blue sky thoughtfully, "she never did sing much when we were together . . ."

Their conversation was interrupted by a shout from Sharon, telling then that the food was ready. Lunch was a lavish affair. It consisted of curried lobster, avocado pear, rice, green bananas, and a green salad. The conversation was pleasant and dealt with Jack and Sharon's move to Jamaica. Realizing that Jack and Bill had planned a close debate over what must be one of the most boring subjects ever, after lunch the two women went on a tour of the gardens, leaving the men to restart their verbal sparring match. The discussion started slowly as the effects of the meal left them lethargic. After a few attempts they gave up and both fell asleep about the same time. The silence and deep snores went on for nearly an hour as they drifted into deep wells of dreams and secret wishes. Jack's dream swept him into the world of internal controls. He drove through these controls that were represented as roads winding through a mountain with precipices at one side marking great danger. Trying to maintain control of the car in the face of this danger was both exciting and frightening. Bill's dream was different. He was lying on an air-bed on a calm sea with a Red Stripe beer in one hand and a radio somewhere playing the Dennis Brown classic, *"Love Me, Love Me Always."* Ruth was always singing this song . . . what a sweet melody . . . .

When this impromptu siesta came to an end, they both felt more lively. Jack gave Bill a tour of the house which added to the short, but much needed break from their discussions. After settling back down onto the veranda, the conversation continued with Bill saying,

"Let's get back to this question of creativity. Being creative is about new ideas, new thoughts. It's about being one jump ahead of the opposition. I've seen this first hand; a board meeting became the venue for a little piece of inspiration. It suddenly occurred to one particular director that the individual computer applications for payroll, pensions, personnel, and performance management were all based around what could be one employee database. He asked why these systems weren't integrated and based on one database. When no one was able to answer this question, a project feasibility team was established that led to the take-up and implementation of what started out as a basic idea. Scaled down versions of this sort of thing happen every day at work. I've seen one administrative clerk ask why she had to go through a weekly routine of typing data into her system from detailed returns from a particular section. If this section were computerized then she could simply strip off relevant parts of the database into her system on a regular basis. An automated solution could give much better results. Again after assessing feasibility, this idea was adopted. One final example relates to a main supplier that was proving unreliable. The official control procedures required a lengthy retendering process to find a better supplier for the contract on offer. One bright spark suggested we buy out the supplier, improve its operation, and then retain the subsidiary as a reliable source, delivering raw material directly into the production process.

"Controls should be about assisting this process of generating new ideas. If procedures only allow project feasibility studies to be initiated by defined persons and then require a complicated routine that ends up with most new ideas being shelved, there'll be little or no progress. However the procedure may simply say that all new ideas should be welcomed and assessed in broad outline. It may go on to encourage these ideas by suggesting ways that can assist the search for creativity, perhaps including brainstorming and buzz groups. The conflict between art and science comes back into the frame where we seek to work within these two spheres. In our discussion, this means balancing intuition and formal analysis.

"We need controls that recognize the importance of creativity. There are hard systems and soft systems. Hard systems, or *hard minds,* involve budgets, accounts, productivity statements, variance reports, and so on. Soft systems involve things like judgment, motivation, energies, team spirit, *warm heart* issues. We have a good track record of establishing controls over these hard systems but little understanding of soft system controls. We audit hard systems in the form of the financial statements but spend little effort auditing the value-based systems or soft systems. The basic dilemma facing most managers is they want to push ahead, make progress, succeed, and get into the future. However, the auditors want to issue statements about internal controls for periods gone. You know, audit and management speak entirely different languages; look to the past under the accountability banner, while seeking a future in the guise of better performance. Hard systems fall under the science of management where we measure success via the balance sheet and profit and loss account. Soft systems is a value-based art where we consider the worth of a company via the value it has to investors (i.e., the share price). This is why it's so hard to comment on internal control outside the financial arena. Society has struggled with this idea of mandatory control reporting and you can see why.

"The problem is we should be able to issue reports on what we've done and how we've established arrangements to ensure we're doing things properly. I predict that, in the future, people, including customers, will judge companies on their track records and their reputations. Sleaze-free, ethical companies will publicize their achievements with pride, while scandal hit ones will have to work hard to retain their client base. Eventually, *The Great Public* will be able to work out which companies provide which products, from the often complicated maze of associated companies. Reports on internal control can address these arguments. The directors should establish suitable systems of control to ensure policy frameworks are adhered to, assets are protected from fraud, information systems work, and quality products are delivered. This shouldn't be a matter of compliance with vaguely worded regulations that no one really understands or supports. It's more about the board of directors and audit committee wanting to make this report on how they manage risks as it fits with their value base.

"We agree that creative management is about the future while accountability is about looking at the past. It's about different perspectives. David K. Hurst et al.(3) have looked at top management teams and organizational reward, and have devised a model that's in Figure 6.6.

"Can we be happy with the past and excited about the future? In this way can we reconcile the auditor and manager's mind-sets? Developing this point, we need to recognize the dual nature of things. You said this yourself, Jack, in your Jekyll and Hyde

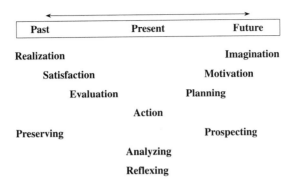

Figure 6.6 Creative management model.

dilemma, the carrot and stick, the art and science argument, and the hard and soft approaches. Maybe even the left side versus the right side of the brain. There's no one answer. This dual nature of managing is also found in the idea of hard minds and soft hearts used by Richard Tanner Pascale who argues:

> Hard minds pertains to a bottom line orientation—the financial performance . . . In contrast "soft hearted" values pertain to intangibles that are tied to higher-order ideals affecting employees . . . they act as a counterbalance to tangible financial goals.(4)

"Hard minds/soft hearts challenge companies to be caring yet realistic."

Jack came in, "I was starting my work on controls from the individual perspective. You've taken this as a society-wide concept. We need to bridge this gap at some stage, don't you agree?"

"Yes," Bill nodded, "but did you know that we can also deal with the personal position. I have read arguments that suggest some people are internals and others are externals. Eugene F. McKenna has considered the use of psychology in business and has written that:

Certain people (externals) feel that the outcome of their efforts is controlled by forces and events external to themselves, such as chance, fate, and powerful figures in authority; while others (internals) are convinced that control is an internal matter related to their own efforts and talents.(5)

"I guess we need to train people to become internals and view control as a dynamic manageable force. The worrying factors relate to stress. Externals may feel stressed, where they don't like being subject to forces that they've no control over. If they don't care, then this is okay. If they would like better control over their lives and cannot achieve it, then there may be an imbalance that leads to stress. Where people are internals, then they may still suffer. This happens when they cannot accept that parts of their environment cannot be controlled or that mistakes can occur where they make bad decisions. Again stress is about not being able to reconcile these issues.

"Jack, you reckon that control is like a gravitational pull that retains order and consistency. This contrasts with your satellite model where control is information that shines on things as an external force. Now I want to ask how space travel fits with your gravitational model, where it fails to keep people on planet Earth?"

"Right. A difficult question," Jack replied. "I use these metaphors not as perfect examples but just to illustrate basic points. If you force me, I can say that gravity, or control, seeks this order but allows exceptions that work with the gravitational pull, allows free space travel, and then brings back the astronauts or probes with information that helps us here on Earth. So controls set parameters, say to keep your feet firmly on the ground. But we allow and encourage creative exceptions to get people to fly away and bring back vital information (i.e., to breach controls and experiment). I can adjust my control model to retain the gravitational pull but keep the satellite. I'll simply point it toward the universe, and not only pointing downward, to shine out and seek new information as an additional aspect of control. So gravitational control pulls us together and promotes order; satellite controls seek new experiences and inspirations based on creativity and exception. We probe new opportunities, we look for disorder and new patterns that we can use to add to our existing patterns as seen in Figure 6.7."

Bill, getting excited, took up this argument, "There's a call for conflict to be introduced into organizations to assist this search for newness. Creativity is based on change. Let me write down how change appears in three main guises. We can call this Figure 6.8.

"Where the board of directors and chief executive officer (CEO) resigns, the organization may spin out of control and old policies are thrown away as political in-fighting occurs. Through this conflict, a new direction is established and hopefully we're

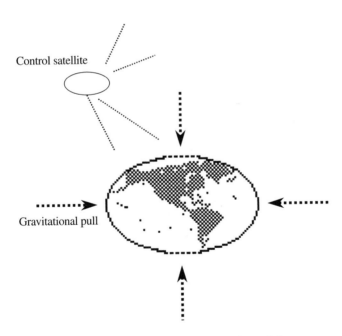

Figure 6.7 Combined control model.
(See also Figures 2.10 and 2.11)

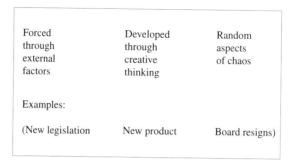

Figure 6.8 Organizational change.

better able to deal with change. Each of these three forces drives the change process. We need then to establish controls over these three processes and ensure that they lead to an organization that is better able to cope with change. We must ensure we cope with external forces, encourage creativity, and use conflict to develop managed chaos. Some argue that where we take chaos to the edge, we repattern and create new systems. Where it falls over the edge, we end up with anarchy and systems disintegrate and fail.

"The other side of the coin argues that without conflicts complacency and full stomachs lead to disaster. Auditors need order, consistency, and good conflict management to feel comfortable. If they don't have these, they publish adverse reports. Good managers want conflicts to challenge norms and keep the organization moving ahead. Employing people merely to administer procedures won't work. They must be creative, challenging, and demanding so that disagreements tend to lead to better decisions. Agreeing to agree leads to stagnation and failure. We need to turn the control concept on its head and look for creative controls, creative accounting, and creative auditing. If you cannot build this concept into your definition of systems of internal control, the manager and the auditor will never be able to communicate meaningfully. Complacency is the enemy of success.

"We try to move away from stability toward instability, but stop before we get to the edge of chaos and systems disintegration. Remember, stability is taken as sameness. Doing the same things the same way doesn't lead to progress. It repeats past mistakes and keeps us in our comfort zones while the competition is surging ahead. What we're looking for is systems to better cope with the strains and stresses of the changing environment as shown in Figure 6.9.

"Meanwhile we install controls so we know what we're doing at all times. We can employ a new CEO who asks 'why do we do that, why aren't we doing this, and what the hell is going on?' In this way we can inject conflict but not pure chaos. Some see order within chaos and seek quantum leaps of inspiration.

"One warning though: There are still people around who adhere to the old views and see change as a threat. They embark on a drastic search for stability. Control here is more about maintaining one's position in the face of adversity. This is personal control but destroys real control because it means the organization isn't allowed to go with the flow and meet its objectives. One bottom line on this topic of creative destruction is the view that order or best fit, while looking good on paper, may in the long run stop an organization from progressing. This is a dilemma for the old style controller as it suggests that too much control isn't good for you.

"I realize now that this is where the control freak in me went wrong. I tried to dominate my environment without realizing some

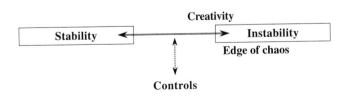

Figure 6.9   Systems adaptability.

things cannot be controlled in this way. This leads to stress and a feeling of being out of control, which leads to further stress. The sheer magic of living breathes life back into things and being able to relax when things go well. But also seeing opportunity when confronted by problems makes excess stress a thing of the past. We must have some stress or we wouldn't get out of bed in the morning. But where we feel out of control, excess stress causes health problems, sick leave, and a way of opting out of the situation.

"The body says, 'I don't like this,' or, 'I'm going to complain,' and the mind starts to go into a loop of problems that can't be reconciled. What I want versus what I've got, and it short circuits. You know, I'm now able to diagnose myself and see where I've gone wrong. I guess the power of positive thinking is a control in its own right."

"Look, Bill," Jack came in, "the self-control concept has to work. It's the only way of making control happen—to give people responsibility and train them in techniques to account for this responsibility. I said that control starts from the soul. We can take the control chart as a comparison that suggests control is a journey through upper and lower bounds, the road to success."

Bill continued, "But this model can be replaced by your organic one. Remember the one where control is seen as a series of concentric circles that start with you, your soul, and continues outward as in Figure 6.10.

"The circles in Figure 6.10 must be kept in balance and work at all times. The task then is to maintain this equilibrium—to ensure we integrate the needs and concerns of each of the parts of the circles as each fits into the other, communicates, and is interdependent. The journey becomes one of maintaining balance and reconciling competing forces. The task isn't to arrive at these goals but to experience the journey. As John Lennon said:

Life is what happens to you while you're busy making other plans. (6)

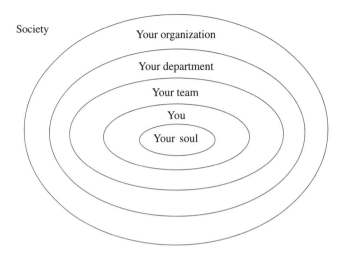

Figure 6.10   Concentric self-control.
(See also Figures 2.5 and 7.6)

"What I speak of isn't a mystery. It's to do with energies, motivations, and searching for success and happiness. It's the opposite to being sad, withdrawn, and uncommitted. Everything starts with you, Jack. Whether you perceive yourself as in control and act accordingly. Self-talk (where you tell yourself that you're in control, your team works, your department is successful, and this makes the customer happy) is a powerful weapon. Self-talk translates reality into words that impact on your being. It's really talking to your soul. The best managers spend a little time with their feet up on the desk, their eyes closed, just thinking. They're saying to themselves, How are we doing? Have I got the right people on board? What's my vision for the future? How far away are we from this vision? How do we get there? Do I feel energy from staff? Am I giving them enough of my energy? Do our processes work? Can I get them better placed to deliver? What about our procedures? Am I happy with them?

"We need to empower ourselves and feel that we'll succeed. You know, we can learn a lot from our friend, Danny-Dread. Control must start with the individual and how that person feels about himself and the organization. The great boxer, Muhammed Ali, once said:

> To be a great champion you must believe you are the best. If you're not, pretend you are.(7)

"This feeling must come from you and not some formal control procedure that dictates how you must feel."

Jack leaned forward, cupped his hands under his chin, and said, "Your idea of change means that systems start to disintegrate and are replaced by newer, more dynamic ones. I can see this. In fact there's no such thing as no system or no method; it's just that these systems are organic and go through phases. It puts a new slant on the auditor's work. Many auditors view compliance as a key issue and report that procedures aren't being adhered to and controls have broken down. What's more apt is for us to consider how a system has changed and what has fallen into place to compensate for these changes. There's always a system in place, but it may not meet official standards or for that matter it may not be well controlled. I remember one audit of payroll that I carried out in my past life as an auditor. The payroll manager held together an old inefficient computerized system that was always breaking down, and in no way gave the type of information that they needed to manage the service. You had to go back to the software supplier to get any sort of useful reports, which they had to specially prepare. On the first day of the audit, I asked him how many people were on the various payrolls. There were no aggregate figures available and the manager spent an hour listing from memory the total number of employees on the seven or eight different payrolls. The section was in a state of constant crisis with staff rushing around trying to sort out problems as and when they arose. The official system and procedures had been replaced by a 'sticking plaster' job where staff papered over the holes in the system. A great part of the system was dependent on the payroll managers and their detailed knowledge of the way processing worked. It was truly chaotic. At the same time, there was still a system in place that had developed over the years, based on memory, tight communications between staff, high levels of teamworking, and a fire-fighting approach to each new crisis. Staff had developed the response-based skills to compensate for deficiencies in the process."

"Interesting," Bill said, taking up this point. "We can build some freedom into controls so long as we know where and when it's a good idea. There's no blanket answer but we can think it through if you like. We can adapt this approach to work out how much personal freedom and discretion to allow. The creativity bit is similar as there are parts of the organization such as marketing, design, or research and development, where people need to free float and think about ideas outside of rigid procedures and supervision. However, this wine, talk, and music style doesn't need to happen everywhere in the organization.

"We separate ideas people from those that take the ideas and make them happen, from those who simply implement these procedures based on the new ideas. It all depends on what's required and who we employ. But we've got to be careful about breaking the first rule of creativity, that is, not making assumptions. Where we form too tight a classification, we may restrict a whole group of people who we may, perhaps wrongly, feel don't need to be creative."

The discussions were interrupted by a visit from Sharon's neighbors who joined the group and conversation turned to local matters. Bill learned that Sharon was doing a research project at the University of the West Indies into health care in the Caribbean. She was on loan to the university and in fact, it was she, and not Jack who had decided to settle in Jamaica for a while. It seemed that Sharon was not impressed by Jack's lack of progress on his book and his detailed knowledge of every bar in Mo'Bay. As the group settled down, politics and the state of the nation became the topics under review. It provided some relief from the journey through controls, which like all long journeys can become tiring and repetitive. You meet dead ends, you go down familiar roads, and at times you may go too fast or too slowly.

After the visitors left Bill suggested, "You say that I don't deal with creativity and control from an individual's stance. But creativity can be a personal thing. We accept that creativity must be encouraged for active change to happen. But, we can establish a standard where new ideas can be assessed and moved forward. Initiators can pass ideas over to people who will take a level-headed view on value, return, and feasibility. This suggested separation of ideas and projects isn't new.

"It can get deeper. Creativity can alter and adapt models of reality. Controlling a person's thoughts, views, and ambitions has repercussions. Getting them to create, setting firm guidance, and assessing what they provide is praiseworthy, but are we moving into the realm of manipulation? Should organizations be controlling their employee's thoughts? The word control can have negative meanings, such as to dominate, manipulate, or rule over.

"We must be very careful not to get closer to this type of model when getting people to become creative. Another problem with controlling creativity is that at times we've no place to start. Problem solving can be quite precise where the problem is isolated, analyzed, options considered, and innovation used to develop a way forward. We can set procedures and so control the process. But creativity can be about throwing all previous thought away and starting afresh. Our procedures start with the defined problem, but creativity can be about restating problems. So we give the creative person or team a problem and leave them to sort it out. Our procedures may state that a week on, we should request the results, only to get back an opinion on a completely different problem they've decided to work on."

"To be honest," Jack entered the debate, "in all my days as an auditor and in most investigations I've done on top management's behalf, there's one common factor. The problems under review are normally caused by failings in the same managers who referred them to me in the first place. Not a popular conclusion when these top managers have set the auditor on what is little more than a witch hunt. To receive a problem for review but redefine it as a management failing, or to develop a new idea that implies top management is inefficient, can be very unsettling. People are wary of creativity because it tends to upset the status quo; they use controls to keep a lid on too many new ideas. This is the worst abuse of the internal control process possible; to establish controls that contain people for ulterior reasons."

"What is it that Luciano says?" asked Bill.

"Oh," Jack looked taken aback, "You mean Luciano, the Jamaican singer. Yes, he calls them ulterior motives; personal gain."

"Okay," Bill returned to his reasoning, "Back to the individual. One problem we have is where people in an organization have developed unique views that cannot be properly reconciled. Some refer to these as mind-sets, others call them mind-maps, while still others sum them up as organizational culture. Creativity can be about getting the right mind-map to address an old problem from a new perspective.

"We move then toward controls over the mind-mapping processes and how different people relate to reality in different ways. One problem faced by most organizations is to get some form of consistency in these visions of reality. Creative solutions have little use where they fall outside the common view of reality. Control here is about keeping people within the bounds of reasonableness. Pure chaos reigns outside these bounds, but, as we have said before, allow them to go as close as possible to the edge without falling over. Not an easy task. Mind-maps mean people feel comfortable with their definition of reality. If this vision is shared by others, then we don't have to ask a person to go it alone to make progress. Sometimes a team approach to creativity helps as different people who share these mind-maps explore new possibilities. Being in a group causes one to devise a reference frame that all members can relate to in some way or other.

"Networking can help promote creativity. Many companies have established social clubs to assist this function. One question we may ask is, where do we concentrate our creative energies? What should we get our people working on? We can work with your ideas about risk. You've said that risk is about assessing the likelihood of something occurring that gets in the way of our progress. Even if it's subjective we need to set some kind of scale. I'll draft Figure 6.11 that we can use here.

"So when something's unlikely, there's 10 percent or less chance that this risk will materialize. The challenge is to assign percentage values to ideas. Where we use it with an assessment of relative importance (i.e., macro or micro issues), we have a dynamic way of assigning resources in Figure 6.12.

"It's clear then, that we need to deal with important issues that have a high level of uncertainty attached to them. So, we aim to spend our creative time at point 1 of the model while points 2 and 3 may compete for our attention. Point 3 relates to important issues that we have sound information on or aren't so hard to deal with. Again, while point 2 issues are in doubt, they're not key to organizational success because they're micro issues. Point 4 matters pose

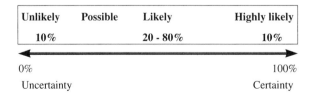

Figure 6.11   Risk index.

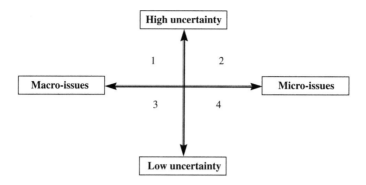

Figure 6.12   Risk squares.

no real problem and may be dealt with by using standard procedures. The important point is that organic change causes these
points to swivel and refocus rapidly. The challenge is to keep up
with these changes and constantly adjust the scores so that they're
up-to-date. If creativity isn't targeted at the right issues, there's little point in developing it. We can use risk to assess the degree of
attention that's given to each area, but there's no finite solution.
The human condition means that once again we must speak about
the art and not science of risk assessment. I like your reference to
Robert Pirsig on the way different people see things differently:

> Some things you miss because they are so tiny you overlook them.
> But some things you don't see because they are so huge. We were
> both looking at the same thing, seeing the same thing, talking about
> the same thing, thinking about the same thing, except he was look-
> ing, seeing, talking, and thinking from a completely different di-
> mension."(8)

Looking at the view toward the coast, it was clear that the sun
was starting its plunge into the sea and the vivid purple sunset that
each evening brings. Sunset would happen in around an hour or
so. Jack instinctively brought out the carefully prepared cocktail of

rum punch and ice cubes. The refreshing aroma set the scene for a winding down of the day's events. The two couples sat around the veranda and let the perfumes from the surrounding gardens float across them. Jack waved towards Bill and asked, "Bill, do you want to sum up some of the things we've said today?"

"Yes," Bill said, "why not. I know that you like to work to a structure when you've spoken in the past, Jack. But it's different for me. I'm not writing a book and my conversation can float around as new ideas come to me. Summing up may be a good idea and, if you like, I can firm up some of the things I've said.

"Creativity would appear at first sight to contradict the control concept. Since organizations must now be creative to survive, we have a dilemma, which is solved by incorporating the spirit of creativity into the control process. How do we do this? Is there a creative process that we can study, understand, and allow for with the emphasis being on allowing freedom to fail, experiment, and change the terms of reference? All that appears to mean we become out of control, which I call OoC. But can we control the OoC climate? If so, then we become essentially in control, or EiC. EiC relates to wider organizational outcomes, which we need to develop a model to deal with. We also need to discuss the barriers to creativity that narrow-based control systems form with their emphasis on roles and authority. We can fit this in with your managerial control system, so long as we can make it adaptive. Maybe we need to talk of the managerial control framework in contrast to such a rigid view. The one remaining problem to solve is the paradigm shift where we work to different mind-sets and so lose the all-important reference frame or aim that binds our managerial processes. Unfortunately, we cannot sacrifice the EiC basics, because accountability and fair play must always be in place.

"We should be thinking about many things when developing controls. Can we turn externals who feel they've no control over their environment into internals? Isn't it simply a question of providing guidance? Also, if we manipulate people and try to brainwash them, is this really a good idea? Can we change people without brainwashing them by giving them more confidence, allowing them more control, encouraging them to see links between processes and risk profiles? Control over others must involve allowing them to control themselves within a frame set by the organization. Give people scope to express themselves, to make sure they, and not some unseen force, can make a difference.

"We must also think about the influence of groups, which can affect behavior greatly. Ownership of ideas means a lot, as coercion can lead to fear, which leads to group solidarity and maybe hostility toward management.

"Turning to complexity, adaptive organizations learn their way into the future. Organizations use economic, societal, and political systems that follow certain rules. But complexity theory means that systems can evolve order out of chaos, with some arguing that this is fundamental to growth. Here, new outcomes can result, although it's hard to control the journey or know the final destination. It's more a journey of discovery.

"But the more you seek to control this journey, the more you remove the inherent creativity. We cannot see the outcomes until they happen, which is a little worrisome for top management. Instead of asking the standard control question, how do we design organizations to yield successful outcomes, we are turning more toward a view that we make sense of our experiences to develop complex organizations. It's about soft systems, you know, emotions, intelligence, and a passion for efficiency throughout the entire organization, not just in isolated corners."

Jack stared at Bill for a few seconds. He is as bad as I am he thought, an actual talking machine.

"I think of creativity in three different ways," continued Bill, "One is organic where ideas grow naturally from the changing environment. Two, it can consist of incremental growth where we develop building blocks of ideas, each taking matters one step further. The third model involves a quantum leap from one condition to a seemingly unrelated one, through an insight into new associations that weren't seen before. We can set control standards over these three models to encourage them as follows:

- *Organic.* Nurture, encourage, fertilize, coax, allow change in direction, and work out what feeds this growth. Use climbing rods to assist direction but more than anything, allow freedom to explore.
- *Incremental.* Set a foundation and provide tools and building blocks to help design and manage structures as they emerge.
- *Quantum.* Encourage new insights, don't worry about looking ridiculous, and take on people who have this skill. They see associations that others are unable to. Capture these new ideas and give them to practical people to develop.

"Let's revisit the control chart and your problem of the out-of-bounds area. The standard control frame appears in Figure 6.13.

"The act of comparing the set standard to actual performance and working out a variance is meant to instill control. The problem is that we never look outside the limits for creative new ideas in Figure 6.14. The control in Figure 6.14 appears as limits on

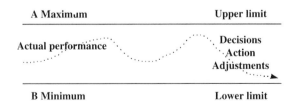

Figure 6.13   Standard control frame.
(See also Figures 2.1 and 3.9)

248

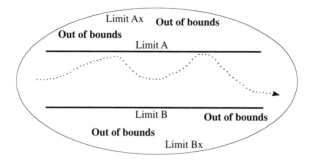

Figure 6.14 Back to the out-of-bounds area.
(See also Figures 2.3, 6.1, and 6.15)

performance A and B, which contains activity to set standards. So our actions are contained within artificial boundaries to achieve control. How do we adjust the control frame to enable new territory, that's out of bounds, in Figure 6.15 to be discovered? There's no right answer, although one approach would be to allow creative probes to test limits A and B when it's felt right to do so in Figure 6.15.

"We still contain the main activities within A and B but allow a deviation based on creativity at levels Ax and Bx. At first sight this

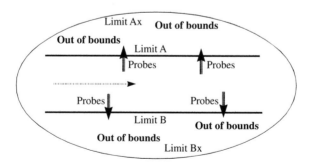

Figure 6.15 Controlled creativity.
(See also Figures 2.3, 6.1, and 6.14)

will appear to be encouraging chaos, but it's still set some sort of standard. The three problems posed by this model are:

1. Who is allowed to deviate?
2. How do we feed lessons learned from these probes into the main AB model?
3. How can we tell whether a new venture is worth pursuing?

"These three questions become three challenges, where the only real answer is to use control criteria that caters for these three questions. You know that I'm a control freak, Jack. I like conclusions and answers and formal criteria that I can use to assess problems. So let's capture the search for creativity and control using ten basic principles:

"**1.** *Build onto existing control frameworks.* Make controls a composite whole. Controls consist of drivers that ensure the right things happen and constraints that ensure problems are kept to a minimum. Creativity requires a focus on the driving controls that allow people to experiment, to an extent. The idea is to promote success (drivers) and avoid failure (restrainers) wherever possible as shown in Figure 6.16.

"Where we take a holistic view of control, we ensure things fit together and work in harmony. We need to adapt the managerial control system in a way that it doesn't restrict people unnecessarily. So use the hard-mind soft-heart equation to balance and set directions. New ideas and new projects are encouraged, but they must in the end be financially viable and based on an agreed budget.

"**2.** *Base deviants around the change process.* Where we can make 'soft decisions'? Precise operations need precise controls, and the people involved in this work area must set standards to stay on a straight path. Softer areas such as research and development, marketing, and strategy analysts must use controls as drivers and not

```
┌─────────────────────────────────────────────────┐
│                   CONTROLS                       │
│                                                  │
│   Restraining Forces          Driving Forces     │
│   ──────────────────          ──────────────     │
│   Model A                     Model B            │
│   ◄──────────────             ──────────────►    │
│                                                  │
│   Avoid Problems              Promote Novelty    │
│   Errors                      Achievements       │
│   Inefficiency                Efficiency         │
│   Problems                    Solutions          │
│   Failure                     Success            │
│                                                  │
│   Push Strategy               Pull Strategy      │
│   Compliance                  Lead by example    │
│   Assessment criteria         Rewards            │
│   Authorization               Encourage          │
│   Risk assessment             Allow freedom to fail │
│                                                  │
│   Tackle Failures             Work toward success │
└─────────────────────────────────────────────────┘
```

Figure 6.16   Push-pull strategy.

restrainers and so may have Ax and Bx frames. Allow greater freedom in areas where it makes sense. Don't let people use inappropriate reference frames. An accountant carrying out complicated final account consolidations can't really be told to do it any way she wants, so long as she's happy. Allowing deviation is based on need; it's not that it suits the person but that it suits the situation.

"We can set people up in roles that have little operational responsibility and give them a 'think tank' role. That is, time to work through complicated problems free from day-to-day work pressures. Each top executive team needs a little bit of genius to work on any vexing problems, which is why the role of deputy chief executive is so important, so long as this person can relate things to reality.

"*3. Build performance indicators that reflect the deviant attitudes.* Use these to supplement the more traditional productivity-based ones, so we can use a measure of ideas generated and, or developed, even where they haven't yet led to increased productivity. They may be based around better communications, a motivated workforce, less staff turnover, and eventually better performance all around. We set performance standards as targets but accept innovative activity that falls outside them. Meanwhile, we need to set minimum standards that stop someone slipping too far behind. A comprehensive performance scheme can handle all these variables and not just target one aspect of performance as Figure 6.17 suggests.

"Performance management is a key control over the way staff deliver and needs to reflect creative activity and not just basic norms. It's about taking things a step further and looking at things with new eyes as suggested by Albert von Szent-Gyorgyi:

> Discovery consists of seeing what everybody has seen and thinking what nobody has thought.(9)

"One hallmark of creativity is experimentation, looking at things anew, and this means some risk. Mistakes can be made and what were thought to be opportunities, may turn out to be blind

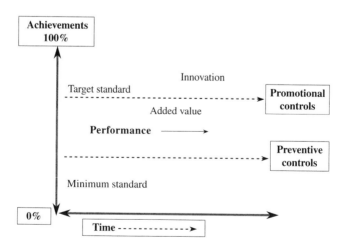

Figure 6.17   Performance controls.

252

alleys. A person situated high on our performance chart may plunge toward the bottom, minimum standards level, as a new project fails to get off the ground. Simply reprimanding them provides a disincentive to further experiment. To simply get staff to turn up for work, clock in a 9 to 5 day, and leave, isn't enough. You get the point. Performance management should allow staff to excel. That isn't to say that it should impose great pressures to solve major problems in a flash. Again, this position will turn into a disincentive in due course. Setting impossible targets can lead to great stress. Figure 6.18 can help here.

"Creativity can result from exerting pressure on people who enjoy a challenge. However, where this isn't the case and the person feels threatened by these pressures, it could be disastrous. Therefore we cannot impose creativity on employees; it can do more harm than good in the long run. It's also an idea to get people to work in teams and build confidence and so lower the pressure. So some computer design teams rope in the highly motivated systems

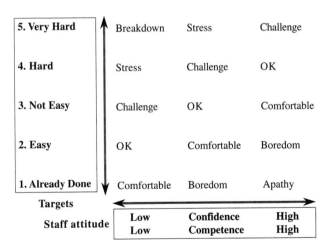

Figure 6.18 Setting the performance standards.

users and lock them into a room with an instruction to come out with a workable system.

"**4.** *Make accountability paramount.* This can be done by the use of those decision sheets that you've already mentioned. People who work within the deviant frame should record their decisions, not to check on them or hold them back, but as a series of records that together tell the story of the project. They can also be used for unblocking thinking: By reviewing the path taken so far we can look for new ideas and different paths. Maybe some of those creative probes in Figure 6.15 can be discovered. Many people seek evidence that supports their case, which is why it can be better to separate the search for ideas from the development of them. We can tell people to go away and bring back a solution, but everyone must be able to justify their actions, if required to. There's just no way past this point.

"**5.** *Work out what constitutes a decision.* Where resources have been assigned, reassigned, or the project has altered since it was last reported, we may feel that a decision has been made. A creative idea must lead to a decision that affects the organization. We still need to get authorization to commit funds or alter a course of action, and there must be some form of referral system for getting initiatives agreed. Ideas belong to someone, as do decisions that are made. Papers and reports recording these matters must be signed, dated, and owned. They don't appear out of thin air.

"**6.** *Leave some room for risk.* The control chart that we've been using sets an upper and lower limit and this is important. The creative probes are based on taking off the shackles of traditional corporate controls. We've refocused our controls to allow some flexibility and movement, but there's still good control. Allowing some risk leaves things a little up in the air. We can't have it both ways. It means we must write off errors, failures, and the various go-back-to-starts. The extent of the financial risk is the budget that the person or team in question has. Other risks relate to staff morale, customer relations, and product reputation. Here, we need fallback people to carry out damage limitation where this happens; that means employee relations, the press office, quality assurance, legal counsel, and the human resource officer, who can swing into action if anything goes badly wrong. We also need early warning devices to pick up real problems. Having said this, problems can provide energy for solutions and these solutions can be part of the way an organization advances. We can use our problems to energize and recognize better futures. Things may appear to be going wrong, but we must have some tolerance to business risk.

"People need support, not when things are going well, but when they are starting to break down. Each failure gives an insight into how to avoid future problems. This experience is positive and should be treated as such. Assigning a project to someone gives them authority to produce the goods, but should also allow room to fail and learn what not to do next time. This is the essence of learning.

"**7.** *Allow a wide assessment framework.* We cannot say that we encourage ideas from staff and project teams and then establish a tight assessment criterion that means nothing gets through. It is disheartening to create a great initiative, only to be told to write a report that, when written, sits on a desk for months. Assessment isn't the same as blockage. If we block ideas that people have spent time bringing out, we will never be creative. The more checks and balances, the more chance that the idea will sit in a filing tray. A broad brush assessment may be made before it's given to a project team to develop, with deadlines for delivery. If people at the top of organizations want to see these projects come to light, it will be on their agendas and they will happen.

"If we employ people who know what they're doing and are committed to the organization, we can trust them. Trusting them means we allow them to go with a decision that feels right. We need only ask them to search for evidence that supports their feeling as well as that which shows they might be wrong. We can trust them with this although there is no harm reviewing the evidence they provide.

"**8.** *Make sure you can keep driving.* How many times have you had a good idea or seen colleagues generate great initiatives only to get bored and discard them. This early infatuation winds down when boredom sinks in. We should ensure we drive through what could be good ideas so that they get to fruition if they really are that good. Brief infatuation leads to so many false starts when the person in question gives up bothering and finds it easier to stick to the main road. Where we require feedback and where top management requests ongoing progress reports, then there's less chance this will happen. We don't want people to simply flirt with ideas—flitting from one to the other. We want them to fall in love with an idea that they want to see happen.

"People are employed for their talents, not just for going through procedures. When they express innovation, these ideas belong to the organization and they must be taken to their conclusion. We don't reward people for coming up with a whizz-bang idea, we reward them for the hard graft in getting sense from these ideas and making sure they can be turned into real projects. Prima donnas prance around the office making useful suggestions that never take off. A good control is to make the person firm up his ideas with a commonsense list of practical considerations, before being passed for development. New ideas mustn't only look good, they must feel good. I've seen many people sit around a table and criticize work but come unstuck when they are asked to present their ideas for sorting things out.

"**9.** *Develop a success orientation.* Opportunities are only useful inasmuch as they add value to the organization and its customers. The focus should be on success and progress, not just new ideas for their own sake. This is where controls come into their own. To demand that there's some direction to the idea, that it doesn't just add to the person's CV (curriculum vitae), but that it means something to the organization as a whole. It must pass this basic test to be of any use. Where we get this success, make sure trumpets are blown and people know about it.

"Ideas can generate results so long as they are used in a structured manner. This means taking the idea and creating a better reference frame armed with this new knowledge. It may operate like Figure 6.19.

"Where the new idea results in a new and better procedure, we have an end product. Where the idea sits in the mind of the initiator, who cannot explain what it is or what it can be used for, then we have a problem. Controls over creativity should insist that we develop a new procedure wherever possible. We need to ask people to explain why a new idea works and how it relates to a better interpretation of reality.

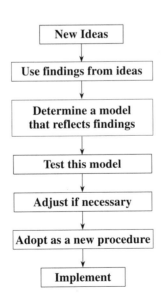

Figure 6.19 Implementing ideas.

"**10.** *Think about compliance as an issue.* We must use compliance very carefully. The compliance process where we come down on staff and lock them into a confined set of activities doesn't really promote creativity. Checkers and inspectors can make life hell for people who want to push ahead and deliver. At times, the compliance drivers represent a viewpoint that simply reinforces an imposed corporate procedure. There's nothing wrong with this procedure if it's done constructively. The problem arises where it refocuses the manager's energies away from customers and product delivery, let alone any form of creative activity. This downside represents a stark warning to all compliance teams.

"Well, Jack, that's my ten-point solution to the problem of controlling creativity. How about that?"

Jack pursed his lip, "Well done, there's a lot in what you've said. These ideas will fit well into my models of control. I guess what you're saying is that managers are responsible for controlling their staffs. A constraining culture means the manager comes down on staff and forces them into set confines. They in turn suffer under this hardship, until they can find another job and leave. However, if people are left alone to do what they like, they are more comfortable. But, managers lose by not being in control, by being overruled by their staff and not being able to get involved with their work. What we want is a definition of controls that means all sides win. Staff have freedom to act and the manager is able to manage this concept. New ideas are encouraged by the manager who acts as a coach, and staff are given the freedom to think. Control isn't a win-lose concept, it's built on a win-win principle. People are able to innovate, the manager's in control, staff are in control, and everything is okay. Controls are not about witch hunts, excessive documentation, multipart approval procedures, or constant referrals to senior management for basic decisions. It's more about empowering people, allowing failures, supporting them, telling them the criteria for new projects, and not being threatened by creative people. We want to get to energy and results directed so that they add value to our corporate mission. It's about seeing an art in business, a light that shines on progress and success. There's an invisible control, like your gravitational model, in allowing staff to share your vision."

Jack topped up Bill and Ruth's drinks and sighed, which signaled an end to the day's discussion. Bill sipped his drink thinking that these conversations were hard work. Stretching the mind wasn't easy and certainly seemed harder after a large glass of rum punch.

Ruth looked at Bill with a curious smile on her lips. "Do you always go on and on like this, Bill?" she asked softly.

"Not at all. In fact I rarely have so much to say. It's just that Jack and I have decided to embark on this verbal journey to help me rewrite the company manual, which is what we've been doing for the whole time I've been here."

Ruth appeared satisfied with this, and the rest of the evening was spent in more talk about life in the Caribbean. Eventually, Jack, who had been drinking rum punch, arranged a taxi to take Bill back to the hotel and drop Ruth off at her parent's house a few miles down the road.

Bill asked, "Would you pick me up tomorrow, Jack?"

"Of course. That will be the last day of your vacation and our discussions. We can cover the final topic then."

"Ah ha," laughed Bill, "the long awaited internalized control facility. Yes, I look forward to it. The final solution . . ."

SEVEN

A Corporate Internalized Control Facility

This chapter is about implementing the solutions discussed in the previous chapters. Practical, workable advice is provided on how organizations can move forward and facilitate improved control and accountability.

"GOOD MORNING, BILL," Jack said, for what would probably be the last time. "How's Ruth?"

"Hello. Ruth's fine. Apparently her parents are buying a restaurant right next to the sea a few miles outside Mo'Bay, just past Rose Hall. Ruth's going to quit her job at the hotel and help her folks run the place. I think it'll work out fine. We went around there last night. The site includes a bar and games room. It's even got a garden area going right up to the sea front where they're going to put tables, chairs, and night lights. Ruth's so excited she can't wait to get started."

"Excellent, Bill. Sounds like a fine business venture. Let's hope it's successful. Anyway, back to you. You're off home when? Tomorrow evening?"

"Yes, the flight's at 7:35 P.M. and I have to check in two hours before then. I'll spend tomorrow morning packing and buying a few gifts. You know, not having a family means there aren't many people back home to buy things for. Don't you miss the states, Jack?"

"I make a return trip every now and again. So I do keep in contact. To be honest I feel that this island's my home for the time being. Well, what shall we do with you today? Have you got any special requests?"

"Not really. We need to get through the final topic which I guess we can do anywhere. I wouldn't mind going for a drive. I might even buy a few of those reggae CDs. Maybe a Bob Marley CD or who's that other guy I like?"

"Dennis Brown. Well, Bob Marley died some time ago, but his records are still on sale. Dennis Brown's also dead. You know that they say the good die young. But don't worry, there's a new guy called Luciano who's taking the music forward. I tell you what, let's make it a day out and drive down to Kingston, the capital of the island. We can visit the Bob Marley museum and check out the record shops at a place called Half Way Tree. It's a long trip but I think we'll have finished our discussions by the end of the day."

This said, they set out on the road to Kingston. As if to gather strength for their last great discussion, they started off in silence. Bill had done most of the talking yesterday and Jack wanted to give him a chance to finish off, if necessary. This wasn't required as Bill sat back and assumed his listening position in the car as he flipped on the tape.

"Well," announced Jack, wondering where to start. "We've rambled on and on about controls. We've developed models and ways of assessing where we are and we've referred to many references and diagrams that adds to our theories. We've covered subjects such as:

- Concepts of control
- The importance of procedures in achieving control
- Using information systems
- Understanding financial management
- Value for money and quality
- Getting to grips with fraud and abuse
- A bit about creativity

"I believe that a good understanding of these things will help staff appreciate, install, and maintain effective systems of internal control. Control, then, is something that each and every employee must get a handle on. If this happens all will be well. If not, we must impose controls on our people and watch them suffer as a result. The battle then ensues. We seek compliance, staff rebel, and we set up our infamous compliance team to enforce controls. The war on controls becomes a war on staff. What a way to run an organization! My approach is to get people committed to control through training and facilitation. It's simple. We set up a small facilitation team and achieve control by internalizing controls, if you get my meaning. We give people faith in themselves and faith in their systems of internal control."

Bill frowned, assumed a stern voice and demanded, "Jack! Let's set some rules for today. No more philosophizing, no more deep and meaningful quotations, and no more detours through the winding roads of theory. Just stick to good old-fashioned suggestions for establishing this so-called control facility. You can stop preaching now—I'm converted. We need systems of control and we need executives who are big enough to say they're happy with them. I now need to know how we can get to this position. Practical, workable things that can be put to use back at work . . ."

"Okay, Bill, hold your horses. I know I go on a bit, but what I say helps me work through the issues and find light at the end of the tunnel. Back to controls. Let me get some sort of structure for today. We need a list of things to cover. We're arguing that we need a corporate internalized control facility and we may as well call this the CICF."

"Fine," Bill replied, "but can't you ever use simple examples. Just for today. Something that I can sell to my people back home."

"An example, eh? Okay, let me see. Yesterday, I had my neighbors' kids in my pool. Remember?"

"That's right," smiled Bill. "I guess you're practicing for when you get your own?"

"Could be," answered Jack with a smile. "Let's say I had a bigger pool and quite a few kids had turned up. I'd need to think through some things. Is there anything I need to do to control this situation? Maybe. I could give them a written list of rules, such as no diving, no jumping in, only use the deep end if you're a good swimmer, use the bathroom before you get in the pool, and so on. I could ask them to read this list and sign that they have, then let them get on with swimming. This is what most companies would do. How do you think they'd respond?

"Well, they may not bother to read the rules and also they may feel that you're trying to spoil their fun by coming down too heavy."

"Exactly. Or, what I could do is get them together when they arrive and ask them what could spoil their enjoyment and what could make their day even more fun. They could come up with ideas relating to safety issues such as in the extreme, drowning. We could ask them to go through each risk and work out whether it's big or not. I could then give them a break and tell them to have some ice cream in the kitchen and think about how to tackle these problems. On their return we could list their ideas and then get them to abide by them. They're sure to come up with stuff like banning dangerous acts like diving and jumping in, depending on how significant the risks are. Also they could come up with suggestions for making the day more fun such as using snorkeling gear, organizing games, and so on. The key is to make the entire exercise of identifying risks and controls inclusive and enjoyable."

"Your point being?" asked Bill.

"This is the essence of control facilitation. Get your people to identify risks to achieving their objectives. In this case having a fun day in the pool. Let them discuss how to manage these risks and come up with suitable procedures. Then get them to use them. We could appoint one child as a monitor to ensure everything is okay and make sure an adult is close by in case of problems. So they're checking their own compliance and they own the procedure, having come up with it in the first place. That's it, Bill, control facilitation from start to finish. Risk awareness, self-assessment of systems of control along with good compliance checks. All done and agreed by the users working as a team."

"You know, Jack. I don't want to be difficult, but this isn't new. A lot of companies are running control workshops. I read about them in my management journal. People get together in groups and go through a checklist of controls that should be there."

"You're absolutely right," Jack pursed his lips and responded, "It is happening but most initiatives use the control beam approach. The workers see it as a one-off exercise; checking their risks and controls, that they do and then forget about. Many of them can't really see the point. It's just another requirement. The forms produced are used by the directors to report on control and everyone's happy. What I'm after is embedded control. You know, our gravitational model where people are doing this as part of their routine work. Let's move ahead to some ideas I've been working on. I believe that in years to come what bothers us now will not be an issue and managers and work teams will be assessing operational risk and control all the time. I've sketched this out in the next four figures—Figures 7.1 to 7.4—where we have a four-stage approach to developments over time.

"In stage one the organization has a clear mission and so develops a strategy to achieve its goals. The success is measured by the performance framework that's set and action is taken based on this information so that we continually refocus our strategy. In Figure 7.1, we ignore risk and take a traditional approach to managing our business. Most organizations, I'd like to think, have moved on from this stage.

"Stage two is where risk is assessed as a separate exercise when we set strategy. Most organizations are here and it fits with our control beam model where it's seen as something removed from our normal processes. It may be done by, say, a risk management team that is given this responsibility. Many organizations are at this stage. They would do a risk assessment once a year as they formulate their annual plan and then more or less forget it.

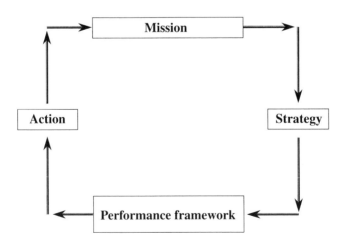

Figure 7.1 Stage one: Traditional.

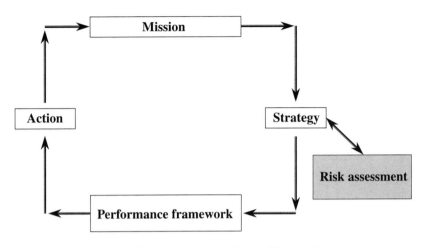

Figure 7.2   Stage two: One-off exercise.

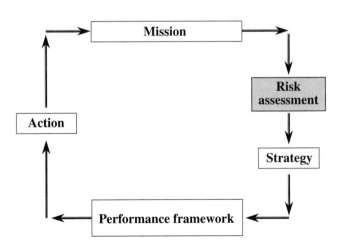

Figure 7.3   Stage three: Integrated.

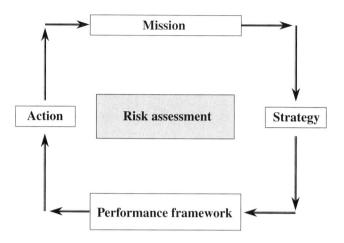

Figure 7.4   Stage four: Embedded.

"We make progress at stage three where we move the risk assessment task into the management cycle and get it integrated to an extent. Some organizations are starting to get there but it's dependent on people seeing it as really important to their work. It's seen as part of the management cycle but still as a separate exercise. The good thing here is that, as the cycle is revisited during the year, risk assessment also happens. The downside is that it's still seen as a distinct exercise.

"One final view is much more progressive than the others. Stage four is when we've actually arrived, where risk assessment is found within the center of the cycle, affecting everything. In fact, the four aspects of management, you know mission, strategy, performance, and action, are the response to risk and how it's managed. That is, the management cycle becomes the risk management process. Over the years the more successful organizations will start to move toward this new direction and internalize the message. This is exactly what I mean by internalizing control."

"This is great, Jack," said Bill, "I like having a goal to aim at. If you can write up all that we've discussed so far—you know, risk and control concepts, procedures, fraud, VFM, and creativity—and give each member of staff a copy of this book, then we'll have arrived. Our people would understand the issues, internalize things, and we'll have achieved control. Simple."

"Not really," Jack said, "It won't work like that. You have to sell it and get top management support. To my way of thinking, you have to go through five stages. Let me list them.

1. Set up the CICF. Get a resource to oversee and help action the entire thing.
2. Undertake corporate level risk assessment. The directors have to get together and decide their priorities and overall risk management strategy. This action starts the whole thing off.
3. Run risk awareness seminars. Seminars should follow to spread the message and get people on board and prepare them for the next steps.
4. Organize control risk self-assessment workshops. This stage is the detailed level work where we get teams to isolate their operational risks, establish controls, and think about compliance as an issue.
5. Link all of these activities into assurance reporting, since we need to get steps 1 to 4 reported as part of our duty to report on our systems on internal control.

"I think, Bill, it'd be a good idea to go through each of these five items today to finish things off. What do you think?"

"Go for it buddy," Bill replied with a smile. Our last great journey."

"Okay," Jack said with an air of accepting this challenge."

SET UP THE CICF

"As with all good initiatives," Jack continued, "there must be a clear sense of direction. A mission statement and a formally authorized charter helps in establishing the team. The precise role will vary depending on the organization and the way the facility is viewed. There's no one way. But to get an idea of what I mean, I'll give you a mission statement I've devised as an example:

> To facilitate the design, maintenance, and reporting on effective systems of internal control and assist all employees in developing good risk assessment and control techniques.

"We could go on to develop more detailed responsibilities that expand on the mission statement. Again this would vary with the type of business but may cover issues such as:

- To promote an awareness of risk and its implications throughout the organization.
- To provide advice and support for all levels of management and employees at whatever grade regarding the assessment of risk and control techniques.
- To liaise with review teams on their work on internal control.
- To liaise with the training manager on the development of competencies in this area.
- To help people responsible for corporate procedures to communicate the standards. This may include the human resource manager, legal counsel, information systems manager, security officer, health and safety manager, equal opportunities manager, chief financial officer, purchasing manager, and others.

- To advise the chief executive on the success of the various CICF programs.
- To furnish reports to the audit committee on the program of work of the CICF.

"In meeting these responsibilities, the CICF needs certain privileges and powers. These may include the rights to:

- Access to all information that supports the various programs.
- Access to all people targeted by the program.
- Maintain the confidentiality of clients using the services of the CICF.
- Independence in designing programs and reporting progress on them.

"The focus is firmly on facilitation. Responsibility for being in control rests with every person who works for, or deals with the organization. The CICF is only there to help them discharge this responsibility, nothing more. Bear in mind that it's more and more difficult to stick to traditional control models where creativity, empowerment, and autonomy are now the norm. The CICF is simply a source of expertise for help in reconciling this equation: autonomy versus control.

"It should make things easier and help the organization feel comfortable that it's in control. It should have a pivotal role, bringing together all those hard working people in the organization who play a role in promoting the right control environment. The CICF doesn't take away any responsibility from key players. So internal audit continues to carry out independent reviews of controls and make recommendations to improve systems where necessary. Audit or review teams may look for compliance and report instances of noncompliance. External audit will review systems as they affect the financial statements and test those figures stated in the accounts. Personnel will ensure staff are trained to do their job either through external or internal programs. The purchasing manager will set standards about spending and how this should be done, while the security manager will likewise set standards for physical security. These activities put together constitute the control environment where people know what they're doing, set standards in this respect, and are able to deliver against these standards. The CICF simply provides a focal point for pulling these activities together and ensuring that there's someone to turn to for help. Figure 7.5 may be used to illustrate the suggested position of the CICF in an organization.

"The CICF formally reports to the chief executive officer (CEO). It also issues reports to an independent audit committee who should oversee the entire thing. The audit committee in turn may care to issue its own reports to the main board. The CICF has links with external audit and internal audit and keeps them apprised of its activities. I actually think CICF should be part of the

Figure 7.5 Corporate control facility—structure.

internal audit set up as an additional service to the planned system reviews and special investigations, because the auditors have the right skills for the task. Another way of viewing the CICF is to argue that it brings together all the forces that affect the control environment. We can repeat our model of personal and organizational control and add the CICF to it in Figure 7.6.

"CICF brings a cohesion to each of these components so that the overall thing makes sense. The resourcing question is difficult. I believe that the CICF should employ the least number of staff to make it successful. This may end up being one or two full-time people with this facilitation role. The essence of facilitation is organizing resources and it doesn't take a whole army of people to do this. I would hate to think that a team of CICF officers would be established to sit around and wait for work to arrive. Resources should be brought in, seconded, borrowed, poached, and generally got hold of as and when required. The final point is that the CICF manager needs a high degree of skill and judgment and the right personality to command respect across the organization. The need for extra

Figure 7.6   Concentric control.
(See also Figures 2.5 and 6.10)

staff will become obvious if it really takes off. One further point: If we're going to develop an open learning facility we would have to think about PCs, CDs, Internet access, videos, publications, and other required support material. The CICF would need a defined budget to get established and defined resources. Since it's costing us money, we need to establish the benefits of adopting a CICF, which include:

- Better risk and control awareness.
- Good procedures and increased working efficiency as a result.
- Better value for money.
- Expertise available to employees.
- Better staff morale through the self-control concept.
- More chance of compliance with procedures.
- Management of fraud and irregularity.
- Defined infrastructure for reporting on internal controls.
- Improved systems of internal control generally.

"We should really go through the standard routines for launching a new CICF, where we have a published mission statement, newsletters, logos, office space, help desk, brochures, and e-mail messages. We need to ensure there's easy access to the services. Presentations to staff on a section by section basis can be one way of getting the message across."

UNDERTAKE CORPORATE-LEVEL RISK ASSESSMENT

Many self-assessment initiatives fail because they are just that, another initiative on top of everything else. Top management take no interest and staff are already overloaded at work. Even if we can get a director to sponsor the thing, it may still fall over, because the director sees it as another bit of work that adds to the stress levels. Some even feel they're being set up, as it's really hard to get new programs working in busy organizations. The only way forward is to make the directors do what they are best at, that is setting and driving a clear direction. This means we start with a board level assessment of corporate risk that's facilitated by the CICF. We need to get the directors together for a morning and get them to:

- Understand the importance of systems of internal control and the role of the CICF
- Appreciate the requirement to report annually on these systems
- Think about what assurances they receive about controls
- Agree on the top corporate objectives (say limited to five)
- Agree to a definition of risk that works for them
- Brainstorm the main risks to achieving these objectives (say limited to two to three for each objective)
- Classify the risks using a basic paradigm (Appendix E)
- Rate the risks in terms of impact on the business and likelihood if not managed properly
- Define the directors' overall strategy for managing these risks
- Work out which corporate processes they most rely on for managing these risks
- Agree on a program for creating better awareness of risk throughout the organization and how operational risk can be assessed and dealt with, bearing in mind their corporate assessment, their overall risk policy, and the need to receive reliable assurances

"The record of this exercise becomes the organization's outline risk register that is the starting place for the annual report on internal control. If we can publicize this exercise, it sets a clear direction for the rest of the CICF program, that is, risk awareness and the operational workshops. It also lays responsibility right at the door of the directors. And we're ready for stage three, the risk awareness seminars."

RUN RISK AWARENESS SEMINARS

"I tell you what," said Bill as he flicked through Jack's reference file, "I've seen risk awareness programs at several companies. It's quite straightforward. You tell your people about risk and why it's so important, and increase their understanding generally."

"I agree," Jack replied. "It's nothing new. But it can go wrong. One thing that can happen is that people attend and are bored to death by someone going on and on about this topic."

Bill glanced at Jack and grinned.

"Okay," Jack shrugged, "I know I go on a bit too. One interesting thing I've developed is a technique for getting people properly involved. It's an assessment tool that allows us to focus our efforts before we do the seminars. Instead of just setting up risk awareness sessions and getting people to attend, we need to take a step back and go through our real aims. Once we've decided on our aims, and remember a lot comes from the board level direction in stage two that we've been through, we can do some more. We can prepare a three-level profile for our staff. Here we work out how risk awareness is seen by management and staff. Do they feel that they simply have to attend the sessions (*have to*), or that it would be useful for work (*should do*) and/or they want to attend because it would be enjoyable as well as useful (*want to*). I'll write this down with aims for the program on the left and the three different perceptions across the top in Figure 7.7.

"Risk seminars go wrong because they don't focus on key aims and they don't ensure that they fit with a bigger picture—that is,

Aims	Have To	Should Do	Want To
1. Understand nature of risk	√	√	√
2. Assess importance of controls	√	√	√
3. Appreciate assurance reports	√	√	√
4. Look forward to workshops	√	√	√

Figure 7.7   Three-level risk awareness profile.

to get people to see how it adds value to their jobs and that it can also be fun. They also don't fit into the next stage—to get people excited about the facilitated workshops that'll follow. If the risk seminars are boring and stuffy, then your people will think of loads of reasons why they can't attend. But we can sell these ideas because they have to do it, it will impact their work, and it will be fun. If we can judge where our staff stand, we can work out how much we need to do to make it a success. So, if we hit all three drivers over the four stated aims, then it has much more chance of being successful."

"I guess in the end, people will do what they are told to do!" Bill said, "Attendance at the seminars should be mandatory."

"You could do this," Jack said, looking upward as if seeking inspiration from above. "But remember our work on internals and externals? If people want to do something because it's both useful and fun, you give them control. You respect their self-worth and boost their confidence a lot. You don't want your staff to be dependent and only do things because they have to or to win your approval. Move away from this submissive view and let them decide what's good or not. Ignoring this point means we risk failure or just lukewarm support, which equals the same thing."

"But what will you cover in these seminars?" Bill asked, while checking the tape.

"I don't think we can really design the seminars as this will vary per organization. But I guess we could note a list of points like:

- Do some background work. Arrange seminars along divisional or section lines and find out about their work roles. Send out a precourse questionnaire to find out where people fit into the twelve box assessment tool we've used—the must do, should do, and want to analysis over the four aims. We want to end up with ticks in each of the twelve boxes as an overall aim of the seminars.

- Make clear the seminar objectives. The four aims can be used as a starting place. We'll want to assess whether we've met them at the end of the event.

- Ask the course members their views and concerns about the seminars. Record these and deal with any important apprehensions.

- Link it into the directors' initial assessments. Get a top director to introduce the thing, define risk and the risk policy, and set the tone at the outset.

- Start with an exercise based on risk. This could be anything from everyday life that they can relate to. What's the risk of say inviting friends to dinner? What could go wrong and how can we ensure success. They can have fun isolating risks, how they may be managed, and the importance of controls. The fact that perfection is impossible will also come out.

- Get through the theory quickly. Present theory in a user-friendly way and refer them to handouts if they want to explore things further. Remember that people get bored very quickly when you just tell them things. One tip is to relate the material to whatever example was used at the start.

- Make sure you make clear where the organization stands and where the five stages of control facilitation come in. And allow time for questions throughout the morning.
- Get them working in groups on a work-related exercise so they can see how operational risks may be assessed, measured, and tackled. Make sure they understand their role and how they fit into the way assurances on control and compliance are fed back to the directors for reporting purposes.
- Close on a high and get some team spirit going. Check whether their expectations have been met and how they feel about things. Link it into next steps and make sure they understand how the facilitated workshops will be run and what we want from them.
- Thank them and don't run over the allotted time.

"That's it. Stage three done. We've hit the four key aims and got them sold on the idea that this program will be fun and we're ready for stage four, where we get stuck in their detailed systems and controls."

ORGANIZE CONTROL RISK
SELF-ASSESSMENT WORKSHOPS

"We arrive now at the most important subject of workshops. My view is that a great deal of development that's done has little value to an organization. Much of it consists of attendance at a half-day event, working through a few set exercises. But it's very hard to get added value into the way the person contributes to the organization. So much of what is covered during the workshop is lost soon after it's ended. Some people declare they've had instant revelations and promise to seek new and improved approaches to work, only to forget everything shortly thereafter. Some disagree, but I feel that development should relate to procedures that are used at work, that is, how best to work, an understanding of methods and approaches, and a commitment to improving the adopted standards. It should be related directly to what's being done at the office, production line, or with the customer. This is why we need to ensure a systematic approach to the workshops that makes sense and is worthwhile."

"Okay," Bill mumbled, "Enough preaching. Let's get back to reality. How would you set up these workshops so that they make sense?"

"I'll go back to the five-stage approach. We've got the team going. You know the CICF team. The directors have set a visible direction on risk assessment and control. Senior and middle management and staff now understand what risk is about and why it needs to be managed and reported on. Flowing from this is the detailed analysis of risk by work teams involved in the function or process. On one level you're telling them what the business executives see as their priorities and on another level you want them to tell you what they feel is important. So we have top down and bottom up communication. That will meet somewhere in the middle, which is where CICF is located. The workshops will aim to do several things, such as:

- Get work teams to agree on their objectives.
- Get them to identify and rate risks to the achievement of these objectives.
- Get them to assess whether the corresponding controls are adequate.
- Formulate action plans to address problem areas.
- Provide an insight into the control environment in place.
- Report upward on the foregoing aims.

"These six components will do the job. But the way it's done will depend on the organization. The main feature is the way it's facilitated, which is where the CICF team comes in. Two facilitators should ensure that the team understands what's needed and that they're able to bring out the best from each team member. In the first workshop they need to agree to their objectives, brainstorm risks, and then score them as high, medium, or low. The next short workshop, say the following week, should deal with these risks by accepting them, relying on existing controls, or improving the control activities, including any contingency arrangements. The gap in between allows team members to talk through the issues and take a break from the intensive analysis. The main point is that the ideas, inspiration, agreements, and action plans should come from the team members. All set within the organization's corporate direction. Couldn't be simpler."

"You sure?" Bill asked.

"Sort of . . . well, not really. You know a lot could still go wrong. If people can't see the net benefit, they will not be inspired by it. If the facilitators are poor, then it will fail. If they're good facilitators but have little expertise in control models, then again, we'll lose it. If the directors see it as a bit of a game to keep the regulators and stakeholders happy, then there's little point continuing. If the organization has a compliance and blame culture, then there'll be no trust in the process. If soft skills such as the way people relate to each other are not seen as part of internal control, then we will have missed a major aspect of managing risk. If the workshops' outputs are used to set the auditors in motion to check up on areas where the teams have expressed concerns, then we come back to the same conclusion. As you see, a lot could go wrong, which is why it may be a good idea to get the internal auditors into the CICF. They have the skills and know how and they can ensure the audit process fits into the new empowered approach to control. All they need is facilitation skills and a clear focus on organization aims for this form of self-assessment. I can't really go any further. Each organization needs to find its own solution. There're no short cuts to this."

"Okay," said Bill, "this can be done. Facilitation is just about getting people to work through the set exercises. Pretty straightforward."

"No, Bill, it's more than that. Much more. It can make the difference between success and failure. Facilitation isn't just listening and encouraging, although it is a start. I'll give you my views on running these workshops:

- Set a goal for the entire program and be able to explain it convincingly so that it makes sense and is worthwhile. Appreciate how the corporate assessment of risk impacts on the team, or process, being dealt with. Explain common terminology and concepts. Start this process with some material that is sent out beforehand, getting them to think about the workshop and assessing risk. You could encourage them to start talking about it a week or so before they all turn up.

- Understand where the team fits into the organization and get members' individual expectations and concerns written up. Reconcile it with the overall program and corporate risk assessment, and clear up any inconsistency and worries.

- Get the team to commit their energies to the workshop and contribute fully. This item is really about giving them responsibility for working through the half-day but also recognizing that they may agree and set rules of conduct to help progress the event and retain the self-worth of each and every individual team member. Don't undermine the managers that also attend. In fact, it's best to discuss the event beforehand with the managers.

- Structure the event and give them a clear sense of direction. Make it challenging but fun. Keep people focused on the aims and ask them to keep within its scope so that it doesn't overrun. Be sure team members identify what's within their responsibility and what falls elsewhere.

- Capture objectives, ideas, issues, and comments from the team members. Get these in a sensible order and get the group to agree on relative importance and classifications. Or, get a vote that reflects where group members stand. Start and finish with the team's objectives and how we can help ensure these are achieved.

- Ensure that the group progresses toward clear outcomes that they feel represent their views and points made. Fit these into the big picture and make sure it's fed into decision points that impact on the way risk is addressed, that is, identified and managed.

- Ensure that the workshop is integrated into the assurance reporting process and provides a reliable account of self-assessed controls in the process, section, or project in question.

- Deal with any outstanding issues that must be referred elsewhere for consideration and action. And ensure the team is aware of what's being taken outside of the workshop.

- Keep the group informed of developments after the workshop.

- Try to maintain a positive atmosphere with a focus on value-added input. Make sure the team is able to tell others that they'll get a lot from these workshops and it's an all around pleasing experience.

"Quite a bit to think about . . ." added Jack as he finished devising yet another list.

"What," asked Bill, "about the big mouth who just can't stop talking? You know, it happens every time you get people together. Someone wants to take over."

"Okay," Jack replied, "Where you've got someone like that, give them lots to do. Don't ignore them or try to embarrass them, or the group may become resentful. If they want to get involved, then use this energy to get the group going. But allow others to come in as well. Don't see them as a threat. Some people get bored unless they're contributing a lot. As a facilitator, rise above personalities and get everyone involved. Tell you what, I'll put some of these tips in Appendix C."

"Fair enough," Bill said with a frown. "But can we get some kind of structure to work to?"

"It's about facilitation. The group can set their own structure for their workshop if they like," Jack replied.

"I don't disagree. What I mean is something the group can rally around. Some common ground. You, yourself, said that facilitation is not just listening."

"If you insist," Jack said with a sigh, "we can develop a model for use in these workshops. You remember our mango model (Figure 2.15)? The one where we bought mangoes for Ruth. This is a good enough way of moving the group along and it'll fit into the assurance bit that we need to cover next. Just by adjusting it a little, it can become a new model that we'll call Figure 7.8. Figure 7.8 can be used to focus the event. So we can spend the first part working out the overall aim and key goals for the team (part A). Let them tell you what they are, limiting the goals to four or five. The team can then brainstorm all risks to the achievement of these goals (part B). This done, they can assess how big these risks are and how likely they are to occur (parts C and D). This gives a score and if we choose the top five risks for each goal, then we can take a well-earned break. The next stage is to come to grips with the way we manage these risks (part F) and whether there're any gaps that need to be dealt with in our action plans (part G). And the action plans are incorporated into our overall strategy. If we give this

Overall Section Aim...

Team's Key Goals	Risks	Impact H M L (3) (2) (1)	Likely with no controls (0-1)	Score	Risks Managed	Action Plan
A	B	C	D	E	F	G
1						
2						
3						
4						

Figure 7.8   Risk register.

form out at the start, then we can keep referring to where we are on it. As the event progresses, each person writes down their scores, which we aggregate at each of the stages A to G and capture at the front, on a large wipe board. They can vote on the assessment bit (C and D) and vote on things they don't all agree on. In the end, they'll have done a self-assessment, like a sort of self-audit and we have a document that can be used as evidence of this process. Some call these documents Risk Registers. How about that for structure, if that's what you were looking for?"

"No complaints there, buddy. It's just that you have to be careful that you don't turn everyone into an auditor, that's all," replied Bill.

"Funny you should say that, Bill. The way to make people comfortable is to avoid talking about risk and control. Instead talk about significant issues and how they are managed, which is really the same thing. Risk and control are audit words. Concerns or issues and how we take care of problems and exploit opportunities are words that people can relate to more. They're not foreign. So if you like, we can ban terms like objectives, risk, control, and assessment and talk in a down-to-earth way about simply taking care of business."

LINK INTO ASSURANCE REPORTING

"The board of directors must report on their systems of internal control," continued Jack. "Users of the annual report and accounts can take comfort in these words from the organization—words that mean the report can be relied on and their interests are being protected. This is so important. It means society can trust their corporate bodies. But directors who make these reports, not because they feel pressured to do so by a vaguely worded external guideline but because they feel it right and proper to do so, should be admired. Their report should really make clear:

- What the organization understands by its system of internal control
- The directors' policy on risk management and innovation
- How risk awareness is provided to staff throughout the organization
- How operational work teams self-assess risk and corresponding controls
- How we've painted our organization red, amber, and green (Figure 7.9)
- What initiatives are in place to ensure controls are monitored and complied with
- What action plans we have to tackle high-risk areas
- How internal and external audit contribute to our ability to deal with risk
- How control as an issue is dealt with as an integral part of working for the organization

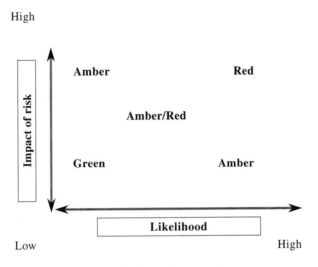

High

Figure 7.9   Risk profile.

- Where people can turn for help in improving their controls

"The bottom line is to report how these initiatives come together to form a comprehensive system of internalized control. And not only that, the Risk Registers can be used to demonstrate this. They can even be audited. Remember, the CICF simply furnishes reports on their activities to the CEO, audit committee, and main board of directors. Internal audit continues to independently review systems, functions, and controls. The CICF is simply an extension that complements this all-around effort to get risks understood and the corresponding controls right."

"Spot on, buddy," Bill suggested, "But outside of the philosophy, what will this really mean?"

"Good God, Bill! You just need a final solution, don't you? Can't you just go with the flow and accept the concept? Man, you're squeezing every last drop from this thing."

"I'll take that as a compliment. Anyway, what can you give me on this?"

Jack had to laugh. Bill was simply impossible, although he did detect a new lightness from his friend. "Okay. A final solution, eh? Let's get a drink and put this to bed for good."

"Hold up, Jack. Let me get a drink of iced jelly." Jack watched as Bill jumped out of the car and walked over to a wooden cart with boys selling iced jellies. He tipped the fruit to his lips and drank heavily. He looked so at home, joking with the people at the stall, telling them he had spent so much on jelly coconuts and that he would be better off planting a coconut tree and harvesting them. Back in the car, Jack resumed the discussion.

"Let's take a step back and think about what we're trying to do. The directors need to profile the organization and get a handle on what's okay, what's not, and what needs doing. Simple so far. People like external audit, regulators, inspectors, and internal audit can tell us about systems of internal control, but only in terms of work they have done that impacts on specific systems and specific controls. For a large organization this isn't enough. We need to get the people who are actually doing the work to assess things, that is, answer the three questions what's good, what's not, and what action is needed. A little bit like Danny-Dread's approach. If it were possible we'd get a giant paintbrush and paint the organization in red for high risks areas, green for low risk areas, and amber for the rest. Then we'd redo this painting every time something happens to change the profile. Let's look at Figure 7.9 that illustrates how risks may be assessed and categorized.

"So we paint the organization in this way. Green means things are okay and there's no real unmitigated risk. Amber means we may accept the level of risk we're exposed to but need to keep an eye on things. Red means we need to take action right away to sort things out. Our risk strategy is then set by this information. Remember our five-stage plan starting with setting up the CICF. We can start from the directors' assessment of risk and plot the areas in our profile. We then need to get information from the self-assessment workshops. We'll get this on processes that run across the organization, like a budgeting system, and the teams that deal with functions or projects that will be separately assessed. If we can score each operation and system, then get a range where the top quarter is red, the middle two amber, and lower quarter green, then we have a starting place. This allows us to plot what parts of the organization fall into the red, amber, and green zones. Action plans for the red zone's issues should then be developed while we need to keep monitoring the amber zones."

"I like it," said Bill raising his eyebrows, "but, is this really integrated into our systems?"

"It can be. We can get our action plans to fit into our strategies. In this way it forms part of our decision-making process. Action that needs to be taken, by whom, when, and where. That's it, Jack, the final solution."

The ensuing silence gave a pleasant relief from the hectic talk that had been the norm. Jack glanced across at Bill who had closed his eyes for a brief moment. Good, thought Jack. He's off to sleep. That must mean the end to all of this. A weariness suddenly swept over Jack. This week had been so exhausting. So much talk, so much concentration, and so much hard work. Bill scratched his head and after a few thoughtful minutes found his voice.

"I'm not trying to be funny, Jack," he said. "but you've only taken us to level three of your development scale. That is integrated risk assessment as part of the management cycle. But not to level four where it's embedded as part of our day-to-day life. These workshops are separate events. They're extra and fall outside of our normal work. That's just like your satellite model of control. How do we get to level four where it's set within our processes?"

"Kiss mi granny goat!" exclaimed Jack, "The more you get, the more you want. I'm gonna buy you a drink. I know I need one."

TAKING IT TO LEVEL FOUR

They pulled up outside a bar in St. Ann's Bay and Jack dragged himself out of the car with Bill following. Sitting on a tall chair around a large highly polished bar, Jack, sipping a soda, looked a little despondent as Bill sat next to him studying his bottle of Red Stripe beer.

"Here," Jack finally said, sliding a small bag across to Bill, "I've made up a few reggae tapes for you to take home. It's got some Wailing Souls songs on it including your favorite song, 'Firehouse Rock.'"

"Great," Bill said. "Much appreciated. I like this stuff, it gets to me. You know, it's a bit like country and western music, full of life stories."

"Reggae music is like a pulse that beats across the island," Jack said. "It's made by the people for the people and it kind of keeps things together with inspirational messages and loads of humor. I'm hooked on it. Listen to this Garnet Silk tune on the bar radio. It's got such a melody and punch. Nothing beats it. Some say the bass line's like a heartbeat that just keeps going. And when it's hooked up on a big sound system, it's out of this world."

"Look," Bill said, "about our discussions. You really don't have to go any further if you don't want to. I know it's a little tiring for you. All this thinking and talking."

"Not at all. I have the answer to your question. At least, what I think is the answer. For what it's worth, I'll give it to you as soon as we get back on the road. We don't have too far to go now by the way."

Back on the road Bill switched on the tape and Jack returned to his task.

"If," he said, "you were to take an experienced internal auditor and put him or her in a new job in the organization, what would you expect from this person?"

"I'd want them to work hard and perform."

"Yes. But, would you expect a good appreciation of risks and how controls can be designed and installed to help mitigate them?"

"I see what you mean. Then the answer is yes."

"Okay. Good. Now let's return to the typical employee. This person doesn't have a specialist appreciation of risk and control okay? So employees need to attend awareness sessions and be told how to assess their work areas. What if we use the gravitational model of control and suggest that it's not a specialist area? If so, it would mean building this understanding into your staff's competencies. Have a look at my Figure 7.10, which I'll take you through.

"We can use this approach to develop a range of competencies covering things like risk awareness, self-assessment, control techniques, fraud, retaining creativity, information systems, and financial management. In fact all those things that we have discussed over the last few days—that is the overall control environment.

"It's systematic, which means it's in line with the requirements of the organization and perceived gaps in staff competencies.

Figure 7.10 Training model.

Learning goals are defined and the ensuing training program and exercises are designed to deliver these learning goals. Meanwhile, we seek an input from employees about their present skills and what they would like to see in the program. Hence the line linking competencies Present In Staff and the Learning Goals. We complete the training and assess the value from feedback received from staff, managers, and others. The results help us refocus the courses in future.

"If each of the foregoing steps aren't taken, training will have less impact and may fail altogether. If, however, we can ensure that the CICF helps set this systematic approach to development, then we're halfway there. The worst position is to rope in a team of trainers who deliver a standard one-off course on control and risk, never to be seen again.

"The main role of the CICF is to have an input into each stage of the systematic approach to training and ensure managers and their staff are able to build relevant competencies, analyze training needs, and commission the relevant development workshops. It is debatable whether the head of CICF should carry out this training, although there's nothing in principle that stops it from happening.

"An open-learning approach is also useful. Here we don't set up formal training programs but we establish facilities available to all staff. These consist of interactive CDs, videos, distance learning material, team or individual exercises, Internet access, case studies, and handbooks that can be referred to as and when required. People can then drop in at their convenience and use the facilities. There're many people who like to work alone or at their own pace.

"We may as well admit that the empowerment concept is here to stay and relies on the manager assuming a different role, where he or she encourages performance by one-to-one input into the employee's own development. We still concentrate on knowledge, skills, and attitudes but know that these can only be changed by the person concerned. It's more than training, counseling, or simply setting targets and monitoring. Can we maintain control by getting people to recognize the areas they need to develop and deal with this? Again, this model isn't the old command and control framework based on past performance but a futuristic model where we get employees to reach for their own competencies.

"We arrive now at the various courses that would fall under the training function of the CICF. There are many different set programs that can be on offer. Remember, however, the best type of training is that which has been tailor-made from the training needs analysis process. What we can do is set up our training events based around the topics that we've covered since we started this, er . . . this seemingly unending discussion. So we'd set up sessions on:

- The nature of risk and risk management
- Control techniques
- The managerial control system
- Fraud and its implications
- Getting to grips with corporate procedures
- Building your own operational procedures
- Maintaining creativity within a controlled environment
- Security and other corporate standards
- Protecting your automated data
- How to carry out a complete review of controls
- Establishing your own compliance routines
- Making yourself the key to control
- Managing the ethical environment
- Value for money and quality
- Financial systems and controls
- Ensuring accountability
- Using information for control

"It'll take forever to go through each of these programs in detail. In one sense this defeats the objective as each one should be designed to reflect the business needs and the staff who're employed by the organization. I'm a great believer in interactive exercises that people can work on as a way of making the event more enjoyable and deliver the learning goals with greater impact. I guess I can say a little about each of these courses and include them in Appendix D.

"We can build on the courses in the list and develop learning goals for each individual session. The approach to delivering the sessions will be a mix of:

- Input—imparting knowledge using visual aids and explanation
- Discussion and brainstorming—using the flip chart
- Syndicate group exercises—with feedback and evaluation
- Tasks—to reinforce the learning
- Videos and so on

"The courses can be further developed into stage 1, 2, and 3, where stage 1 level of difficulty may involve a half-day course, while stage 3 may run into several days. All possibilities can be explored. We can also provide videos and open learning material (i.e., notes) to support each course and these can be referred to by course members as a record of what happened during the course and as a revision tool. The videos and CDs may have to be left in the CICF and viewed through a booking system. Further exercises may be provided to consolidate and expand the work covered.

"If we use this more advanced approach, then I guess the head of CICF should be a competent trainer. There're people who can deliver training well in contrast to those who are better suited to just doing presentations. But we must also remember to locate training within the everyday realities of working life or it'll be too artificial. As such, it's best to bring in the right people to do the right parts of the training programs. We need a course chair to be present throughout the event and, as we've said, this may be the head of CICF or one of the CICF staff. But specific sessions will be done by specialists. For example, sessions on purchasing, information systems (IS), and human resources would be done by the purchasing manager, IS manager, and personnel manager, respectively. Sessions explaining the role of internal audit would be presented by the chief internal auditor, or representative, and so on—you get my meaning. This training reinforces the CICF's role as one of facilitation, not being experts in everything that goes on in the organization.

"As I said, control training is nothing new, and many organizations have adopted self-audit or control risk self-assessment programs to get internal control on the business agenda. Companies are training their managers and issuing checklists that can be used to assess whether basic controls are in place. There's an entire risk industry that promotes the use of proactive risk management across organizations. All I'm doing here is trying to get people to view controls as an integral part of their work and not a foreign language that they dip into from time to time. It's not just about senior managers having to attend a half-day seminar on control risk and then work through a series of low level self-assessment checklists. I want all staff to have a basic knowledge of control concepts, skills in applying internal controls, and attitudes that support a controlled environment, and know how to get help in acquiring these new competencies."

A CORPORATE RAINBOW

"We're pretty close to Kingston now. I wasn't going to go this far but if you like, I'll give you my bottom line on the whole thing. I warn you it's philosophical and fluffy."

"I guess," Bill replied laughing, "we may as well go over it, Jack. A fluffy bit to finish. Why not?"

"Okay," Jack said, "let's do it. Let me tell you about the organization's rainbow. Hold on. I'll explain. Three things make up the corporate risk profile that'll come from our control facilitation work. Let's leave out the general risk awareness stuff and concentrate on the directors' assessment of risk, workshops on the corporate processes, and the operational work teams' risk assessment. If we can bring these together we have three parts of a What's Hot/What's Not Rainbow in Figure 7.11.

"So our bottom line is to get all three parts of the organization to understand each other and agree on what's important, what activities and projects go into the red, amber, and green bits. Reconciling this means the organization is united in the way it sees and tackles risk, which is no mean feat. This is the real value add from the work of the CICF. Getting people working from one common perception. Essential, but so very, very difficult. You know, getting to this point creates a lot of tension as we try to get the views to make sense as a whole. But once we've got there, it means so much.

Figure 7.11   What's hot/What's not rainbow.

People on the shopfloor know what drives the board, the board meanwhile understand the stresses that their staff have to manage and how well corporate processes fit into this rainbow of views, drivers, and energy. Bill, this is an ideal for any organization to get to. And all through control facilitation."

A WARNING

"There's one final word of warning. Many people resist change. Others perceive control as an intrusion and resist any moves in this direction. We must break down these barriers and seek driving forces to create a culture where managers and their staff take responsibility and see no problem seeking guidance in establishing systems to help them meet these new responsibilities. But we must be careful about giving too much detailed advice as we may create victims of managers who cannot function without double-checking with CICF.

"There are forces that oppose control, including lack of support from top management, incompetent staff, fear of failure, excessive work pressures, boredom, poor communications, staff mistrust of their managers, lack of staff motivation, and fear of reprimand for noncompliance with procedure. Where these forces are strong, the CICF needs to work with the chief executive officer on initiatives to create an environment where it can work. If not, there will be excessive negative conflict and the CICF will eventually turn into nothing more than a hit squad; checking, criticizing and reporting on employees as part of the internal disciplinary machinery. The other problem is where the CICF is used by managers to avoid blame if things go wrong. Again the CICF will not really work in organizations that have an ingrained blame culture. Take this as a warning that the idea won't work in some companies and in some circumstances. It's just a fact of life, that's all.

"Well, there you have it, Bill. My preferred solution."

"Excellent!" Bill suggested, "But what about my Out of Bounds Probes?"

"Your what?" asked Jack looking surprised.

"You know. Figure 6.15 on controlled creativity. We discussed it yesterday."

"No problem. We could include that then."

"I tell you what," Bill replied not looking happy at Jack's answer. "You've been talking about my challenge. Managers like me getting into the control thing and having a go. Well, let me give you auditors and consultants a challenge. You've moved from reviewing controls to reviewing risks and controls and then facilitating this idea across the organization. Lately, you've asked that this be set within an overall risk management strategy. So you work to two dimensions: risk and control. How about adding a third dimension? I'll sketch it out for you, Jack, in Figure 7.12.

"So you need to deal with all three in your audits and your workshops. Isolate risks, work on controls, and then ensure people have and use their creative probes. Get people to make progress by thinking out of bounds and taking some risk. Build this into the

Figure 7.12   Three dimensions of audit.

audit process. You know, expand your assessment criteria to include these things. Include in your terms of reference for your audits something like, What is the system for promoting creative progress by staff? And in your risk assessment workshops ask yourself whether creative problem-solving techniques can be used to deal with barriers to managing risk. You can even go into things like negotiation skills. Here you ask, In what areas should the team be encouraged to make creative (risk-managed) progress? The scope is limited only by your imagination. Quite a challenge for your profession, eh?"

"It is." Jack looked thoughtful, "Maybe it's something we can think about for the future."

The day spent in Kingston, a lively place where people spent their time keeping busy with vibrant energy, was quite enjoyable. It was such a contrast to the laid-back tourist resorts on the tranquil north coast. The visit to the Bob Marley museum and record shop proved successful and Bill returned to the car with a bag full of CDs.

The journey back was much quieter as Bill relayed his concerns about getting support for this new approach in his company, which had proved very difficult in the past. As the miles swept past and they got closer to Mo'Bay, Jack sensed that a final word was required. Responding to this Jack said, "Control starts with self-control, that is, ensuring there's enough stress to represent a challenge, but not too much stress that cannot be handled. People who feel they're in control can deal with stressful situations. People who feel that they have little or no control over their environment may well suffer from stress. They enter a cycle of problem-worry-problem-worry and so on.

"Meanwhile, coaching sets aside the traditional management styles and replaces it with help and self-development. We challenge norms, look to the future, and encourage mistakes as part of the learning process so that our controls incorporate these concepts but provide for some accountability.

"We've said that the essence of control is still self-control and the learning process. I guess it's all part of the emotional intelligence that we now hear so much about. Why do so many people feel they would never want to work for anyone or that they hate their job? They're victims and feel lost to the forces that affect them and their environment. But to take control and have a possible dream to work to sets a frame for self-control. Not the kind of formal control that represses and restrains by instilling fear, but the kind of force that envisions this dream and sets free the spirit to take steps to ensure it happens. The fun and excitement of arriving at the dream should be all-consuming, based around the organization's values.

"Control does work within this reference frame, although it must have a charm and ease that attaches to the way people work. Boundaries and barriers are acknowledged, but the main focus is on releasing one's energies to roam free and seek this vision. We tend to do what we have to do to survive at work and then wish we could do other things as a form of escapism. What if we could incorporate these wishes into our everyday work? Wouldn't this provide the energy that distinguishes a vibrant person from an employee moving through a procedure in a zombielike fashion. Energy is about fun, discovery, fulfillment, and challenge. As we make mistakes we learn about ourselves—formal appraisal systems are located in past performance against a set standard. Appraisal should be about self-discovery and a desire to develop. The manager as a coach assisting in this journey is important, not as a mistake spotter, but as a guide and source of inspiration. If we know where to go, how to get there, and what problems to look out for and tackle, then all it takes is a reason to travel this route (i.e., motivation). Energy directs the extent to which we throw ourselves into the task and this energy must come from within. It comes from an earnest desire to express ourselves. Its power is deep as it's the difference between a person who has lost the will to live and someone who sparkles with life and vitality. It's not based on physical fitness but a love of life and a clear focus on realistic outcomes. We take control as systems that support and help direct us, which moves us far away from the traditional view of this concept. It places us closer to a philosophical model where we need to reexamine our motives and visions. Can we ask organizations to operate on this level? And can we teach ourselves to view controls in this way? The control chart appears a somewhat mechanical interpretation of reality based on adopted standards, measuring devices, information systems, and past performance as the guide to current decisions. How do we measure spiritual well-being and internalized energies? These conceptual forces are so important that we must try, and this effort requires a different mind-set than traditional approaches. Control is then an uplifting process that locates one to higher planes and not a pressure lid that contains any form of originality or freedom of expression. This is the challenge, and this is the problem with no final solution, just a journey of discovery that takes one closer to understanding how to tackle the problem, rather than fixing things. A major preoccupation of our society is the quick fix. Society feels that all issues must be controlled. That is why people view the real world as closer to pure chaos than a series of simple solutions. Anyway, Bill, that's me done. Let me know how you get on back home."

"So," Bill said choosing his words carefully, "you say it's all about realizing your dreams? What's your dream, Jack?"

"You know, I think I'm there. The tapes we've made will help me write my book and this right now is my dream. And you've given me so much help here. I'll never be able to thank you enough. If I get our conversations typed up, you know, from the tapes, then all I need to do is tidy it up and we're more or less there. I could make up some presentations packs of slides to go with it."

"Jack," Bill held up a hand in protest, "you can't be serious. You can't write a business book consisting of a series of conversations.

It's never been done before and people would think it's silly. Forget it, buddy."

"Not true. Books are about communicating with the reader. If I can get my message across, then I'll do it. I want to do something new. Not just a standard boring text."

"You won't get it published," replied Bill.

"Yes, I will!"

"No, you won't!"

"Yes, I . . ." Jack stopped, laughed, and continued, "You really need to get yourself a wife. Then you'd have someone to argue with. Okay, Bill, you tell me. What's your dream then?"

"I think this week has made a lot of things clear to me. You may joke but I really need to settle down, without making the mistake I made with my first wife, trying to control what can't be controlled. I know that now. Life's short, Jack, and I'm not going to risk letting good people pass me by. Not any more . . . I'm going to take charge of my life."

They arrived at Bill's hotel. Jack promised to keep in touch and thought that he really would miss their talks and debates. Over a last drink at the hotel, Bill likewise said that he had enjoyed their long journeys together. Ruth joined them shortly after and Jack wondered whether there would be a sad farewell between them this evening. As it became dark and the shadows of the nearby trees lengthened, Jack drove out of the hotel for the final time and headed up toward his home in the hills of Mo'Bay Town.

EIGHT

The Letter

This chapter completes the journey so that all loose ends are properly tied up.

J ACK TURNED TO the clerk at the post office counter and said, "You sure this is for me?" looking at a letter she had just handed over to him. A sharp nod confirmed that it was his, although he did not recognize the handwriting. Jack stepped back into the shade to avoid the midday sun, which burned down on the center of Mo'Bay town. He opened the letter and immediately saw that it was from Bill in New York. The sanctuary of a nearby bar provided the relief from the sun Jack was looking for, and over a cold Red Stripe, Jack read through Bill's letter:

Dear Jack,

I hope all is well.

Could not get through on e-mail hence this letter.

I must say I enjoyed our long talks on a subject that seems to involve so much. The more you find out about controls, the more there is to learn. As you have said, there is no real solution—it's simply a never-ending journey much like the one from Mo'Bay to Kingston.

Anyway, I've seen a leaflet about your soon-to-be-published book and it's great to think you've finally finished it. Congratulations, you finally realized your dreams, my friend.

Let me give you my own good news.

I returned to my company amid a great deal of commotion. Apparently, during my vacation, the chief executive had brought in a new compliance officer who was going to check that people were using the new standards manual once it was finalized and implemented.

I made a formal presentation to the board using the slides pack you kindly sent me and made a case for this corporate internalized control facility. I even prepared a paper with diagrams and so on. My presentation went down really well and the board were more or less sold on the idea straight away. The fact they had to sign a statement on control this year helped a lot.

Anyway, they went for it and it turns out that the new compliance officer, Sue, is a qualified trainer and is pretty suited to the facilitation role. The CICF will be part of an expanded internal audit and we've already got dates for the board-level assessment. Can you send your presentation pack to me if possible?

I'm now in charge of CICF, which we call Internal Audit and Risk Facilitation (IARF) consisting of Sue and two internal auditors and we are getting on just fine.

Ruth and I have been on the phone most days. And, just to let you know, I'll be arriving in Mo'Bay shortly for a return visit. In fact, I've arranged to see Ruth and I'm going to pop a certain question. I think I'm ready for this now. How do you feel about being my Best Man?

I'm not sure that we need to embark on any more journeys through the world of controls, I think we have been there and done it. Maybe we can find another subject for discussion—what do you think about conducting special investigations as an interesting topic?

Best regards,
Bill Reynolds

And see you in a few months.

Well, thought Jack with a smile, this journey does have an ending after all.

APPENDIX A

The Managerial Control System

The managerial control system represents the fundamental processes that must be in place to control any operation. The systems school of thought uses General Systems Thinking to help define these processes and the way they link together to form a complete system. When reviewing what may be viewed as a business unit (i.e., a defined set of resources under a manager working to achieve a defined objective) then we may consider the adequacy and effectiveness of the macro-based managerial control system. This is done by considering whether the various attributes (as set out in the following) are present. Potential weaknesses may be identified where any of these attributes are lacking.

The areas that form the managerial control system (MCS) are:

- Objectives—a clear statement of goals
- Strategic analysis—an efficient way of achieving the goals
- Structuring—the way resources are deployed
- Human resource management—a process of acquiring the required resources
- Quality standards—the standards applied to the operation in terms of quality and quantity
- Procedures—the way work is undertaken

- Operational activities—the activities themselves
- Marketing—the way that clients' needs are defined and met
- Management information—the information required to manage the activities

OBJECTIVES—CONTROL ATTRIBUTES

Main Issues

All operational activities must work to a clear objective. The role and responsibilities of a department, and therefore the relevant manager, must be agreed at the outset and should be understood throughout the organization. Any problems with role definition affect the entire operation and can have a major adverse affect on performance even if the control systems are good.

Main Risks

The main risk that attaches to inadequate objectives is that substandard performance may easily be masked even though the operation itself may be well controlled with staff working efficiently. The problems arise when, because of poor role definition, the impact of the resulting services is not able to fully contribute to the overall welfare of the organization. It could be a case of vague role definition or that the manager is not working to the terms of reference originally agreed when the activity was first resourced. Control mechanisms promote the achievement of the control objectives that must be in place for systems' objectives to be achieved. If business objectives are unclear, then it follows that systems objectives will likewise suffer with the resulting adverse consequences. This flow of objectives forms the basis on which the available resources are applied, and in this respect is totally dependent on the formal terms of reference for the particular operation.

PRINCIPAL CONTROLS

- Formal document setting out terms of reference.
- Charter: documented, agreed by the organization, signed, kept up-to-date, short, precise, reflects current position, components and subcomponents, authority and responsibilities shown.
- Objectives publicized
- Set out in job descriptions
- Set out in strategic documents
- Understood by all operational staff
- Communicated throughout the organization
- Performance targets based on achieving objectives
- Objectives contribute to the overall welfare of the organization
- Management by objectives (MBO) techniques where objectives are broken down into tasks and goals
- Objectives regularly reviewed and reassessed
- All activities linked in some way into these objectives
- Objectives based on overall organizational objectives
- Training and developmental programs linked into objectives
- Approved budgets linked into objectives

STRATEGIC ANALYSIS— CONTROL ATTRIBUTES

Main Issues

The next part of the managerial control system relates to the process for effecting strategic analysis. Management textbooks contain much detail on this subject and we may note here that all operations must employ an effective strategy. In one sense the managers' primary role is to define this strategy and ensure that it is fully implemented. In addition, it must be subject to a continuous review and adjusted accordingly so that it is up-to-date and vibrant. The main issue that arises is based around the need to install the mechanisms that underpin strategic analysis.

Main Risks

The failure to define a formal strategy leaves a gap between the objectives and the way these objectives will be met. This gap may be seen as the process of directing the available resources in such a way as to maximize their impact so as to achieve value for money from these resources. A lack of strategic analysis means a lack of direction and no clear method through which to seek continual improvements in the way services are provided. In this situation there will be no formal process for ensuring that the operation is successful in terms of service delivery, and operational weaknesses may not be addressed by management. A constant state of crisis management is usually symptomatic of a lack of strategy.

Principal Controls

Goal formation

- Based on objectives
- In line with organizational values and policies
- Consistent with social responsibilities

Analyze internal position

- Process for isolating strengths
- Process for isolating weaknesses

- Process for isolating opportunities
- Process for isolating threats

The foregoing based on a formal management information systems (MIS).

Analyze external position

- Process for isolating political factors
- Process for isolating economic factors
- Process for isolating social factors
- Process for isolating technological factors
- Process for isolating legal factors

The foregoing based on a formal MIS.

Identification of strategic gap

- Staff performance problems identified
- Other resource problems identified
- Inefficiencies identified
- Poor service delivery (including complaints) identified

The foregoing based on a formal MIS.

Evaluate alternatives

Process for stimulating the production of alternatives and weighing each one based on a formal MIS.

Select strategy

Process for discussing and authorizing the best strategy based on a formal MIS.

Implement strategy

- Comprehensive and formally documented strategy circulated to all staff and agreed by senior management.

- Meetings with staff to discuss the strategy and any training implications.
- Clear change management procedures aimed at systems, structures, culture, and the staff.
- Milestones and tasks assigned to staff with deadlines and budgets built into the performance appraisal process.

Review current strategy

- Regular reports of progress on strategy and staff achievements
- Effective action where strategy is not being progressed
- Effective action where strategy is not achieving the intended results
- Effective action taken to update the strategy on an ongoing basis
- An adequate MIS to support the foregoing review process.

STRUCTURING—CONTROL ATTRIBUTES

Main Issues

The way an operation is structured in terms of the definition of staffing roles can have a major impact on the success of the resulting services. If this component is not properly managed then, regardless of the skills and commitment of the staff, frustration and inefficiency will be the net result. Control is enhanced where the organizational structure flows from the main strategies and allows the human resource aspects to be efficiently planned.

Main Risks

Examples of some of the control risks from a poorly planned organization structure include

- Poor task definition leading to duplication of effort and overall confusion
- Inappropriate spans of control leading to over- or underemployed managers
- Vague reporting lines making it difficult to establish accountability
- Activities that have no defined person formally responsible for their success or otherwise

In the main, the risks relate to inefficiencies in the way staff are employed. It is also very difficult to implement strategy if the underlying structure has not been adjusted to reflect the new strategy. The main problems result from structures that have not been regularly updated.

Principal Controls

- Defined structure flowing from the strategic analysis process
- Ongoing restructuring to reflect changes in strategy
- Ongoing analysis of jobs to ensure that they reflect the requirements of the defined structure
- Constant review and updating of job descriptions (JD)
- Person specifications that reflect the requirements of the job with minimum qualification and experience levels
- Periodic job evaluations to ensure the grade equates to the work being performed
- Staff working to the requirements of their JDs
- Clear reporting lines that are used in practice
- Officer accountability established
- Use of delegation wherever possible with built-in reviewing arrangements
- Appropriate spans of control that ensure that the managers' skills are fully utilized

- Correct mix of technical staff and no obvious skills gaps
- Use of project teaming where appropriate along with adequate associated controls
- The relationship between staff from these and other link operations clearly defined

HUMAN RESOURCE MANAGEMENT— CONTROL ATTRIBUTES

Main Issues

Staffing may be the single most important factor in the managerial control system and could make the difference between a badly run service and an efficient one. Reviews of staffing are not concerned with individual personalities and performances, but deal with the processes that underpin the human resource management (HRM) aspects of management. The HRM components may be broken down into a defined system as shown in Figure A.1. Each of the items in the system must be carefully planned and implemented by management who should not leave it up to chance.

Main Risks

There are many risks where the HRM process has not been adequately planned, and some include

- The wrong type of staff employed
- Demotivated workforce
- Poor performance
- High levels of disciplinary activity
- An inappropriate culture

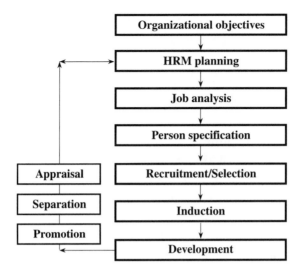

Figure A.1 Human resource management cycle.

- Managerial frustration
- Staff incompetence
- Constant breaches of procedure
- High levels of errors and corrections

Principal Controls

Organization objectives: HRM policies set within the framework of organizational objectives.

- Specific HRM policies set within the framework of overall organizational HRM policies
- HRM policies fully documented

Manpower planning: An ongoing process for

- Assessing future HRM demand
- Assessing existing resources

- Assessing future internal supply
- Assessing future external supply
- Isolating a supply gap in terms of numbers and skills
- Plans for bridging this gap
- Keeping the plans up-to-date

This plan should be published and properly implemented. It should result in the supply of the right staff and may cover recruitment, training, redeployment, development, automation, and improving staff performance. The plan should be kept under constant review.

Job analysis: Management should establish a process for providing a continuous assessment of the working arrangements to ensure that each post properly reflects the requirements of the operational strategy. The types and levels of skills and experiences must be reassessed wherever strategy changes or problems are evident. JDs may have to be amended in line with these changes.

Personal specification: The type of person required to discharge the duties of the various posts (which may have been redefined) should be codified within a person specification. This should be linked to recruitment or selection and staff development to ensure that current and/or proposed postholders meet this specification.

Recruitment: Clear recruitment procedures should be identified in line with organizational policies. This may involve recruiting through

- Internal staff
- General advertisements
- Professional journals
- Recruitment agencies
- Links with educational establishments
- Job fairs

Formal shortlisting arrangements should include the manager who is responsible for the new recruit.

Selection: All matters on the person specification should be considered.

- The line manager should be involved.
- Specialist skills should be fully tested by including the right people on the interview panel.
- The selection process should be adequately resourced.
- The selected individual should be given full details of the requirements of the job and type of control culture that they will operate within.
- All personal references and certificates should be confirmed by an independent third party.

Induction: Arrangements for carrying out suitable induction training should be in place.

- Introduction should be geared to acclimatizing the newcomer as quickly as possible.
- A probationary period should be required so that either side may terminate the contract at short notice. This period should include regular performance reports and action taken where necessary.

Appraisal: A formal performance appraisal process should be in place.

- It should be based on targets that in turn should be based on operational strategy.
- Where targets are not available, then a daily record of work activity should be made by each officer and presented to the line manager for review and action where necessary.
- Wherever possible a time-charging system should be in place with each task given budgeted hours by the manager.

Reports on actual/planned hours should then be available for consideration by management.

- Management must also be included in a similar procedure.

Training: A suitable staff training program should be in place based on the following:

- Performance appraisals wherein performance gaps are isolated
- Training programs directed at closing these gaps
- Review of the results of training
- General professional training for the services being provided
- An approved training budget in line with overall training needs
- Regular in-house skills-based training carried out by senior staff
- A link between training and the person specification
- Additional training where a new procedure is being implemented
- Comprehensive record of courses that staff have followed and results where appropriate
- Appropriate management action where staff have dropped out of training courses or have failed any qualifying examinations

Development: In conjunction with staff training, each member of staff should be on a clear developmental program, which may include

- Performance appraisals
- Experience gaps identified
- Work rotation
- Secondments where appropriate
- Additional work responsibilities wherever possible

- The use of delegation wherever possible as long as there are good controls over quality and access to management at short notice
- Line management's close involvement in individual career development

Separation: It is necessary to establish firm procedures for picking up on poor performance, and these may take the following pattern of events:

- Targets set on quality and quantity of work
- Review of the achievement (or not) of these targets
- Training directed at performance problems
- Counselling where performance cannot be corrected
- Disciplinary action where the failings continue for unreasonable periods, or the person's behavior is inappropriate

Generally, managers should have the ability to deal with staff who are not able to perform to the required standards.

Promotion: In contrast to poor performance, managers should be able to reward good performance as follows:

- Files that record specific achievements
- A system for recognizing outstanding performance
- A method of linking promotions to good performance
- A method of providing good performers with exposure to more interesting and demanding work
- A clear link between rewards and any performance appraisal scheme

Review: Management should establish clear mechanisms for reviewing the way HRM policies impact on the efficiency and effectiveness of the operation. Organizational policies should not provide a barrier to performance, and where this occurs, then action must be taken to remedy the situation.

QUALITY STANDARDS—CONTROL ATTRIBUTES

Main Issues

Quality cannot be ignored by managers and they are charged with defining and implementing appropriate quality standards. Quality is about doing things right all the time and depends on sound procedures. Operational activities have to be carried out with reference to a predetermined standard set by management. In this context, standards are set in terms of quantity and quality and they must be communicated to staff before being reviewed. A continual struggle to improve quality standards should also be part of management's goals. Quality assurance in its true sense is achieved through the implementation of the managerial control system detailed later in Figure A.4. A more narrow view of quality control is dependent on effective review systems that look at the way work is performed. This review may consider the performance of staff per se or management may review the extent of compliance with quality standards.

Main Risks

Some of the risks associated with a lack of good quality standards are as follows:

- Poor work performance
- Excessive supervisory review and correction
- Inconsistencies in the application of operational procedures

320

- Conflicts between quantity and quality
- Poor performance appraisal standards and an inability to set performance targets
- An environment that is unable to support quality goals
- Inability to provide a quality service or product

Principal Controls

Management must install quality systems and as already mentioned, this factor affects all activities. However, several specific processes contribute to quality assurance and examples are listed as follows:

- Managerial supervision and review of staff activities.
- Standards for operational performance.
- Checks on staff output that are not merely concerned with correcting poor products but have the wider role of determining the underlying causes and how they may be rectified.
- Managerial concern for quality where this is promoted at every opportunity.
- Commitment to achieve quality assurance standards.
- Good documentation and efficient filing systems and working papers. High standards should be set in this respect.
- A zero error policy built into performance targets with associated review checks.
- A zero client complaints policy built into performance targets with associated review checks.
- The principles of quality circles applied, allowing bottom up communications from work teams feeding into the managerial process.
- Comprehensive external and/or internal reviews commissioned by management to promote improvements in operations and services.

PROCEDURES—CONTROL ATTRIBUTES

Main Issues

All operations are carried out with reference to procedures. Where these have not been carefully considered, planned, documented, and implemented then they will depend entirely on individual members of staff. Sound operational procedures that reflect the way management wishes work to be performed are essential to the proper maintenance of control. Procedures should be used to direct operational activities and may be used to promote creativity and discretion where necessary. However, they may be used to contain staff and ensure that they work to consistent standards. The choice depends on the particular activities and type of staff employed. Within this model, some matters are subject to formal detailed procedures while others are simply set within the framework of general policy statements. We may establish a dynamic process for using procedures as shown in Figure A.2. The manager must review the way the system is being defined and applied.

Main Risks

Where procedures are inadequate, then problems will ensue and these include

- Management will not be able to define how an activity should be undertaken.
- It will not be possible to identify staff training needs.
- It will not be possible to review staff's work.
- It will not be possible to define how particular operational services interface with link systems due to unclear procedures.

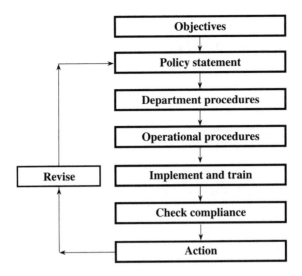

Figure A.2 Managerial direction.

- Staff will not have their operational roles clearly defined.
- Clients will not understand how their services are being provided.

There is a resource implication in defining and drafting clear operational procedures and keeping them up-to-date. However, the risks associated with the lack of documented procedures are great and as such, should be fully addressed.

Principal Controls

Objectives: Each procedure should have a clear link into the systems objective that is being sought.

Policy statements: Procedures should work within corporate policies that have set the overall framework.

Departmental procedures: Clear procedures should apply to the whole department, section, or operation. These should promote equity across the organization.

Operational procedures: For each main activity undertaken clearly documented procedures should apply that must be

- Comprehensive
- Up-to-date
- In line with the realities of the activities
- Consistent with job descriptions

Communicated: The procedures should be properly communicated to all staff even where they are working in a different area:

- Upward communications should arise where staff have a major input into what is officially set out.
- The procedures should be produced in a suitable format by using colors where appropriate along with clear print. All staff should be given up-to-date copies.
- There should be a formal avenue for getting management to respond where staff are experiencing problems with a particular procedure.

Training: It is essential that in-house (or external) skills training is undertaken where

- Technically difficult procedures are in use.
- Procedures are changed.
- They are not being applied properly.
- New starters are in the post.

- The current standards with which the procedures are being applied are inadequate.

Compliance reviewed: There must be an effective method that allows managers to satisfy themselves that procedures are being adhered to and this may include:

- Management commitment to compliance
- Documentation that supports the application of a procedure
- Supervisory review
- Spot checks particularly for remote locations
- Special control teams that undertake regular compliance tests
- Occasional comprehensive reviews of compliance
- Compliance built into job descriptions
- Disciplinary action where noncompliance occurs

Management action: Management action should ensue where the standards set by the various procedures are not being achieved:

- This action should be geared to setting a culture that promotes the use of good workable procedures.
- Job descriptions should include the requirement to comply with procedures. They should also include the requirement to seek improvements to procedures.

OPERATIONAL ACTIVITIES— CONTROL ATTRIBUTES

Main Issues

The operational activity may be seen as "the things that are done" in the area under review. The whole premise of reviewing the managerial control system is that it has a fundamental effect on the services being provided. It is necessary to derive a control system (or series of systems) for the operation being performed by breaking the processes down into natural stages in line with the flow of work. Systems objectives are identified along with the associated control objectives before the appropriate control mechanisms can be applied during the evaluation stage.

Main Risks

The main risks to the operational element of an organizational activity should be related to the inability to achieve the five key control objectives that are concerned with:

1. Compliance with procedure
2. Reliable information
3. Protecting assets
4. Promoting economy and efficiency
5. Achieving objectives

At all stages of the operation, these objectives must be secured as well as the relevant systems objectives attached to that stage.

Principal Controls

Reference should be made to the various textbooks and internal control questionnaires (ICQs) that detail suitable operation-specific control mechanisms relating to specific areas such as inventory, personnel, debtors systems, expenditure systems, budgeting, final accounts, banking, and so on.

MARKETING—CONTROL ATTRIBUTES

Main Issues

Most management textbooks include extensive material on marketing, and these should be consulted. Competition affects all aspects of a business and most activities work in line with the principles of a strategic business unit. The main point is that all services must be competitive and provided to meet client expectations. This concept applies equally to in-house services because managers should have the ability to select the supplier who best meets their needs. This is the reality of competition and managers who do not appreciate this factor will risk losing their client base even where they are internal clients working for the same organization. Marketing controls are part of the managerial control system and these should be in place along with the other fundamental managerial processes. It is not possible to provide a service where clients' needs have not been ascertained and provided for as part of the service delivery process.

Main Risks

Where marketing issues have not been adequately considered, then a number of problems may result including the following:

- Dissatisfied clients
- Poorly defined product
- Competition from similar service providers
- Isolation from the realities of the organization
- Complaints from clients
- Disputes over internal recharges

- Demotivated staff
- Services contracted out to competitors

Principal Controls

Some of the relevant control attributes may be listed:

- A clear marketing strategy based on good marketing information
- Marketing research properly resourced
- Service level agreements
- Complaints procedure
- Standards for responding to clients' inquiries such as:

  time taken to respond to memos
  time taken to address a complaint
  time taken to answer the telephone
  amount of detail provided to clients on request

- Brochures that set out the services provided and how these might be secured
- Continual reassessment of the services or products that are provided in line with feedback from clients
- Continual reappraisal of the costs of providing the services and how these might be minimized by improved efficiencies and the application of best practice
- Continual assessment of competitors' services and how they compare to what is on offer
- Regular client surveys to see if they are making full use of the services being provided
- Employee code of conduct and checks to see if the requirements of this code are being satisfied

- Regular meetings with operational staff to discuss marketing-related issues and how improvements may be sought

MANAGEMENT INFORMATION— CONTROL ATTRIBUTES

Main Issues

A total systems approach should be applied where the information system is seen as part of managerial processes and is interfaced into the operation that it supports. It is not possible to assess an information system without considering the way it fits into an operation with clear business objectives. The type and extent of controls over the MIS are dependent on the objectives being achieved, which in turn is linked to the services being delivered.

Main Risks

Where the MIS is inadequately controlled, then it may not produce information that is:

- Reliable
- Accurate
- Timely
- Secure
- Promoting accountability
- Promoting operational efficiency
- Promoting operational effectiveness

Many important controls rely on the information supplied to management as part of the review process. The implications of poor

MIS may reduce the overall impact of many other controls and so lower management's reliance on them.

Principal Controls

The following controls represent the minimum that should be considered when assessing a MIS:

- There should be a documented IS (information systems) strategy that has been defined to support the operational strategy.
- This in turn should be supported by an IT (information technology) strategy that covers:

hardware requirements	software requirements
networking arrangements	database solutions
internet working	intranet working

- The strategy should define the type of systems architecture being developed and how it links into the existing organization-wide architecture. New developments should fit this strategy.
- There should be clear policies on controlling personal computer-based systems covering acquisition, input, processing, file, and output controls.
- There should be a defined officer responsible for the integrity of the information.
- There should be clear guidance on complying with data protection requirements.
- The information systems outputs should be linked to the reporting needs of the operation and all reports should be accurate, complete, timely, secure, and useful.
- There should exist a reporting system that accounts for the operational activities on a periodic basis to senior management, including relevant statistics and performance indicators.

- Activity reports in terms of the budget and spending to date should be produced periodically at least each quarter and action should be taken on adverse variances.
- Management reports should be based on the exception principle, where variance from standard is used to highlight potential problems.
- A computer replacement policy should be in place to ensure that all equipment is up-to-date and efficient. There should also be adequate security over the computers and information that is held.

CONCLUSION

One model of control argues that control is seen to shadow the management process as an additional system superimposed over and above this process to ensure that activities are carried out

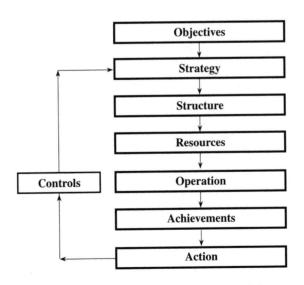

Figure A.3 Traditional control model.

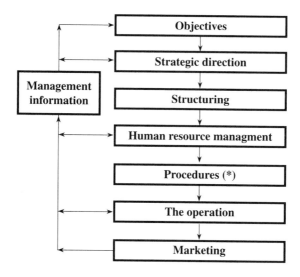

Figure A.4   Managerial control system.
(See also Figures 2.12, 4.1, and D.1)

properly and objectives achieved as shown in Figure A.3. The alternative model in Figure A.4 simply argues that the management process constitutes the absolute control process, which is impossible to separate from management's main activities.

We can surmise that at least 80 percent of control is exercised via the management processes while the remainder falls in line with the more traditional type of controls that are based around the actual operation (incorporated within operational procedures [*] in Figure A.4). All managers and employees should consider the extent to which the MCS has been catered for in their areas of responsibility and should likewise ensure that they have a good appreciation of the inherent risks and associated controls therein.

APPENDIX B

Three Strikes and You're Out: Putting Compliance into Perspective

THE MEANING OF COMPLIANCE

Compliance is behavior that promotes the defined approach and standards adopted by an organization. It recognizes the need to work within an established corporate and operational framework, in whatever form this takes. We can argue that an organization is a collection of united activities that is moving in the same direction. That is, it is moving through time along a predetermined road. Both the action and road chosen should result from a strategy designed to ensure objectives have been set and will be achieved. So long as the organization moves along this road, all will be well. By definition the road has boundaries on either side that must be observed. Boundaries may relate to policy, staff conduct, corporate standards, or operational procedures. They appear throughout the highest and lowest levels of any organization. Compliance simply means keeping within these boundaries.

THE IMPORTANCE OF COMPLIANCE

We have said that compliance means keeping within set boundaries while moving toward organizational goals. In this context, it is important because

- The organization must set a direction for managers and their staffs.
- This direction must be predetermined (a corporate strategy).
- Without boundaries employees may go in different directions.
- By default, boundaries indicate what is acceptable and what is not.
- As a self-managing system, boundaries, once set, will guide employees with no need for further intervention.

If we accept the need for boundaries, then we must accept the importance of complying with the restriction (and guidance) they entail. The organization believes that employees are working within set standards and its success depends on this belief. Where employees are not, it indicates either

- Infringement means we will not be successful.
- The boundaries are inappropriate, so compliance will not lead to success.

Whatever the case, the foregoing scenario suggests there are problems that need to be addressed. Simply allowing noncompliance to occur unchecked cloaks these problems, and in the long term is unacceptable.

THE REVIEW FUNCTION

We have said that boundaries may relate to policy, staff conduct, corporate standards or operational procedures. They may have international recognition, such as quality assurance (QA) standards, or simply be an internal product. They may in turn be subject to periodic accreditation from an external review body. Whatever the set standard, we could inform staff, publish the documentary guidance, and leave it at that. Alternatively, we may make line or middle management responsible for checking whether these standards are being applied in practice. A further approach, that is the subject of this paper, is to establish an additional tier of monitoring by also making compliance the responsibility of an internal review unit. The review unit may be given many different titles including

- review unit
- compliance unit
- quality assurance unit
- inspectorate unit
- audit unit

One comprehensive model appears as Figure B.1. Here the manager is responsible for ensuring compliance within the corporate policy framework set by the board. Supervisors make regular checks as part of their front-line management role. An internal review unit also carries out reviews or inspections and reports back to an independent body within the organization (or a more senior manager for the area in question). There may be an external body (e.g., external audit) that also assumes a monitoring role. Ideally, the external body reviews and hopefully relies on any work done by the internal review unit. Meanwhile the organization relies on any assurances given by the internal review unit and acts on any recommended action again from the review unit.

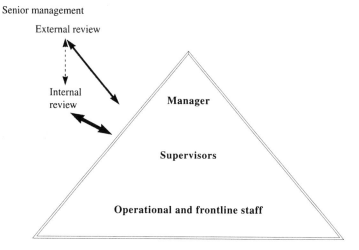

Figure B.1 Review structures.

THE THREE STRIKES ARGUMENT

This appendix defines and recommends a conceptual framework for internal review units that are involved in compliance issues. Its name (three strikes) derives from the judicial view that criminals (people who infringe criminal law) are not only dealt with according to the severity of their infringement, but are also dealt with in accordance with the frequency of these infringements. That is, each infringement is handled with increasing degrees of severity. People are given a chance, then a second chance, and then "they're out."

The parallel we draw in dealing with breach of procedure within an organization would appear as follows:

- Chance one—let's help you sort things out.
- Chance two—what's going wrong? Let's further clarify things.

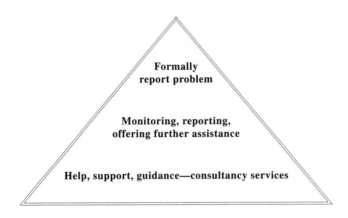

Figure B.2 Reporting three strikes.

- Chance three—we will remove the cause of the problem (perhaps the person most responsible).

Moreover, we can establish a diagram shown in Figure B.2 that review units can use to implement the three strikes model.

Let's tackle these three levels in more detail. We'll take them in reverse order:

Level 1—Help, Support, and Guidance Consultancy Services

A newly established compliance/assurance unit should have as its main objective the following:

- Ensure all relevant standards are secured and documented.
- Identify all parts of the operation affected by these standards.
- Establish the way in which selected (high-risk) operations are complying.
- Review the extent of compliance.

- Provide ongoing advice and support to management in establishing compliance mechanisms.

Level 2—Monitoring, Report, Further Assistance Offered

As we have assisted managers in establishing and maintaining set standards, we may expect some degree of continuing problems. In this case the review unit is needed to

- Review the way in which selected (high-risk) operations are complying.
- Review the extent of continuing noncompliance.
- Recommend action steps to manager that need to be take to ensure compliance.
- Copy the agreed action (and target dates) steps to senior management.
- Inform manger of consequences of continuing noncompliance.
- Follow-up action taken and review progress.

Level 3—Formally Report Problem

Despite all efforts to support standard setting and monitoring, we may come across blatant breach. We are still concerned about explanation (and justification) but the theme of the reviews alter and follow a more formal line, for example

- Follow-up review—any further examples of noncompliance.
- Make a formal investigation of noncompliance and responsible person/s.

- Provide a formal report to the senior manager and head of personnel.
- Attend any formal forum that considers the findings of the compliance review.

CONCLUSION

The foregoing approach is designed to recognize the distinction between types of noncompliance with set standards. Noncompliance could be because the standard is not fully established, the standard is inappropriate, compliance is not seen as an issue, people adopt different customs, or there is evidence of maladministration, negligence, or irregularity. There are problems for compliance units working within such a multifaceted environment. Reviewers must adopt an appropriate response to the situation. There are inherent conflicts within the review role in this respect.

It follows that we look toward yesterday (what went wrong and why?) as well as tomorrow (where do we go from here?). Assisting and guiding is different from blowing the whistle on unacceptable behavior. These two roles may be captured as a double-headed figure as shown in Figure B.3.

The Three Strikes model comes to our help in suggesting an eight-stage set of guiding principles for compliance units, along these lines:

1. We are here to help get standards up and running.
2. We will support management in this task.
3. We will continue to provide assistance where there are continuing problems.
4. We will report progress on compliance issues to senior management.

Figure B.3   Inherent conflicts.

5. We will monitor problem areas until these problems are resolved.
6. We will investigate occasions where noncompliance is happening for no good reason.
7. We will formally report managers who have a blatant disregard for standards.
8. Meanwhile, we will continue to monitor and support all areas where compliance is important.

Compliance team members who are able to understand and work within this model will have no problem providing a professional service. But, it is up to the head of service to set this direction and ensure these principles are incorporated within their work role.

APPENDIX C

Top Ten Imperatives for Facilitators

1. *Explain expectations.* Make clear what the group is there to achieve and how long it has for the workshop. You are using their valuable time, so don't misuse it.
2. *Take a back seat.* Give responsibility to the group for meeting the set objectives. They, and not you are important. Explain, ask, listen, probe, and record.
3. *Secure equitable involvement.* Empower the group to agree to their rules of conduct and monitor themselves. If you treat them as adults, they will behave as adults.
4. *Get something going.* Reinforce the concept of continuous improvement and the futility of searching for perfection. Sense and sensibility are crucial to success.
5. *Step over puddles.* Suggest tools that may help the group achieve its goal where asked for, but do not impose or offer, as this creates victims, not action. Tools for creative problem solving fits here.
6. *Tackle obstacles.* Neutralize barriers to group performance by getting the group to recognize and deal with them. Encourage the managers to let go of their power.
7. *Unlock energy.* Get the group members to release their energies in a positive way. They may feed off your enthusiasm.

8. *No hidden extras.* Make clear the need for accountability, proper documentation, and formal assurance reports from the group on their risks and controls. Don't apologize—it's a fact of life.

9. *Continue after and thereafter.* Encourage the group to continue the analysis after the workshop has closed as an ongoing process. Action planning takes time while risk assessment and management should be part of their daily routine and not depend on your presence.

10. *Extra, extra read all about it.* Encourage add-ons (like team-building, shared understandings, and better knowledge of the work) if this happens. And let the entire thing be an enjoyable and uplifting experience that is talked about.

APPENDIX D

Training Courses

COURSE TITLE: Basic Control Awareness

OBJECTIVE: To provide course members with a basic awareness of the principles of control and the overall control environment so that they are able to work efficiently within this environment.

Session

Introductions and learning goals

1. Defining control
2. Your responsibilities
3. The corporate internalized control facility (CICF) and control initiatives
4. The role of internal and external audit
5. Managing high-risk areas through risk assessment
6. Working with procedures
7. Systems objectives, control objectives, and control mechanisms
8. Accountability and fraud
9. When systems break down
10. Getting yourself in control

Course summary and review

COURSE TITLE: Induction Training (Controls)

OBJECTIVE: To ensure new employees have a good understanding of the control environment established by the organization and that they are able to work efficiently within this environment. (Note: This course entails a few sessions set within an overall induction training event.)

Session

Introductions and learning goals

1. What we mean by control
2. How the organization establishes control
3. Your role and responsibilities
4. The CICF
5. Available training on control issues

Course summary and review

COURSE TITLE: The Managerial Control System

OBJECTIVE: To provide course members with an understanding of the managerial control system and enable them to adopt the standards implicit within this system, which is shown in Figure D.1.

Session

Introductions and learning goals

1. What we mean by the managerial control system
2. Objectives and strategies
3. Structuring your resources
4. Human resource management

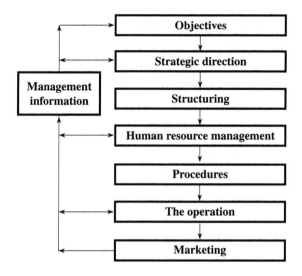

Figure D.1 Managerial control system.
(See also Figures 2.12, 4.1, and A.4)

5. Procedures
6. Controlling your operations
7. Marketing and feedback
8. Information systems
9. Assessing the arrangements
10. Creativity and adaptability within the MCS

Course summary and review

COURSE TITLE: Fraud and Its Implications

OBJECTIVE: To provide course members with the knowledge, skills, and attitudes required to manage the risk of fraud within organizational standards.

Session

Introductions and learning goals

1. Definition of fraud
2. High-risk areas
3. Background to organizational standards
4. Defining roles and responsibilities
5. What to do about allegations
6. Your role in investigations
7. Background to police action
8. Background to internal discipline
9. Interviewing skills
10. Prevention

Course summary and review

COURSE TITLE: Coming to Grips with Corporate Procedures

OBJECTIVE: To provide course members with a good understanding of corporate procedures so that they may appreciate the importance of compliance.

Session

Introductions and learning goals

1. Your duty to comply with corporate procedures
2. What falls under this heading
3. Human resource policies and procedures
4. Financial regulation and procedure
5. Physical security standards
6. Information technology (IT) security
7. Project management standards
8. Purchasing codes and practices
9. Equal opportunities
10. Health and safety

11. Inventory control
12. Business ethics
13. Cash handling
14. What to do about noncompliance

Course summary and review

COURSE TITLE: Building Your Own Procedures

OBJECTIVE: To provide course members with the techniques required to enable them to assist in the process of reviewing, preparing, and maintaining adequate operational procedures.

Session

Introductions and learning goals

1. The role of procedures
2. Reviewing procedures by reviewing processes
3. When to start from scratch
4. Establishing and flowcharting underlying processes
5. Seeking improved work flows
6. Drafting the document
7. Getting people committed; avoiding the paper chase
8. Assessing usability and value
9. Reviewing and updating procedures
10. Ensuring compliance

Course summary and review

COURSE TITLE: Maintaining Creativity within a Controlled Environment

OBJECTIVE: To provide course members with the ability to innovate within a structured environment and release their creative energies while maintaining control.

Session

Introductions and learning goals

1. What is creativity and why is it important
2. Overcontrol and the dangers of stagnation
3. Using conflicts to the edge of chaos
4. What happens when things get out of control
5. Adaptable and flexible controls
6. Creativity and accountability
7. Project control techniques
8. Ideas and how to use them
9. Using teams and personalities
10. A final word—reconciling control and creativity

Course summary and review

COURSE TITLE: How to Use the CICF

OBJECTIVE: To provide course members with an understanding of the role of the corporate internalized control facility and how it can help them do their job.

Session

Introductions and learning goals

1. Start with self-control
2. The concept of the CICF
3. Services on offer
4. When and where to use the CICF
5. Ending with self-control

Course summary and review

COURSE TITLE: Security Standards

OBJECTIVE: To provide course members with the knowledge, skills, and attitudes required to implement the organization's security standard.

Session

Introductions and learning goals

1. The importance of physical security
2. Protecting your organization
3. The role of the security officer
4. Your responsibilities
5. Physical access restrictions
6. How to spot breaches of security
7. Assessing your current arrangements
8. Using resources off-site
9. The organization's assets register
10. What to do about fraud

Course summary and review

COURSE TITLE: Protecting Your Automated Data

OBJECTIVE: To provide course members with an understanding of IS/IT security standards and enable them to work efficiently within this environment.

Session

Introductions and learning goals

1. Information and why it must be protected
2. Background to corporate IT security standards

3. The role of the data protection officer
4. The importance of password control
5. Assessing whether you are at risk
6. Security and your private life
7. Contingency planning and backups
8. Network security, remote access, and the Internet
9. Reviewing your arrangements
10. What to do about fraud

Course summary and review

COURSE TITLE: How to Carry Out a Complete Review of Controls

OBJECTIVE: To provide course members with the knowledge, skills, and attitudes to enable them to undertake complete reviews of systems of internal control.

Session

Introductions and learning goals

1. What we mean by systems of internal control
2. Why reviews are required; case studies
3. Getting help from internal audit
4. Planning the review
5. Ascertaining current control systems
6. Evaluating the control arrangements
7. Testing for evidence of strengths and weaknesses
8. Seeking improvements
9. Getting staff committed to change
10. Reviewing what we have done

Course summary and review

COURSE TITLE: Establishing Your Own Compliance Routines

OBJECTIVE: To provide course members with an understanding of compliance with procedure and how it can be established and maintained.

Session

Introductions and learning goals

1. The importance of compliance
2. Ensuring procedures work in the first place
3. The start is staff commitment
4. Making sure procedures are understood
5. Setting up compliance-checking routines
6. Allowing errors; keeping things positive
7. What to do about major breaches
8. Dealing with fraud and corruption
9. Allowing for creativity
10. Making procedures fun

Course summary and review

COURSE TITLE: Making Yourself the Key to Control

OBJECTIVE: To provide course members with an understanding of the methods of being in control of themselves as the key to establishing systems of internal control.

Session

Introductions and learning goals

1. The self-control model
2. Finding out where you stand; signals of burnout
3. Managing stress; finding happiness at work

4. Managing conflicting priorities
5. Coaching not managing
6. Managing your time
7. Listening skills
8. Using body language for control
9. Controlling your emotions
10. Becoming a creative control freak
11. Compliance with procedure; making sure you are up-to-date
12. Working within a healthy environment; plants and colors
13. Internalizing control
14. Putting the self-control model to work

Course summary and review

COURSE TITLE: Managing the Ethical Environment

OBJECTIVE: To provide course members with an appreciation of the ethical framework of the organization and enable them to work efficiently within this environment.

Session

Introductions and learning goals

1. The roots of ethics in business
2. The organizational position
3. The internal disciplinary code
4. Different perspectives—enforcement versus encouragement
5. The dangers of sleaze; case studies
6. Assessing your position on ethics
7. Making the right decisions
8. Accountability
9. Whistleblowing—rights and responsibilities
10. Establishing your own ethical code

Course summary and review

COURSE TITLE: Value for Money and Quality

OBJECTIVE: To provide course members with an introduction to the topic of value for money and ensure they can translate these principles into quality standards.

Session

Introductions and learning goals

1. The concept of value for money (VFM)
2. Ensuring efficient processes
3. Ensuring effective processes
4. Measuring quality
5. Measuring performance
6. Assessing success
7. Seeking constant improvement
8. The link into standards and procedures
9. How to tackle operational problems
10. Taking an integrated approach to service delivery

Course summary and review

COURSE TITLE: Using Control Circles

OBJECTIVE: To provide course members with the competencies underpinning the design, use, and review of control circles that seek to add value to systems of internal control.

Session

Introductions and learning goals

1. The concept of control circles
2. How to set them up
3. Using teamworking
4. Getting good ideas
5. Dealing with errors and poor performance

6. Spotting systems weaknesses
7. Preparing reports on systems improvements
8. Selling ideas through presentations
9. How the CICF can facilitate control circles
10. Maintaining the circles; integration and acceptance

Course summary and review

COURSE TITLE: The Theory of Risk and Contingency

OBJECTIVE: To provide course members with an understanding of risk assessment and how it can be used to direct controls at high-risk areas.

Session

Introductions and learning goals

1. The concept of risk management
2. Linking risk to business objectives
3. Key control objectives
4. Going through an assessment process
5. Transferring risk; techniques
6. Insuring against risk
7. Tackling risk through control; prevention
8. The dynamics of changing risks
9. Using the computer to assist risk management
10. Seeing the wood for the trees

Course summary and review

COURSE TITLE: Financial Controls

OBJECTIVE: To provide course members (with no background in finance) with an understanding of financial management as a key aspect of the system of internal control.

Session

Introductions and learning goals

1. Discovering the world of debits and credits
2. Basics of financial accounting
3. Basic of management accounting
4. The role of internal audit
5. The role of external audit
6. The corporate standards on financial regulation
7. Understanding the year-end financial statements
8. Using the budget as a key control
9. Project appraisal; financial implications
10. How to use open learning to increase your knowledge

Course summary and review

COURSE TITLE: Ensuring Accountability

OBJECTIVE: To provide course members with an understanding of the concept of accountability and ensure that they are able to work efficiently within this environment.

Session

Introductions and learning goals

1. The meaning of accountability
2. Being responsible for resources
3. The technique of delegation
4. Establishing codes of conduct
5. Financial regulation in outline
6. Representing the organization
7. Maintaining a record of activities

8. The role of audit services; internal and external audit
9. Getting a balance with autonomy and supervision
10. Getting rid of the fear of failure

Course summary and review

Course Title: Using Information for Control

OBJECTIVE: To provide course members with an understanding of information systems as a key aspect of the system of internal control.

Session

Introductions and learning goals

1. Defining the management information system (MIS)
2. The end user computing concept
3. Decision support systems
4. Using information in the control cycle
5. Using SMART (specific, measurable, achievable, results-oriented, and timely) targets
6. Exception reporting
7. Data profiling and the detection of fraud
8. Data protection security standards
9. Contingency and backups
10. Developing your information system for control

Course summary and review

APPENDIX E

A Risk Paradigm

Business risk consists of all those influences that interfere with one's ability to achieve organizational goals. A typical approach to the assessment of business risk tends to involve isolating key objectives, then deciding on how best to manage these influences. While being quite straightforward, it does reinforce a free-floating approach to identifying and managing business risk. Formal frameworks to assist this task are generally discouraged, because each organization needs to adopt an approach that best suits its environment and unique business needs. This appendix provides one framework that can be used to focus the risk management process. Like most management tools, it should be applied in a way that makes sense within the context of the organizational setting in question.

Our approach to assessing risk is to set a four-tiered hierarchy of key areas covering health and safety, ethics, stakeholders, and excellence. The ability to recognize the main drivers of corporate accountability sets the tone for dealing with risk. These drivers comprise matters that need to be addressed in order of priority. As one is achieved, the next one comes into the frame. The Risk Paradigm is illustrated in Figure E.1.

Figure E.1   Risk paradigm.

EXPLANATIONS

The four main drivers are explained in more detail in the following list:

- *Health and Safety*. Organizations must protect the welfare of their staff, customers, suppliers, and environment. This basic standard should appear as a first priority before all others. Death, injury, and distress must be avoided at all costs and in any assessment of risk, it is important to determine whether there is any risk to the health and safety of employees and others from the set business activities. Serious accidents can put an entire business out of action temporarily or permanently, if the organization is at fault at all.
- *Business Ethics*. The next level of risk assessment concerns the reputation of the business in terms of its corporate integrity. Problems such as fraud, breach of procedure, illegal trading, financial misreporting, and poor due diligence adversely

impact on the public perception of the organization. We need to assess whether the risk of these things happening is being properly addressed.

- *Stakeholders.* One main aspect of risk assessment relates to the needs of stakeholders, that is, the owners, financial backers, government, customers, and all those people affected by the way the organization performs or fails to perform. The assessment should relate to corporate objectives, targets, profitability, sustainability, and performance generally. Where risks to these matters are not being managed, our stakeholders may lose confidence in the business, eventually leading to its demise.

- *Excellence.* The final aspect of the risk model concerns the *bit-at-the-top.* That extra aspect of business that drives it forward toward excellence rather that just good performance. Some call this innovation, whereas others see it as constructive and dynamic change projects. Whatever the format, we need to assess the risk of not moving forward quickly enough and making new things happen. It may be viewed as the positive side to risk; making better progress and not simply getting rid of problems.

GETTING RESULTS

The risk paradigm attempts to set a structure for risk management. Instead of just defining business objectives and isolating all things that get in the way of achieving them, we start with what's too important to leave to chance, that is, matters of life and death. Then we think about what makes us look bad in terms of ethical matters. Next, we tackle our performance and what our investors and associates expect from us in terms of actual delivery of services, products, and earnings. Finally, we need to push for more than just standard and aim for an extra level that sets us apart from the opposition. Having addressed the foregoing in order of importance, we can argue that we have adopted a structured approach to managing risk.

NOTES

TWO: Concepts of Control

1. M. Power, *The Audit Explosion* (London: Demos, 1994).
2. *Collins English Dictionary*, third ed. (England, USA: Harper Collins, 1997), 349.
3. V. Harper, "My Wife Didn't Have To Die," *The Mail on Sunday* (June 29, 1997): 45.
4. Monty Python, in J.M. Cohen and M.J. Cohen, ed., *The Penguin Dictionary of Twentienth Century Quotations* (London: Penguin Books, 1995), 268.
5. E. Blyton, (1958). *The Secret Seven—Secret Seven Fireworks.*
6. W. Churchill, in J.M. Cohen and M.J. Cohen, ed., *The Penguin Dictionary of Twentienth Century Quotations* (London: Penguin Books, 1995), 79.
7. H. Geneen, in H. Exley, ed., *The Best of Business Quotations* (New York, Watford, UK: Exley Publications Ltd., 1993), 5.
8. R.H. Kilmann, *Beyond the Quick Fix: Managing Five Tracks to Organisational Success* (San Francisco, London: Jossey-Bass, 1984), 14.
9. R.R. Blake and J.S. Moulton, *Building A Dynamic Corporation Through Grid Organisation Development* (Reading, Massachusetts: Addison-Wesley Publishing, 1969).
10. Committee of Sponsoring Organizations of the Treadway Commission (COSO), (1992). *Internal Control, Integrated Framework.*
11. Canadian Institute of Chartered Accountants (CoCo), (1995). *Criteria of Control.*

THREE: Negril and the Art of Using Procedures

1. C.M. Zimmerman and J.J. Campbell, *Fundamentals of Procedure Writing*, second ed. (London: Kogan Page Ltd., 1988), 3.
2. Chuang Tzu, in D. Schiller, ed., *The Little Zen Companion* (New York: Workman Publishing, 1994), 58.

3. C. Northcote Parkinson, in H. Exley, ed., *The Best of Business Quotations.* (New York, Watford, UK: Exley Publications Ltd., 1993), 26–27.

4. Thoreau, in D. Schiller, ed., *The Little Zen Companion* (New York: Workman Publishing, 1994), 49.

5. C. Northcote Parkinson, in H. Exley, ed., *The Best of Business Quotations* (New York, Watford, UK: Exley Publications Ltd., 1993), 36.

6. D. McGregor, *The Human Side of Enterprise,* International ed. (Mcgraw-Hill, 1960).

7. P. Kalinauckas and H. King, *Coaching—Realising the Potential* (Institute of Personnel and Development, 1994).

8. A.H. Maslow, "A Theory of Human Motivation," *Psychological Review* 4 (July 1943): 370–396.

9. N. Blundell, *The World's Greatest Mistakes* (London: Hamlyn, 1992), 73.

10. P.F. Drucker, *The Practice of Management* (London: Pan Books Ltd., 1972), 155.

11. Ts' Ai Ken T'an, in D. Schiller, ed., *The Little Zen Companion* (New York: Workman Publishing, 1994), 118.

12. P. Walker, in A. Eisen, ed., *Positive Thoughts: Living Your Life to the Fullest* (Kansas City, Missouri: Ariel Books, Andrews & McMeel, 1995), 223.

FOUR: Fishing, Witches, and Support Systems

1. D. Meacham, in A. Eisen, ed., *Positive Thoughts: Living Your Life to the Fullest.* (Kansas City, Missouri: Ariel Books, Andrews & McMeel, 1995), 121.

FIVE: Fraud, Corruption, and Lots of Rain

1. G. Vinten, ed., *Whistleblowing Subversion or Corporate Citizenship?* (Paul Chapman Publishing Ltd., 1994), 1.

SIX: Controlled Creativity and Chaos

1. J. Henry, ed., *Creative Management* (Sage Publications, 1991). (Published in association with the Open University).

2. Martin Luther King, in A. Partington, ed., *The Oxford Dictionary of Quotations,* fourth ed. (Oxford, New York: Oxford University Press, 1992), 396.

3. D.K. Hurst, et al., in J. Henry, ed., *Creative Management* (Sage Publications, 1991), 235. (Published in association with the Open University).

4. R. Tanner Pascale, *Managing on the Edge: How Successful Companies Use Conflict to Stay Ahead* (Penguin Books, 1990), 76.

5. E.F. McKenna, *Psychology in Business Theory and Applications* (London, Hillsdale, New Jersey: Lawrence Erlbaum Associates, 1987), 49.

6. J. Lennon, in D. Schiller, ed., *The Little Zen Companion* (New York: Workman Publishing, 1994), 276.

7. Muhammed Ali, in A. Eisen, ed., *Positive Thoughts: Living Your Life to the Fullest* (Kansas City, Missouri: Ariel Books, Andrews & McMeel, 1995), 114.

8. R.M. Pirsig, *Zen and the Art of Motorcycle Maintenance: An Inquiry into Values* (London: Vintage, 1974), 62.

9. A. von Szent-Gyorgyi, in A. Partington, ed., *The Oxford Dictionary of Quotations,* fourth ed. (Oxford, New York: Oxford University Press, 1992), 677.

INDEX